GRADE LEVEL
K-12

A Systemwide Approach to Rigor, Relevance, and Relationships

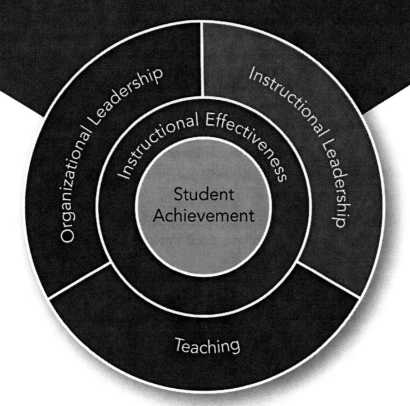

RIGOROUS LEARNING FOR ALL STUDENTS

No part of this publication may be reproduced in whole or in part, or stored in a retrieval system, or transmitted in any form or by any means, electronic, mechanical, photocopying, recording, or otherwise, without written permission of the publisher.

Copyright © 2012 by International Center for Leadership in Education, Inc.

All rights reserved.

Published by International Center for Leadership in Education, Inc.

Printed in the U.S.A.

ISBN-13: 978-1-935300-82-3
ISBN-10: 1-935300-82-2

International Center for Leadership in Education, Inc.
1587 Route 146
Rexford, New York 12148
(518) 399-2776
info@LeaderEd.com

Contents

Overview 1

1. **The Daggett System for Effective Instruction** 5
   Imagine 5
   DSEI 7
   Review Questions 14

2. **DSEI and the 21st Century 3R's: Rigor, Relevance, and Relationships** 15
   From a Student Perspective 15
   The 21st Century 3R's 17
   A Closer Look at the Power of Rigor, Relevance, and Relationships in 21st Century Learning 19
   Schools Not Meeting Student Needs 26
   Relationships 27
   Relevance 29
   Rigor 34
   A Fresh Approach 35
   What Does Rigor and Relevance Look Like in the Classroom? . . 45
   A Closer Look at "Real World" 58
   Review Questions 60

3. **Rigorous and Relevant Instruction** 61
   Instructional Planning 61
   Student-Centered Learning: The Key to Learner Engagement . . 77
   Nextpert: A Tool That Supports Standards-Based Curriculum Integration 87
   A Process for Creating Interdisciplinary Instruction 92
   Review Questions 96

© International Center for Leadership in Education

4. **Rigorous and Relevant Learning in the Digital Age** 97
   Teaching Digital Natives 97
   The Tools of Technology as Tools of Rigor, Relevance,
   and Learner Engagement 98
   Transforming the Way We Teach Digital Natives 101
   Review Questions 109

5. **Relationships Make Learning Possible** 111
   The Critical Importance of Teacher-Student Relationships in Learning 113
   Relationship Framework 114
   How to Build Relationships 121
   Supportive Behaviors 127
   Supportive Initiatives 130
   Student Behavior 143
   Parent Partnerships 143
   Schools That Say "Welcome" 148
   Review Questions 149

6. **Supportive Structures and Strategies for Building Rigor,
   Relevance, and Relationships** 151
   Small Learning Communities 153
   Alternative Scheduling 158
   Teaching Continuity 163
   Building a Team to Support Rigor, Relevance, and Strong Relationships 165
   Review Questions 177

7. **Community Partnerships** 179
   Benefits of Business-Community Partnerships 179
   Why Business-Community Involvement? 182
   Service Learning/Community Service 182
   School-Based Enterprises 184
   Three Examples of Successful Partnerships in Model Schools 187
   Review Questions 191

8. **Creating a Culture of Rigor, Relevance, and Relationships 193**
    Instructional Leadership. 194
    Strategies for Moving to the Next Level of the Rubric 205
    Student Work. 209
    Public Awareness Support. 210
    Pitfalls When Making Change 214
    Facilitating Effective Professional Development. 215
    What's a Gold Seal Lesson?. 217
    Personal Portfolio 238
    The New 3 Rs Powered by Aligned School Systems. 245
    Review Questions 247

Appendix. 249

Overview

The Daggett System for Effective Instruction

The Daggett System for Effective Instruction (DSEI) provides a coherent focus across the entire education organization on the development and support of instructional effectiveness to improve student achievement. Whereas traditional teaching frameworks are teacher-focused and consider what teachers should do to deliver instruction, DSEI is student-focused and considers what the entire educational system should do to facilitate learning. It is a subtle but important difference based on current research and understanding about teaching and learning.

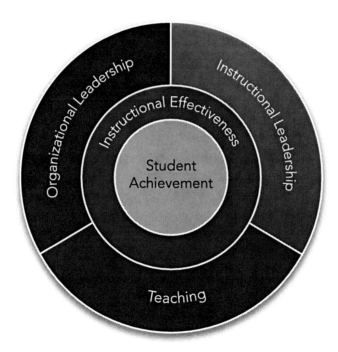

A Systemwide Approach to Rigor, Relevance, and Relationships

The three parts of DSEI are illustrated here. The following are the critical functions of each part of the system. Think about where you, as a professional educator, fit into this system.

Six Elements of Organizational Leadership

- Create a culture of high expectations.
- Create a shared vision.
- Build leadership capacity.
- Align organizational structures and systems to vision.
- Align teacher/administrator selection, support, and evaluation.
- Support decision making with data systems.

Five Elements of Instructional Leadership

- Use research to establish urgency for higher expectations.
- Align curriculum to standards.
- Integrate literacy and math across all content areas.
- Facilitate data-driven decision making to inform instruction.
- Provide opportunities for focused professional collaboration and growth.

Six Elements of Teaching

- Embrace rigorous and relevant expectations for all students.
- Build strong relationships with students.
- Possess depth of content knowledge and make it relevant to students.
- Facilitate rigorous and relevant instruction based on how students learn.
- Demonstrate expertise in use of instructional strategies, technology, and best practices.
- Use assessments to guide and differentiate instruction.

When all parts of the system are working together efficiently, teachers receive the support they need, and students are successfully prepared for college, careers, and citizenship.

Overview

DSEI and A Systemwide Approach to Rigor, Relevance, and Relationships

The focus of this book is to support school leaders at all K–12 levels to take a far-reaching approach in creating or enhancing a culture of rigor, relevance, and relationships (RRR) in their schools.

Chapter 1: The Daggett System for Effective Instruction

Chapter 1 provides an introduction to the Daggett System for Effective Instruction (DSEI) as a foundation for RRR.

Chapter 2: DSEI and the 21st Century 3R's: Rigor, Relevance, and Relationships

Chapter 2 considers how DSEI can drive a more effective implementation of RRR and how you can implement it, both organizationally and instructionally.

Chapter 3: Rigorous and Relevant Instruction

Chapter 3 discusses using rigor and relevance through establishing interdisciplinary instruction and incorporating instructional technology.

Chapter 4: Rigorous and Relevant Learning in the Digital Age

Chapter 4 delves into the importance of technology in education and its role in achieving rigor and relevance.

Chapter 5: Relationships Make Learning Possible

Chapter 5 examines four relationships that make rigor and relevance possible — learning relationships, staff relationships, professional relationships, and community relationships — and how they are applied to a relationship framework.

Chapter 6: Supportive Structures and Strategies for Building Rigor, Relevance, and Relationships

Chapter 6 considers structures to support rigor, relevance, and relationships, including small learning communities, alternative scheduling, and professional development.

Chapter 7: Community Partnerships

Chapter 7 discusses the benefits of business-community partnerships and opportunities for developing them.

Chapter 8: Creating a Culture of Rigor, Relevance, and Relationships

Chapter 8 concludes by taking a look at instructional leadership, interdisciplinary curriculum work, public awareness support, and Gold Seal Lessons.

Appendix

The Appendix lists resources that support and extend the ideas presented in this book.

Chapter 1

The Daggett System for Effective Instruction

Imagine

Imagine that for one day you could entertain your grandparents and great-grandparents who grew up in the early 1900s. Wouldn't it be a thrill to show them where you live and to introduce them to the amazing advances in technology, new modes of travel, appliances and conveniences in the home, and the multitude of improvements that we enjoy compared to the lives they lived a century ago? As educators, we might want them to see what our schools are like — and we would be struck by the sobering realization that school has not changed anywhere near as much as the world we live in and other aspects of our lives have changed.

The major features of school are much the same as they were 100 years ago. Yes, students ride on buses and our great-grandparents walked to school, but the calendar and daily schedule are still the same. The curriculum might include some more up-to-date content, but the basic subjects and topics that students study haven't really changed. Classrooms have whiteboards instead of blackboards and the desks are not made from wood, but our great-grandparents would recognize it all. In many classrooms, instruction is delivered with students listening to lessons presented by their teacher, reading their textbooks, and completing assignments and tests with pencil and paper. Apart from the use of computers in some schools, our visitors from a bygone era probably would recognize it all.

The powerful point for us to ponder from all of this is the fact that the world that our children are growing up in — let alone the world they will live, learn, and work in tomorrow — is immeasurably different from the world that our great-grandparents grew up in. Yet the thing that we call "school" still convenes the town's children and youth for 180 days each year, and it has changed very little in the past century. We cannot expect to reinvent a new form of schooling overnight; but to begin to achieve the standards and expectations we have set for 21st century learners, we must refocus leadership for schooling on a systemic vision that aligns teaching, instructional leadership, and organizational leadership in support of rigorous and relevant instruction that empowers student learning.

Converging Challenges

As Western nations struggle to recover their economic equilibriums following the financial crisis of 2008, China and India are leveraging their size and human capital to become global economic powerhouses. Emerging economies such as Vietnam, Argentina, Brazil, Indonesia, and Panama are increasingly capable of winning greater shares of international business. The ability to compete in the interconnected global economy is primarily leveraged by technical innovation and a highly skilled workforce. A more rigorous and more applied curriculum is needed to drive both levers.

While our schools are working hard at improving, the reality is that the rest of the world is changing even faster, leaving a growing gap. In an effort to close the gap, state-supported initiatives for raising standards and measuring student achievement will require schools to change what and how they teach. The "fewer, clearer, higher" Common Core State Standards (CCSS), anchored by the "next generation assessments" (NGA), will significantly raise the bar for most states to help ensure that every student is challenged to achieve and succeed. Proficiency levels will be set higher. Assessment will measure not just what students know but also what they can *do* with that knowledge. Most schools involved with Race to the Top (RttT) initiatives will need awareness building, planning, time, and support to realize the mandatory 2014–2015 implementation dates of the new learning expectations represented by the CCSS and NGA.

These challenges are driving a greater focus on accountability and a growing demand for proof of effectiveness and efficiency in public education. If *No Child Left Behind*'s Adequate Yearly Progress (AYP) provision laid accountability for results on the backs of principals, today's education policy, including measures such as growth models and teacher effectiveness evaluations, is shifting the burden of accountability to teachers. These shifts are consuming some of our most precious capacity: teachers and principals.

It Takes a System, Not Just a Teacher

Research supports what most of us see as common sense: What goes on between the teacher and the each student is central to high-level learning. Effective teaching is not the end goal, however; it is the means to an end: student achievement.

All teaching is more effective when it is effectively supported. Achieving the goal of improving instruction requires a supportive and aligned system. Stated another way: Although effective teaching is essential, it is not sufficient to maximize achievement for all students. This understanding of the need for an organization-wide commitment is at the heart of the DSEI, a framework for understanding how the key components of a successful school system work together to support leading, learning, and teaching. A clearer understanding of these critical components is critical to make the adjustments and changes needed to support rigorous, relevant learning.

DSEI

For decades, the International Center for Leadership in Education has been an active participant in education reform. The International Center's "on the ground" work with schools has reinforced the view that it takes an entire system to develop, enhance, and sustain effective instruction. Teachers can succeed only when they are supported by focused instructional leadership and organizational leadership.

The DSEI has been significantly informed by:

- **Observing and disseminating best practices.** This is the result of the International Center's 20 years of assisting leadership and teachers, as well as identifying, studying, and showcasing America's most successful schools — including the Successful Practices Network and CCSSO co-sponsored Bill and Melinda Gates Foundation-funded research on America's most effective and most rapidly improving exemplar schools and school districts — at the annual Model Schools Conference and other events.
- **Current and past research.** This has been conducted by some of the most respected thought-leaders in K–12 education, as described previously.

Components of the DSEI

The DSEI helps us envision the key systemic components of learning that must be aligned to improve student achievement. Effective instruction, based on clear, challenging standards and useful data indicating learner needs, establishes the path for student achievement. With that focus, the capacity of the entire system can collaborate for remarkable results — powerful teaching guided by precise instructional leadership and supported by coordinated organizational leadership.

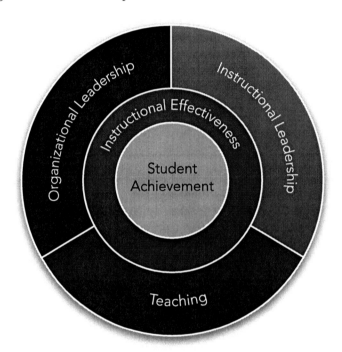

Organizational Leadership

Organizational leadership involves a mentality, structure, focus, and commitment to create the environment in which learning is optimized. The following elements of Organizational Leadership, are the important work of the school system that empowers strong instructional leadership and powerful teaching and learning.

Create a culture of high expectations that communicates and encompasses:

- *Why*: the challenges of changing demographics, a wired and tech-savvy generation of students growing up in a digital world, as well as a global economy in which America must innovate and compete
- *To Whom*: students, staff, and community stakeholders
- *How*: through active and ongoing communications and messaging at staff development events, community forums, and business roundtables

Create a shared vision. The district and school culture needs to be embedded in goals and action plans focused on instructional effectiveness and a common understanding of student success, not just as scholars but as future workers, citizens, consumers, and parents.

Build leadership capacity. Organizational leadership needs to support school leaders and to identify and cultivate the development of emerging future leaders.

Align organizational structures and systems to vision. Once culture, mission, and distributed and empowered leadership are established, Organization Leadership needs to:

- decide which external impediments to instructional effectiveness can be changed or compensated for, and which are beyond the control of the education organization.
- ensure that enabling conditions and structures to support instructional effectiveness are in place.
- identify which factors impacting effective instruction are most effective and efficient

Align teacher/administrator selection, support, and evaluation. Organizational Leadership's role is to adopt "talent management" systems for recruitment, retention, development, and evaluation that are focused on instructional effectiveness. These systems must also reinforce for all staff the instructional vision of the organization.

Support decision-making with data systems. Organizational Leadership needs to ensure that a realistic and efficient data system is used to inform and enhance instructional effectiveness. This includes building "data literacy" among all stakeholders as well as emphasizing the importance of data-driven decision-making.

A Systemwide Approach to Rigor, Relevance, and Relationships

Instructional Leadership

Instructional Leadership is not vested in a position; it is a "dis-position" shared by a like-minded array of staff. It is directly focused on instructional effectiveness and ultimately student achievement. Instructional Leadership can be provided by a variety of people and functions in support of teachers, including:

- principals and assistant principals
- department chairs and teacher leaders
- counselors and social workers
- mentor teachers, teacher coaches, teaching peers, and team leaders
- district and regional instructional leaders

The Instructional Leadership segment of the DSEI concentrates on five overarching elements:

Use research to establish urgency for higher expectations. The first job of Instructional Leadership is to reinforce the vision set forth by Organizational Leadership with research and authoritative testimony that corroborate the urgent need for improvement in student achievement.

Align curriculum to standards. Instructional leaders also need to prepare teachers for the new types of instruction and formative assessment that are at the heart of the Common Core State Standards (CCSS) and the related Next Generation Assessments (NGA).

Integrate literacy and math across all content areas. Literacy and math are the cornerstones of success in college and careers. The CCSS, with special emphasis in the English language arts standards placed on text complexity and nonfiction transactional reading and writing, emphasize the practical applications of literacy. All teachers at all grades and across all subjects need to assume responsibility for this heightened emphasis on broad-based literacy development. Similarly, the CCSS focus on the "Standards of Mathematical Practice," which include process standards such as problem solving, reasoning and proof, and "strands of mathematical proficiency" (including adaptive reasoning, strategic competence, conceptual understanding, procedural fluency, and productive disposition).

Facilitate data-driven decision-making to inform instruction. To meet the needs of diverse learners, teachers must be supported as they use data to measure student growth and to inform and differentiate instruction. Achieving this goal will involve providing teachers with a clearer understanding of student data and how to apply that understanding to actionable instruction and interventions.

5) Provide opportunities for focused professional collaboration and growth. The research clearly shows the importance of teacher selection and job-embedded, teacher-led professional development, along with a continuous cycle of evaluation and support. Professional development is one of the cornerstone "Four Assurances" in Race to the Top: "Recruiting, developing, rewarding, and retaining effective teachers and principals, especially where they are most needed."

Teaching

If Organizational Leadership does its job to establish an overarching vision and mission, to deal with obstacles, and to align systems and build leadership capacity; and if Instructional Leadership ensures that tools, data, and support are made available and accessible to teachers; then the vanguard of instructional effectiveness — teaching — will be well-supported in addressing the many challenges of the classroom.

Drawing on the research on teacher effectiveness and observations of best practices for two decades, the DSEI includes the following six broad elements of teaching:

Embrace rigorous and relevant expectations for all students. Teachers and school leaders must embrace the organizational vision that all students can and will learn and must work effectively together to help every student reach his or her fullest potential. This is the infectious attitude that effective administrators and teachers bring to school every day.

Build strong relationship with students. Research on the characteristics of successful schools shows that teacher-to-student relationships have a major impact on student achievement. The presence of strong, positive, trusting relationships impacts student engagement and therefore fuels students' sense of belonging and commitment to their own learning.

Possess depth of content knowledge and make it relevant to students. While teachers must have strong content expertise in the subjects they teach, effective instruction is more than just a transmittal of knowledge. It is equally the ability to make connections, show relevance, nurture engagement, and embed understanding. The new Common Core State Standards will require this same rigorous and relevant approach to teaching, and the Next Generation Assessments will require students to show their ability to apply higher-order thinking, not just recall of factual knowledge.

Facilitate rigorous and relevant instruction based on how students learn. Every teacher needs a thorough understanding of pedagogy as well as a versatile and comprehensive repertoire of instructional strategies so that they can match teaching approaches with learning objectives, subject matter, and the needs and interests of learners. Teachers also need a clear understanding of today's students who are "wired differently" — who want to see a reason for learning something; who take connectivity and instant access to information and to one another for granted; who multitask; and, perhaps most significantly, who would rather "do to learn" instead of "learn to do."

Demonstrate expertise in use of instructional strategies, technology, and best practices. Teachers must become comfortable and skillful in "wherever learning" strategies. In successful schools, learning takes place in many different ways and places — by completing an individual assignment, working in groups, sitting with a tutor, or learning online; via cell phones, interactive whiteboards, or computers; by completing a lesson with family members around the kitchen table, in a lab, in the gym or band room, at an outdoor education center, at a museum, on a field trip, or when interviewing a guest speaker. Instructional effectiveness extends far beyond the walls of the classroom.

The professional development needed to support teachers in today's learning environments will not be met with traditional workshops or unfocused staff development days. Teachers will need time and a safe environment to practice and develop the skills of effective instruction. Many will need coaches working with them in the classroom to model best practices. And we will have to figure out how to let the school technology experts — the students — lead the way!

Use assessments to guide and differentiate instruction. Good teachers always ask themselves: "Did they ALL get it? How do I know they got it? How do I measure mastery? How do I help those students who didn't? How do I know at any given point in the year if students are on track to achieve? John Hattie's meta-analysis research rates the use of formative assessment data to inform instruction as the number-one factor in instructional effectiveness — a rating of +0.90, or almost two full years of growth in a single year.

The DSEI departs from some of the existing models and frameworks for teaching in several significant ways.

Traditional Teaching Frameworks	DSEI
What teachers should do	What the entire system should do
Teacher-focused	Student-focused
Teachers deliver instruction	Teachers facilitate learning
Vision is set by top leaders	Vision is built more inclusively
Define vision primarily in terms of academic measures	Define vision as strong academics and personal skills and the ability to apply them
Rigid structures support adult needs	Flexible structures support student needs
Focus on teaching	Focus on learning

Other models are excellent guides and tools for what they choose to focus upon, primarily teachers' professional development, mastery of content, and use of instructional strategies.

By comparison, the DSEI's most distinguishing attributes include:

- focus on coherence and alignment at the system/organization level
- focus on instructional leadership grounded in a broad base of analysis and meta-analysis research on instructional effectiveness
- balancing effectiveness with considerations of efficiency (e.g., affordability)
- best practices drawn from partnering with model schools
- a clear focus on rigorous, relevant instruction and student learning

The DSEI leverages more than the teacher in the classroom. It emphasizes vertical alignment (with organizational systems and structures and with instructional leadership) and horizontal alignment (with teaching colleagues and classroom resources) as keys to success. Because teachers are the most powerful influence on instruction, the entire system needs to be focused on making teachers effective. The DSEI provides a coherent focus across an entire education system: Organizational Leadership, Instructional Leadership, and Teaching.

A Systemwide Approach to Rigor, Relevance, and Relationships

To summarize, the DSEI is more than an approach to enhancing instruction and instructional capacity. It is a way of thinking about what we believe about children, schools, and learning that has coalesced at a critical time in American education — a time when standards, assessments, accountability, teacher evaluation systems are intersecting with budgets, the global economy, technological innovation, "wired kids," and public policy debates.

The DSEI builds upon the ideas, inspirations, practices, and research of others, including the best research and meta-analysis on effective instruction and the years of collective experience that International Center staff, consultants, and thought leaders have accumulated and harvested from thousands of American schools. It recognizes the primacy and immeasurable value of great teachers and great teaching and strives to align education systems and functions with what teachers need to be the best support to learners. It does so not only by looking at teachers but also by looking beyond the classroom to inspire leadership at all levels in support of instruction and by challenging all educators to consider what could be with a sense of practical urgency and a buoyant sense of the possible.

The DSEI is a tool to transform a traditional system into one that better supports all teachers and more fully prepares every student for college, careers, and citizenship.

Review Questions

1. In what ways have your professional experiences reinforced the validity of the idea that "it takes a system, not just a teacher"?
2. Does your school culture focus on student achievement as its focus?

Chapter 2

DSEI and the 21ˢᵗ Century 3R's: Rigor, Relevance, and Relationships

From a Student Perspective

Tony Wagner, co-director of the Change Leadership Group at Harvard University's Graduate School of Education, has an interesting perspective on rigor, relevance, and relationships — and it draws on some thinking about learning and teaching from a student's perspective. Wagner tells about his work with a group of administrators, in which he responds to a question on defining *rigor, relevance, and relationships* by initiating a process in which the group of administrators defined those three concepts through collaborative thinking and discussion. In doing so, they began to see weaknesses in the common assumption of defining *rigor*:

> Rigor in the classroom, we began to see, was invariably tied to the larger questions of what society will demand of students when they graduate, what it means to be an educated adult, and how the skills needed for work, citizenship, and continuous learning have changed fundamentally in the last quarter-century.

Wagner described how the group of administrators, who were working together at a week-long institute, continued to find agreement on a working definition of *rigor* and to develop a rubric that they could use in classroom walk-throughs so they would "know it when we saw it."

For the next several days, we conducted learning walks in each of the six principals' schools, K–12. At the end of our 2-hour visits in each school, we debriefed every class we'd visited in terms of whether we thought the class was high, medium, or low rigor and why. After a remarkable two days of work together, the group had calibrated their classroom assessments to the point where there was now frequent alignment among the group about the level of rigor in the classes we observed, as well as discussions about what each principal might say to the teacher to create a more challenging class. Along the way, we had substantially modified our rigor rubric as well. We began to realize that rigor has less to do with how demanding the material is that the teacher covers than with what competencies students have mastered as a result of a lesson.

Seven questions emerged from this work, as Wagner reported in *Education Week* on January 11, 2006. These questions clearly show how a laser-like focus on rigor, relevance, and relationships can bring a whole new purpose and meaning to instruction, both for students and for teachers. The seven questions asked of students are:

- What is the purpose of this lesson?
- Why is this important to learn?
- In what ways am I challenged to think in this lesson?
- How will I apply, assess, or communicate what I have learned?
- How will I know how good my work is, and how I can improve it?
- Do I feel respected by other students in this class?
- Do I feel respected by the teacher in this class?

Wagner and the group of administrators he was working with that week concluded that their work had to change significantly, both at the building level and the district level, if they were going to inspire, transform, lead, and support powerful learning in every classroom, learning that empowers students to experience rigorous, relevant instruction based on meaningful relationships among students and their teachers. Wagner and his institute colleagues agreed that . . .

... meetings at every level had to be more than just for "housekeeping." The principal's or superintendent's meetings are his or her "classroom" and must be models of rigor. And so the group committed to replicating the discussions of what is rigor with their faculty and to a new way of working together. Instead of meeting occasionally for a quick catch-up over breakfast, as had been the case, Art and his principals now meet for a half-day a month in one another's schools on a rotating basis, to conduct learning walks and to present and discuss real case studies related to strengthening rigorous instruction in their schools.

In this chapter we will take a closer look at the concepts of rigor, relevance, and relationships and how they can become the focus of a systemwide effort to transform and sustain effective leading, teaching, and learning. We will use the DSEI as the lens to view the systemic components of a district-level and school-level focus and will identify a set of tools that can be used effectively and efficiently to support a transformation of the 3R's.

The 21st Century 3R's

Since its inception in 1991, the International Center for Leadership in Education's core belief has been that what students need to succeed in the 21st century is an education that is both academically rigorous and has "real-world" relevance. This objective of rigor and relevance is not just for some students; it is for all students. The current context of school reform, as driven by the *No Child Left Behind Act of 2001*, places the International Center for Leadership in Education ahead of its time in gauging the essential goal of public education. As schools and teachers struggle to cope with new accountability requirements, one thing is clear: Simply working harder or doing what we have always done will not yield higher student achievement. Achieving different results requires taking a different approach.

While we often hear the call for rigor and relevance, frequently leaders are adding a third "R" and calling for schools that aspire to "rigor, relevance, and relationships." This is more than a nice alliteration or an updating of the original 3Rs — reading, 'riting, and 'rithmetic. Increasingly, we are recognizing that relationships are critically important to learning.

Relationships do not become a new standard but a way to improved learning and a means to the end of high achievement. The recent work of the International Center has examined some of the most successful high schools in the country — schools that have the challenges of poverty, mobility, and diversity but that still have high rates of student success. In these schools, it is clear that relationships among students and staff are deliberately nurtured and are a key reason for their success. Students feel that the staff genuinely cares about them and encourages them to achieve at high levels. Experience in working with these schools indicates that when schools raise student expectations, they also need to focus on the quality of relationships and support for students. If there is not a high level of positive relationships, students will not respond to higher expectations.

How do you know that high-quality, positive student-teacher relationships exist? The *WE SURVEYS*™ suite was developed by the International Center in partnership with the Successful Practices Network to address questions like this. The surveys focus on leadership, rigor, relevance, and relationships. The *WE SURVEYS*™ are easy-to-use tools that ask students, staff, and community members to share their perceptions anonymously about the learning environment, quality of instruction, and leadership in a school or district.

Aggregate data from the WE™ LEARN Student Survey and the WE™ TEACH Instructional Staff Survey provide insight into perceptions from students and instructional staff on the academic interests and goals of students. For example, the correlated survey responses from students and their teachers in the example below reveals a significant gap in perceptions about a critical aspect of student-teacher relationships. Understanding this data and its implications is a first step in providing relevant instruction linked to student interests.

Percent Agree	Item	Survey
37%	My teachers know my academic interests and goals.	WE™ LEARN Student Survey, Grades 6–12
80%	I know my students' academic interests and goals.	WE™ TEACH Instructional Staff Survey

Through using the *WE Surveys*, leadership teams can analyze data, discuss perceptions, and make decisions on next steps. These qualitative tools can help teachers, administrators, and other staff explore vocabulary and align perceptions on definitions for rigor, relevance, and relationships.

Chapter 2: DSEI and the 21st Century 3R's: Rigor, Relevance, and Relationships

Developing and Sustaining a Systemwide Focus on the 3R's

With the components of the DSEI as a guide, district and school leaders can establish an overarching vision and mission of high expectations, deal with obstacles, align systems, and build leadership capacity at all levels of the system. Using the components of the DSEI's Instructional Leadership component to set the agenda for action, district and school leaders can ensure that tools, data, and support are made available and accessible to building-level leaders and teachers. By establishing these foundational conditions, school leaders can begin to empower teachers and provide the leadership and support to bring rigor, relevance, and meaningful relationships alive in the classroom.

Many successful school districts have used the DSEI teaching elements to lay out a roadmap for a systemwide focus on rigor and relevance. They have provided strong and persistent leadership to set the tone for all to **embrace rigorous and relevant expectations for all students.** Leaders in those districts have developed a culture and climate of trust as they have encouraged all teachers to **build strong relationships with students.** They provide ongoing coaching and support to ensure that all teachers **possess depth of content knowledge and make it relevant to students.**

Successful districts support the effective use of formative assessment data and targeted coaching on differentiated instruction to help teachers **facilitate rigorous and relevant instruction based on how students learn.** Professional development in successful systems that seek rigorous and relevant learning is much more than periodic staff development days and a focus on topics and workshops. They develop capacity and create systems of job-embedded, teacher-led ongoing support that enables teachers to **demonstrate expertise in use of instructional strategies, technology, and best practices.** And successful districts and schools understand that timely, efficient data fuels learning as they **use assessments to guide and differentiate instruction.**

A Closer Look at the Power of Rigor, Relevance, and Relationships in 21st Century Learning

Never in the history of mankind have we seen the magnitude of change that we have experienced in the past quarter of a century. As we considered in Chapter 1, children and young people in our schools are experiencing a school curriculum, pedagogy, and environment that closely resembles what their great-grandparents experienced 100 years ago.

One might make the case that we are actually getting much better student achievement results than should be expected, given that reality.

American social philosopher Eric Hoffer said, "In times of change, learners inherit the Earth, while the learned find themselves beautifully equipped to deal with a world that no longer exists." As we prepare to lead schools and school systems to powerful implementation of rigorous and relevant instruction, it is essential that we have a deeper understanding of the critical factors that make such a transformation imperative. Let's take a look at seven of those factors and examine the implications for this focus on rigor, relevance, and relationships. The seven factors are:

- A Changing World
- Need for Motivating All Students to High Achievement
- Emphasis on Essential Skills/Knowledge
- Shift in Focus from Teaching to Learning
- Reduction of Overloaded Curriculum
- Unified Perspective and Focus
- Preparation for State Tests

A Changing World

Recent advances in science and technology are mind-boggling. Three areas of technological change that have far-reaching implications are information technology, biotechnology, and nanotechnology. While technological innovations bring many benefits, there is little argument that they add to the complexity of our world and increase the skill level that every person needs to function effectively in our society.

It is impossible to forecast exactly where the future will take us. However, it is obvious that as technology continues to evolve, it will alter the workplace and our homes, personal lives, and education systems.

High school graduation must be viewed not as the end of learning, but as the jumping-off point for a lifetime of experiences that will involve both acquiring new knowledge and applying existing knowledge to new situations. This realization provides an even greater sense of urgency for teachers to make learning relevant through technology. It is lifelong learning skills that will help students make informed and intelligent decisions regarding the direction and limitations of technological developments, the use of technology to alter their own lives, and other major financial, professional, and personal questions that they will undoubtedly face. These skills cannot be taught as discrete topics; rather, students learn them through high-quality, challenging lessons that are based on real-world problems and are unbounded by separate school subjects.

Need for Motivating All Students to High Achievement

One of the barriers to higher achievement that teachers cite most often is that students lack motivation to learn what is being taught. The problem might be better defined as lack of student involvement or engagement in the learning experiences being offered. A telling piece of research was published in *The Condition of Education 2002*. This report from the National Center for Educational Statistics reported on student perceptions of meaningful schoolwork, interest of courses, and whether school learning will be important in later life. (See the following bar graph.) To understand the shrinking percentages, we must recognize the changes that have occurred in schools over that time. Since A *Nation at Risk* appeared in 1983, there has been a continual introduction of new requirements as part of an ongoing effort to raise standards. It appears that the result at the high school level has been to make learning less interesting, less meaningful, and less connected to students' perception of the future.

In the spring of 2005, the National Governors Association surveyed teenagers as part of a policy initiative on high schools. More than 10,000 completed the *Rate Your Future* surveys nationwide. In this large sample, more than one third called high school "easy." Two in three students agreed with the statement "I would work harder if high school offered more demanding and interesting courses." More than 70% thought that taking courses related to the kinds of jobs they wanted was the best way to make their senior year more meaningful.

By interviewing and/or surveying students and staff in your school, you can confirm the connection between relevance and student engagement. Students consistently indicate that they do not work as hard as they are capable of doing if they fail to see the relevance of what they are learning. By looking at teaching and learning from the perspective of relevance as well as rigor, and by emphasizing hands-on learning, we can engage students in meaningful and challenging work. Rigorous and relevant instruction motivates students to learn.

Emphasis on Essential Skills/Knowledge

Too often teachers answer a student who asks, "Why do I need to learn this?" with the glib "Because I had to learn this stuff, and now it's your turn" or with the equally weak "You will understand later in life why this is important." Some skills are important for all students to learn in school; but many topics, taught out of tradition or teacher interest, are of lesser importance. Students need to understand what is truly important for them to learn. Teachers need to provide a relevant contextual base for the knowledge and skills they teach to their students. Education is meaningless when it is reduced to an unending list of content topics for which the student quickly learns the facts, takes the test, and then forgets it all. Focusing on a narrower list of priority skills and knowledge makes the importance of learning these things clear.

Rigorous and relevant instruction presents projects and problems that are related to the context. When students experience a problem in context, they are more likely to make connections and thus see the value in what they are learning. Relevance makes rigor possible.

Shift in Focus from Teaching to Learning

In a discussion of low or inadequate student achievement, some teachers lay the blame completely on the students. Teachers who feel this way believe that they are doing a good job. They feel that if the lesson is clear in their minds, organized well, and presented completely, then they have done their job.

This narrow perspective fails to recognize that learning, like communication, is not a one-way street. There is no communication if one person presents a message and no one listens or understands. Healthy communication requires foundational relationships between the parties involved. Communication is most effective when another person listens, understands, and then applies what was heard.

Teaching involves demonstrating skills and presenting knowledge, but learning does not occur until students engage and understand. One of the most powerful ways to change what happens in the classroom is for teachers to think about planning instruction from the perspective of student learning.

An easy way to enable teachers to embrace this perspective is to design student work in the form of problems and projects that link standards and benchmarks from multiple disciplines. By taking this approach, teachers are more likely to shift their focus and think in terms of student learning rather than focusing on teaching.

> WE™ TEACH Instructional Staff Survey: Staff are expected to do interdisciplinary planning and projects. 63% agree.

Reduction of Overloaded Curriculum

Several large-scale studies have confirmed what many educators already know: The curriculum in the majority of U.S. schools is overcrowded. The Third International Mathematics and Science Study (TIMSS) and the International Center for Leadership in Education are among the organizations that have published reports on the subject.

In the most comprehensive effort to quantify the extent of the problem, researchers at Mid-continent Research for Education and Learning (McREL) compiled a comprehensive list of standards and benchmarks found in the major national standards documents. Across all subjects and grades, they identified 200 unique standards, with 3,093 related benchmarks. They then obtained estimates from teachers on how long it would take to teach each benchmark adequately. The researchers calculated that it would take 15,465 hours to cover all of the standards and benchmarks; however, the most generous estimate of the instructional time that students have during their academic careers is 9,042 hours.

Based on these findings, it would appear that although the standards and assessments being put into place across the country are intended to bring structure and clarity to school curricula, they often do just the opposite. In an effort to be comprehensive, far too many topics are labeled "essential," blurring the distinction between high-priority and low-priority topics. Districts, schools, and teachers must make this distinction themselves and attempt to filter the topics that are truly essential from those that are simply nice to know.

> WE™ TEACH Instructional Staff Survey: I spend too much time reteaching what students should already know. 48% agree

The recent national curriculum changes are working to provide a "less is more" approach. The Common Core State Standards are requiring teachers to provide meaning to learners in a more concise and streamlined approach throughout grades K–12. The Common Core Mission states:

> The Common Core State Standards provide a consistent, clear understanding of what students are expected to learn, so teachers and parents know what they need to do to help them. The standards are designed to be robust and relevant to the real world, reflecting the knowledge and skills that our young people need for success in college and careers. With American students fully prepared for the future, our communities will be best positioned to compete successfully in the global economy. (http://www.corestandards.org)

To focus in on what is essential for students, the International Center for Leadership in Education encourages districts to develop and analyze data to answer two questions: "What do students need to know to succeed in life?" and "What do students need to know to succeed on the test?" If a topic fulfills either of these needs, it can rightfully be labeled a high priority. If it meets neither, schools and districts need to reexamine whether it is worth the investment of scarce instructional time.

Administering the WE™ LEARN Student Survey and WE™ TEACH Instructional Staff Survey can help provide a comprehensive approach to gauging perceptions about how well a school is focused on rigor, relevance, and relationships.

Once priorities are set, using strategies such as project-based instruction and inquiry creates learning experiences that can include several standards, thus enabling schools to use time more efficiently to develop students' competence in standards. By using well-designed projects, a teacher can include multiple standards within a single lesson. This also allows for more in-depth instruction and reduces the superficial efforts of "covering" topics with little student retention.

Unified Perspective and Focus

One weakness in many schools is that teaching, testing, school improvement, and resources emphasize different skills and knowledge. A school may have highly qualified teachers, good assessments, abundant technology and library resources, and extensive professional development, but the sum of all of these parts may not lead to high levels of student achievement. Schools need to do more than create the components of effective schools; they must have all of these parts working in alignment and emphasizing similar perspectives. Applying the concepts and levels of rigor and relevance is useful in bringing curriculum, instruction, and assessments into alignment.

Moreover, any organization is more successful when all of its activities focus on a goal and all of its functions are aligned with achieving that goal. Research has shown that the most effective schools have a laser-like focus on curriculum. This unity is easiest to accomplish in elementary schools, since most teachers are common branch teachers. In middle school and high school, however, teachers lack a common teaching situation, and they are deeply immersed in their own subjects. It is difficult for teachers of mathematics, science, and English language arts to share a narrowly focused, common objective. Still, a school can embrace a common focus that cuts across subject areas with rigor and relevance that applies to all subjects.

Preparation for State Tests

The expansion of high-stakes testing programs over the last decade has led many teachers to "teach to the test." Some have criticized this focus as detrimental to "real" learning. However, teaching to the test is not bad — if the test is a good one. States are working to make the tests more criterion-referenced, better aligned with state standards, more valid, and free of bias. These tests are also becoming more difficult, and efforts are underway to create questions that demand complex thinking. The Partnership for Assessment of Readiness for College and Careers (PARCC; parcconline.org) and the Smarter Balanced Assessment Consortium (smarterbalanced.org) are among the groups currently working to provide assessments for the Common Core State Standards. These exams will require higher levels of thinking and application knowledge for students.

There is a common misconception that state tests include only low-level recall multiple-choice questions. The International Center for Leadership in Education's review of these tests has revealed that many do include complex questions, high rigor, and application of knowledge. With the adoption of CCSS and NGA, teachers will need to teach to higher levels of rigor and relevance in order to prepare students for the expectation set by those tests.

> WE™ TEACH Instructional Staff Survey: I use performance-based assessments to reflect how well my students have learned. 88% agree

Schools Not Meeting Student Needs

The challenges of a changing economy and society have been recognized for quite some time. How well have schools responded?

In response to the 1983 publication of *A Nation at Risk*, virtually every state raised its graduation requirements and beefed up its testing program. "Back to basics" was a frequent rallying cry. These efforts, however, concentrated on the same academic, theoretical, abstract teaching areas that had caused the education crisis in the first place. What is taught in schools and the way instruction is organized and delivered often do little to prepare students to assume their adult responsibilities.

The organization of U.S. schools and the U.S. culture itself has become the biggest obstacle to school reform and higher standards. Offering discrete courses taught in isolation, with little connection to other subjects or other learning may be compatible with teacher training and certification, but it bears no resemblance to the integrated way that we use knowledge in life. Furthermore, as a society we have come to view getting students ready for college as the primary goal of schooling. Yet, every year the level of skills needed for employment climbs, while requirements for college entry stay the same — or even diminish — in years when demographics produce a dip in the number of high school graduates and many colleges struggle to fill seats.

One result of a school system that focuses almost exclusively on preparing students for the next grade or level of education is a preoccupation with sorting students. The culture of U.S. schools is to sort and compare students to identify the "brightest." Schools have paid so much attention to comparing students to the average that few have noticed that standards are too low. Ranking at or near the top of the class does students little good if they do not have the skills to compete in modern society. Today, all students need high levels of skills and knowledge to succeed in adult life. Schools must develop a culture of excellence that challenges every student to achieve rigorous and relevant standards.

Teaching through application is a very effective way to engage more students in pursuit of higher standards and to ensure that graduates can use what they have learned. When students see the relevance of what they are learning, they are more motivated to learn. Research has also shown that people retain more of what they have learned by doing instead of by reading or listening. It is not just higher standards that are needed, but the right standards. More emphasis needs to be placed on looking at the specific skills and knowledge that students must acquire.

Chapter 2: DSEI and the 21st Century 3R's: Rigor, Relevance, and Relationships

Every core subject has applications to the real world, yet too often these subjects are reduced to a textbook-driven memorization of facts. Science, for example, is about understanding the natural world. It seems logical that experiences in a science curriculum should give students the direct opportunity to use science skills to make observations in and about the real world. However, memorizing tables and taxonomies and moving through the chapters in a textbook are the more typical activities found in a science classroom.

Relationships

Importance of Relationships

Schools are not simply buildings, curriculum, textbooks, or assessments; schools are about people. Students, teachers, parents, support staff, and administrators work together to create a place of learning called school. In reference to people, we often talk about the importance of finding or developing talented school leaders and teachers who are "high quality." However, having the best people is not sufficient. The International Center's examination of successful model schools shows clearly that relationships among people are what make schools effective.

Education leaders are discussing relationships in schools more frequently. In *Leading in a Culture of Change*, Michael Fullan offers insight into the importance of relationships and explains that leaders must connect with people and lead them toward change. Tom VanderArk, former Director of Education Initiatives for the Bill & Melinda Gates Foundation and current CEO of Open Education Solutions, promotes schools aspiring to develop "rigor, relevance, and relationships," as the foundation supports large urban school districts in creating smaller learning communities.

Ronald F. Ferguson, a lecturer and senior research associate at Harvard, is the creator and director of the Tripod Project. The Tripod Project examines curriculum, pedagogy, and relationships, as well as their impact on student achievement. Ferguson states, "The special importance of encouragement highlights the likely importance of strong teacher-student relationships in affecting achievement, especially for African-American and Hispanic students." Relationships may hold the key for reducing the achievement gap in this country.

School improvement is driven by various experts in government, business, and education who try to ensure that all students achieve high levels of learning. These improvement efforts focus on standards, curriculum, student assessments, accountability measures, classroom management practices, use of technology, instructional strategies, decision-making processes, and school leadership. These improvement efforts are necessary, but they may not be sufficient to create really great schools, particularly great schools that sustain achievement over the years.

The International Center's examination of high-performing high schools provides rich examples of schools that are great not only because of their practices in improvement efforts but also because of the quality of relationships in the school. Having positive relationships in schools will not, by itself, create high levels of student achievement. However, these relationships are critically important, for relationships make rigor and relevance possible. Rigor requires students to make a substantial personal investment in their own learning. Students involved in rigorous learning are deeply engaged in thought, critical analysis, debate, research, synthesis, problem solving, and reflection.

The High School Survey of Student Engagement offers teachers and administrators actionable information on school characteristics that shape the student experience. In 2004 and 2005, HSSSE polled 200,000 students from high schools in 29 states. Since it is a national survey, it provides baseline data to compare student's perceptions in your school with others nationwide. Here are some of the results:

- More than half (52%) had not discussed ideas with a teacher outside of class during the year.
- Three-fifths (60%) had not communicated with a teacher by e-mail.
- However, 70% agreed that they had many opportunities to ask questions about their work.
- Less than half (48%) had frequently discussed grades or assignments with a teacher.
- Half never or only sometimes received feedback on assignments from teachers.

Impact of Relationships on Student Learning

The Tripod Project, introduced earlier in this chapter, examined the impact of curriculum, pedagogy, and relationships on student achievement in approximately 20 schools. The project report shows the results of student surveys used at the elementary and high school levels to assess the levels of student support and teacher expectations.

In *Finding Out What Matters for Youth*, Michelle Gambone and her team from Youth Development Strategies, Inc., examined whether higher levels of student support contributes to higher levels of student engagement and achievement. The results indicate that teacher support is important to student engagement in school. Students who perceive teachers to be creating caring, well-structured learning environments in which expectations are high, clear, and fair are more likely to have greater developmental outcomes.

Relevance

Relevancy Leads to High Achievement

Research in many aspects of physiology as well as education reinforces the importance of using application instruction as a means of raising student achievement.

Modern technology enables biologists, medical researchers, and cognitive scientists to research and better understand how the human brain functions and how people learn. This fascinating exploration of brain neurons and synapses gives physiological documentation to many of the practices of good teaching.

The brain is stimulated through the senses. When teachers create learning experiences that embody new sights, sounds, and manipulations, more learning will occur. The brain records these many stimulations but retains them only as a result of rehearsal, practice, or connection to other knowledge and experience.

Children utilize language and develop patterns of learning very young. Research confirms that the brains of children ages 4–10 are much more active than when children are older. The foundations of learning are therefore established at an early age for students. If high-quality learning does not occur then, later learning will be stunted.

The old adage of learning best by experience is really true. Recent research confirms that more learning occurs when students are immersed in a rich, stimulating environment. Learning that involves a physical component, such as writing or design and construction, results in greater brain activity than occurs simply by listening or viewing. To be effective, education must create these types of stimulating learning experiences. As Renate Nummela Caine has said, "Children learn best if they are immersed in complex experiences and are given the opportunity to actively process what they have learned."

When a student cannot recall a new piece of information, it is because that information never made it into long-term memory. Research confirms that there is a process for converting short-term memory to long-term memory. Research also shows that greater learning takes place when students are challenged and engaged in their learning. Too often, according to Caine and Caine, the rote teaching of facts leads to students becoming intellectually disengaged from the learning process; the brain stops learning. This finding does not mean that students should not be required to memorize information, but that it needs to be done in a manner that keeps students interested, which is often through real-world, integrated tasks.

Application results in better learning. The compilation of research in communication and learning by William Glasser reinforces something that we all know innately: We retain information better when we actually use it.

Students retain 75% or more of what they experience through application. Gathering new information only through lecture results in a retention rate of 5%. Reading can increase that rate to 10%, and adding audiovisual material results in a 20% retention rate. These are the instructional practices applied in most U.S. classrooms. Application of learning is not only a worthy learning objective but also an effective route to greater retention of knowledge and higher levels of learning.

Students in U.S. classrooms have limited exposure to application. In this country, the term *applied* is often used in conjunction with lower-level, less-demanding courses. Parents and educators in search of high-level courses avoid anything that is described as "application." Likewise, teachers do not attempt to include application in instruction.

Other nations, however, equate application with high-level learning and frequently incorporate real-world problems into instruction. Stevenson and Stigler have pointed out the significant international differences in this area. Analysis of William Glasser's The Quality School classroom instruction revealed that only 16% of instruction in a sample of U.S. classrooms could be characterized as application. In contrast, instruction in Taiwan and Japan was 62% and 82% real-world applications, respectively. Contrary to perceptions in the United States, application instruction does not mean a lack of rigor. In the most comprehensive study to date on a comparison of achievement of students across nations, TIMSS tested 500,000 students in 1995 and 1996. The study also compared textbooks and instructional practices. The curriculum analysis component is published in *A Splintered Vision*.

In *Characterizing Pedagogical Flow*, the authors made this observation about U.S. classrooms:

> Subject matter content in general appeared to be represented in more theoretical, abstract, and procedural form rather than represented in practical situations or related to students' experiences.

Chapter 2: DSEI and the 21st Century 3R's: Rigor, Relevance, and Relationships

Research on the tens of thousands of students who drop out of school annually in this country shows that their main reason for leaving is not that they lack the intellectual skills to do the work; it is that they see no connection between what goes on in school and their future. If we are to reach all students to help them develop the level of skills and knowledge that will provide them greater future opportunities, we must make those connections between education and the real world.

Stevenson and Stigler have pointed out that one of the obvious differences among international systems is that U.S. education does not have a tradition of valuing learning through application. Close examination shows significantly higher levels of application in European and Asian classrooms. It is therefore no surprise that U.S. students do not fare well on international tests that emphasize application. U.S. 8th-graders ranked 28th in math and 17th in science on the 1996 TIMSS.

Carefully planned instruction that is aligned with academic standards and taught in a context that interests students leads to greater relevance of instruction. When instruction is more relevant, it not only increases student interest but also helps to deepen student learning through application. When students experience relevant applications, they are better able to retain skills and knowledge and demonstrate proficiency at a later time.

The national curriculum effort in interdisciplinary instruction is High Schools That Work (HSTW), sponsored by the Southern Regional Education Board. This program encourages the adoption of practices that include incorporating academic skills in career and technical instruction, active student learning, and teacher collaboration. Research found evidence to support the hypothesis that meeting curricular goals is related to meeting achievement goals: A higher percentage of students in a school meet the achievement goals when more students complete integrated instruction. HSTW detailed research that continues to show that teachers who use best practices in relating concepts to the real world contribute to higher student achievement.

Perhaps the most compelling research driving the need for application is that most students learn best when instruction emphasizes application, as Conrath reported in *Our Other Youth*. To assist students in achieving high standards, teachers must create learning environments that present students with challenging problems. This work must be aligned with their learning styles, so that they can demonstrate their knowledge and use their skills.

Adding to the research on the efficacy of more application in learning are the findings from community forums and focus groups of parents and business and community leaders. All of these groups expect high school graduates to use the knowledge that they acquire in school when they venture out into the world. Research shows that students learn more when they realize that what they are learning has a practical application to the world of work. Some research findings on how people learn and how to structure successful programs and schools are described briefly below.

Knowledge Is Best Acquired When Taught in Context

Brain research reinforces what many teachers observe: Students retain knowledge best when it is connected to other experiences. One of the key recommendations of the Committee on the Science of Learning states:

> Knowledge that is taught in a variety of contexts is more likely to support flexible transfer than knowledge that is taught in a single context. Information can become "context-bound" when taught with context-specific examples. When material is taught in multiple contexts, people are more likely to extract the relevant features of the concepts and develop a more flexible representation of knowledge that can be used more generally.

From 2004–2010, the International Center for Leadership in Education, in partnership with the Successful Practices Network and the Council of Chief State School Officers, examined 75 high-performing high schools throughout the country. Among the characteristics that defined these successful schools were extensive instruction in context and high degrees of relevancy. These schools were committed to having students acquire knowledge through contextual learning in many forms.

In the United States, with its exclusive focus on preparation for college, the term *applied* has become synonymous with *lower-level*. But the truth is that all students need to be taught not only theoretical and content knowledge but also ways to apply those theories and that content. Overwhelming evidence has established that the knowledge acquired in the typical U.S. school curriculum fails to equip students for the increasing rigors of the workplace.

Children become better problem solvers in direct relation to the opportunities they have to solve problems and to reflect on what did or did not work. Real-world problems do not come neatly packaged in predictable, easy-to-solve formats. We need to provide students with experience in grappling with problems that mirror the world beyond school.

Metacognition Is Essential for Continued Learning

In simple terms, metacognition occurs when a learner takes a new piece of information, examines its validity in relation to what else he or she knows about the subject, and then considers how it expands his or her understanding of the topic. Prior knowledge — including knowledge about one's own strengths and weaknesses and the demands of the task at hand — is important in determining performance.

Metacognition also includes self-regulation, the ability to orchestrate one's learning. Skills such as planning, monitoring success, and correcting errors when appropriate are all necessary for effective intentional learning. Often, metacognition takes place in classrooms, when students consider information and talk about its application. By talking about it, they are forced to think more deeply about the issue.

Interdisciplinary instruction and real-world problems encourage metacognition more than traditional subjects taught in isolation do. Traditionally, the teacher disseminates knowledge, and the students listen and perhaps take notes. Learning should be an active process; instead, many students spend the school day watching their teachers work. To make learning active requires teachers to change the way that they teach.

High Expectations Correlate with Achievement

Any effort to introduce interdisciplinary activities must simultaneously include high expectations for all students. Research shows that students will try to rise to the level of expectation established for them. For interdisciplinary education, this means having high expectations for students' performance in all of the concepts involved from each discipline.

Using interdisciplinary instruction creates learning experiences that can include several standards. This enables schools to use student time more efficiently to develop competence in standards. It also allows for more in-depth instruction and reduces the superficial efforts of "covering" all topics with little student retention.

Interdisciplinary instruction is not an experiment in alternative learning; it is a viable, deliberate strategy to better prepare students for success in an increasingly complex world. For many students, interdisciplinary instruction can also be part of the solution to achieving higher performance on state tests. Interdisciplinary instruction is also consistent with research on learning. It remains only for teachers to look beyond "the way they were taught" and do the right thing for students by giving them rigorous and relevant learning experiences.

Rigor

Rigor means that critical thinking takes place on a regular basis. Instruction should engage students in challenging coursework that stretches them to go beyond just understanding. Instructional staff should hold high expectations for all learners and provide the support they need to achieve.

Knowledge Taxonomy

There is a continuum of knowledge that describes the increasingly complex ways in which we think. The Knowledge Taxonomy is based on the six levels of Bloom's Taxonomy: (1) knowledge/awareness, (2) comprehension, (3) application, (4) analysis, (5) synthesis, and (6) evaluation.

In 2001 Bloom's Knowledge Taxonomy was updated and revised by Lorin Anderson, a student of Bloom's, and David Krathwohl, a colleague, to reflect the movement to standards-based curricula and assessment. Nouns in Bloom's original model were changed to verb forms (for example, *knowledge* to *remembering* and *comprehension* to *understanding*) and slightly reordered. We believe that the original Bloom's taxonomy as shown in our Rigor/Relevance Framework® clearly describes expectations for Quadrants A, B, C, and D. The revised Bloom's elevates the importance of Quadrants B and D and indicates how 21st century lessons should be built. We regard both the original and revised taxonomies as necessary and important.

The low end of this continuum involves acquiring knowledge and being able to recall or locate that knowledge in a simple manner. Just as a computer completes a word search in a word processing program, a competent person at this level can scan through thousands of bits of information in the brain to locate that desired knowledge.

The high end of the Knowledge Taxonomy labels more complex ways in which individuals use knowledge. At this level, knowledge is fully integrated into one's mind, and individuals can do much more than locate information: They can take several pieces of knowledge and combine them in both logical and creative ways. "Assimilation of knowledge" is a good way to describe this high level of the thinking continuum. Assimilation is often referred to as a higher-order thinking skill; at this level, the student can solve multi-step problems and create unique work and solutions.

A Fresh Approach

The Rigor/Relevance Framework, noted above, is a fresh approach to looking at curriculum standards and assessment. It is based on traditional elements of education, yet it encourages movement to application of knowledge instead of maintaining an exclusive focus on acquisition of knowledge.

The Rigor/Relevance Framework is easy to understand. With its simple, straightforward structure, it can serve as a bridge between school and the community. It offers a common language with which to express the notion of a more rigorous and relevant curriculum; and it encompasses much of what parents, business leaders, and community members want students to learn.

The Rigor/Relevance Framework is versatile: It can be used in the development of instruction and assessment. Likewise, teachers can use it to measure their progress in adding rigor and relevance to instruction. It can also help select appropriate instructional strategies to meet learner needs and higher achievement goals.

Defining Rigor

Rigor refers to academic rigor — learning in which students demonstrate a thorough, in-depth mastery of challenging tasks to develop cognitive skills through reflective thought, analysis, problem solving, evaluation, or creativity. Rigorous learning can occur at any school grade and in any subject. The Knowledge Taxonomy describes levels of rigor.

A versatile way to identify the level of rigor of curriculum objectives, instructional activities, or assessments is through the Knowledge Taxonomy Verb List. The Verb List can be used either to create a desired level of expected student performance or to evaluate the level of existing curriculum, instruction, or assessment.

A Systemwide Approach to Rigor, Relevance, and Relationships

Knowledge Taxonomy Verb List

Quadrant A Verbs	Quadrant B Verbs	Quadrant C Verbs	Quadrant D Verbs
calculate	adjust	analyze	adapt
choose	apply	categorize	compose
count	build	classify	conclude
define	collect	compare	create
describe	construct	conclude	design
find	demonstrate	contrast	develop
identify	display	debate	discover
label	dramatize	defend	explore
list	draw	diagram	formulate
locate	fix	differentiate	invent
match	follow	discriminate	modify
memorize	illustrate	evaluate	plan
name	interpret	examine	predict
point to	interview	explain	prioritize
recall	look up	express	propose
recite	maintain	generate	rate
record	make	infer	recommend
say	measure	judge	revise
select	model	justify	teach
spell	operate	prove	
view	play	research	
	practice	study	
	produce	summarize	
	relate		
	role-play		
	sequence		
	show		
	solve		
	tune		
	use		

During the creation of lesson plans and student objectives, selecting the proper word from the Knowledge Taxonomy Verb List can help to describe the appropriate performance. Simply start with a verb from the desired level and finish the statement with a description of that skill or knowledge area. The Verb List can also be used to evaluate existing lesson plans, assessments, and instructional experiences. Looking for verbs and identifying their level will give a good indication of the level of student performance in that instruction.

Defining Relevance

Relevance refers to learning in which students apply core knowledge, concepts, or skills to solve real-world problems. Relevant learning is interdisciplinary and contextual. Student work can range from routine to complex at any school grade and in any subject. Relevant learning is created, for example, through authentic problems or tasks, simulation, service learning, connecting concepts to current issues, and teaching others. The Application Model describes the levels of relevance.

Identifying the level of relevance of curriculum objectives and instructional activities is a little more difficult than determining the Knowledge Taxonomy level because there is no verb list. However, just as the Knowledge Taxonomy categorizes increasing levels of thinking, the Application Model describes increasingly complex applications of knowledge. Any student performance can be expressed as one of five levels of the Application Model.

Why Is This Useful?

One of the principles of effective learning is congruence among curriculum, instruction, and assessment. Make sure that levels of rigor and relevance are consistent throughout a lesson. For example, if a teacher has lofty curriculum objectives in Quadrant D (high rigor/high relevance) but develops instruction and assessments in Quadrant A (low rigor/low relevance), it is unlikely that students will achieve those high expectations. Similarly, if a teacher creates high-rigor instructional activities but uses a low-rigor assessment, the test will not be an accurate indication of what students have learned.

Use the Knowledge Taxonomy Verb List and the Application Model Decision Tree to draft, examine, and modify curriculum objectives, instructional activities, or assessments to get them to the desired level. The Knowledge Taxonomy Verb List lists verbs that can

A Systemwide Approach to Rigor, Relevance, and Relationships

be used to expand into objectives or test questions. The Application Model Decision Tree helps categorize draft objectives or test questions.

Rigor/Relevance Framework®

Knowledge Taxonomy		
6	Evaluation	
5	Synthesis	
4	Analysis	
3	Application	
2	Comprehension	
1	Knowledge/Awareness	

- C — Assimilation
- D — Adaptation
- A — Acquisition
- B — Application

Application Model

1. Knowledge in one discipline
2. Apply in discipline
3. Apply across disciplines
4. Apply to real-world predictable situations
5. Apply to real-world unpredictable situations

© International Center for Leadership in Education

Chapter 2: DSEI and the 21st Century 3R's: Rigor, Relevance, and Relationships

The Rigor/Relevance Framework has four quadrants. Quadrant A represents simple recall and basic understanding of knowledge for its own sake. Examples of Quadrant A knowledge are knowing that the world is round and that Shakespeare wrote *Hamlet*.

Quadrant C represents more complex thinking but still knowledge for its own sake. Quadrant C embraces higher levels of knowledge, such as knowing how the U.S. political system works and analyzing the benefits and challenges of the cultural diversity of this nation versus other nations.

Quadrants B and D represent action or high degrees of application. Quadrant B would include knowing how to use math skills to make purchases and count change. The ability to access information in wide-area network systems and the ability to gather knowledge from a variety of sources to solve a complex problem in the workplace are types of Quadrant D knowledge.

Each of these four quadrants can also be labeled with a term that characterizes the learning or student performance.

Quadrant A—Acquisition

Students gather and store bits of knowledge and information. Students are primarily expected to remember or understand this acquired knowledge.

Quadrant B—Application

Students use acquired knowledge to solve problems, design solutions, and complete work. The highest level of application is to apply appropriate knowledge to new and unpredictable situations.

Quadrant C—Assimilation

Students extend and refine their acquired knowledge to be able to use that knowledge automatically and routinely to analyze and solve problems and create unique solutions.

Quadrant D—Adaptation

Students have the competence to think in complex ways and to apply the knowledge and skills they have acquired. Even when confronted with perplexing unknowns, students are able to use extensive knowledge and skills to create solutions and take action that further develops their skills and knowledge.

Teaching and Learning in the Rigor/Relevance Framework

One way to think about the Rigor/Relevance Framework in day-to-day instruction is in terms of the roles that teachers and students take.

When instruction and expected student learning is in Quadrant A, the focus is on "teacher work." Teachers expend energy to create and assess learning activities — providing information, creating worksheets, and grading student work. The student is often a passive learner.

When the student expectation moves to Quadrant B, the emphasis is on the student doing real-world work. This student work is often more complicated than Quadrant A work, and it requires more time. Learning in Quadrant B is best described as "student work" because students are doing extensive real-world tasks.

When the learning is placed in Quadrant C, it is best described as "student think." In this quadrant, students are expected to think in complex ways — to analyze, compare, create, and evaluate.

The term that best describes Quadrant D activities is "student think and work." Learning in Quadrant D is more demanding, and it requires the student to think and work. Roles shift from the teacher-centered instruction in Quadrant A to student-centered instruction in Quadrants B, C, and D. Teachers still work in Quadrants B, C, and D, but their role is more as a coach or facilitator.

Another way to distinguish learning among the four quadrants is by looking at whether the students "got it right" in terms of how the work will be evaluated. When instruction is in Quadrant A, there is clearly a right answer. When the level of learning moves up into Quadrant C, often there is more than one "right" answer, and the teacher is looking for original work that reflects logical and rational thinking on the student's part. Quadrant C is about rational answers. When the learning is real-world in Quadrant B, instruction often involves having students follow a procedure to do some work, and the right answer requires doing the procedure correctly. In Quadrant D, where the student is working on complex real-world problems, results depend upon whether the student asked all the right questions in order to consider everything that should have been included in attacking the problem.

ICLE believes that when a system is focused on RRR, all students will achieve at high levels. Both rapidly improving schools and high-performing schools have had a relentless focus on RRR and continue to show success.

An example of student performance at various levels follows. Notice that each statement starts with a verb that comes from the appropriate section of the Knowledge Taxonomy Verb List. The expected achievement level for teaching about nutrition can vary, depending on the purpose of the instruction. If a teacher wants students only to acquire basic nutritional knowledge, a student performance set at Level 1 or Level 2 is adequate. If the instruction is intended to have a more significant impact on nutritional habits, then some of the objectives need to be similar to Levels 4–6.

Basic Nutrition

Level		Performance
1	Knowledge	Label foods by nutritional groups
2	Comprehension	Explain nutritional value of individual foods
3	Application	Make use of nutrition guidelines in planning meals
4	Analysis	Examine success in achieving nutrition goals
5	Synthesis	Develop personal nutrition goals
6	Evaluation	Appraise results of personal eating habits over time

Note that each of the levels requires students to think differently. Levels 4–6 require more complex thinking than do Levels 1–3.

Defining the level of relevance of curriculum objectives and instructional activities is a little more difficult than determining the Knowledge Taxonomy level because there is no verb list. However, just as the Knowledge Taxonomy categorizes increasing levels of thinking, the Application Model describes increasingly complex applications of knowledge. Any student performance can be expressed as one of five levels of the Application Model. The Application Model Decision Tree can assist in setting the desired level of expected student performance in application.

A Systemwide Approach to Rigor, Relevance, and Relationships

The Basic Nutrition example that follows is similar to the one in the Defining Rigor section in that it uses nutrition to describe student performance at various levels. Each level requires students to apply knowledge differently.

Similarly, the expected achievement level for teaching about nutrition can vary depending on the purpose of the instruction. If a teacher wants students only to acquire basic nutritional knowledge, a student performance set at Level 1 is adequate. If the instruction is intended to have a significant impact on nutritional habits, then some of the objectives need to be at Levels 4 and 5.

Basic Nutrition

Level	Performance
1 Knowledge in One Discipline	Label foods by nutritional groups
2 Application in One Discipline	Rank foods by nutritional value
3 Interdisciplinary Application	Make cost comparisons of different foods considering nutritional value
4 Real-World Predictable Situations	Develop a nutritional plan for a person with a health problem affected by food intake
5 Real-World Unpredictable Situations	Devise a sound nutritional plan for a group of 3-year-olds who are picky eaters

Chapter 2: DSEI and the 21st Century 3R's: Rigor, Relevance, and Relationships

Application Decision Tree

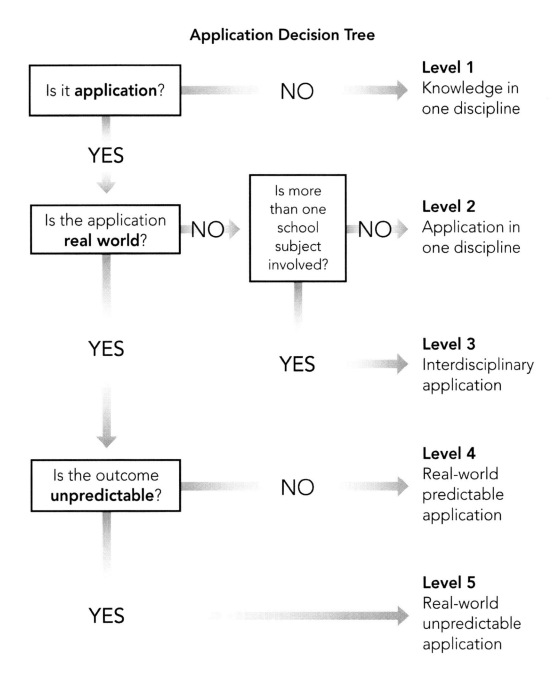

A Systemwide Approach to Rigor, Relevance, and Relationships

Application Decision Tree

Is it **application**?	**YES**	**NO**
	Requires use of knowledge	Requires only recall or understanding
	Requires students to actually use practice steps in a procedure	Requires learning steps in a procedure
	Uses previous knowledge to solve problems, create a design, or communicate information	Requires memorization of facts or formulas
	Asesses performance	Assess content knowledge

Is the application **real world**?	**YES**	**NO**
	Application occurs in same way it is used by adults	Application occurs only in school
	Standards for performance are same as for adult roles	Lower standards of performance are acceptable
	Students have access to real-world resources (tools, references, etc.)	Resources are limited
		Students have extended time to complete the task
	Task must be completed in same time frame as real-world	

Is the outcome **unpredictable**?	**YES**	**NO**
	Application has uncertain results	Application involves routine solution
	Unknown factors involved (environment, people, time)	Parameters are controlled
	Students have individual and unique solutions to problems	All students complete similar designs or solutions

© International Center for Leadership in Education

Chapter 2: DSEI and the 21st Century 3R's: Rigor, Relevance, and Relationships

What Does Rigor and Relevance Look Like in the Classroom?

On the following pages are a series of examples of learning activities organized according to the four quadrants of the Rigor/Relevance Framework. The charts cover four subjects: English language arts, mathematics, science, and social studies. Examples are provided at the elementary, middle, and high school levels.

As a general rule, remember:

- **Quadrant A — Acquisition:** Experiences focus on recall or discovery of basic knowledge.
- **Quadrant B — Application:** Activities provide definite opportunities for students to apply knowledge, typically to a real-world problem.
- **Quadrant C — Assimilation:** Activities are often complex, requiring students to come up with solutions that lead to deeper understanding of concepts and knowledge.
- **Quadrant D — Adaptation:** Learning experiences are high in rigor and relevance and require unique solutions to unpredictable problems.

A Systemwide Approach to Rigor, Relevance, and Relationships

English Language Arts

Student Activities in the Rigor/Relevance Framework

Elementary Examples

Quadrant C Assimilation

- Give and seek constructive feedback in order to improve writing.
- Role-play stories.
- Write a poem about yourself.
- Develop a WebQuest on learning language skills.
- Brainstorm as many words as possible to describe an object.
- Create and decipher coded messages.
- Describe mystery objects to partners to strengthen use of descriptions.
- Create word puzzles.

Quadrant D Adaptation

- Create new words to describe phenomena or objects.
- Publish a brochure.
- Design and create objects related to a children's book.
- Plan a family vacation trip.
- Research an issue and write a letter to the school board, elected official, or local newspaper.

Quadrant A Acquisition

- Create a drawing, picture, sign, or other graphic to represent a word or concept.
- Put words together in sentence format.
- Retell stories.
- Respond to oral directions.
- Participate in word games.
- Develop outlines from a nonfiction presentation.
- Memorize spelling words.
- Create a list of commonly misspelled words.

Quadrant B Application

- Record observations on a field trip.
- Use job-related tools or clothing to stimulate writing and drawing about a career.
- Read, analyze, and share content of local newspaper.
- Present a story through a computer graphics application.
- Communicate with e-mail pals in another country.
- Search newspapers for abbreviations and acronyms.
- Write factual stories of personal experiences.

© International Center for Leadership in Education

Chapter 2: DSEI and the 21st Century 3R's: Rigor, Relevance, and Relationships

English Language Arts

Student Activities in the Rigor/Relevance Framework

Middle Level Examples

Quadrant C Assimilation

- Play word games to identify specific language usage, such as figurative language.
- Research the history of words and phrases.
- Keep a journal of reflection on literature.
- Write a creative story, such as surviving in the wilderness.
- Create analogies to explain an idea.
- Analyze commercials for fact and opinion.
- Analyze a character in a novel.
- Create a new character in mythology.

Quadrant D Adaptation

- Create a Bill of Rights for your school or classroom.
- Write directions for assembling a product or carrying out a procedure.
- Create a rubric for evaluating writing assignments.
- Research and debate a controversial issue.
- Write a folk tale based on contemporary life.
- Analyze and rewrite political cartoons.

Quadrant A Acquisition

- View movies that depict human emotions and behaviors.
- Analyze sentences for parts of speech.
- Look up the definition of the "word of the day."
- Use library reference tools.
- Give an oral presentation.
- Read nonfiction or historical literature.
- Locate and describe technical writing.
- Act out characters in a story.

Quadrant B Application

- Conduct an interview.
- Conduct a meeting using parliamentary procedure.
- Conduct an Internet search.
- Write captions for cartoons.
- Lead a class discussion on a current event.
- Assemble a product following written directions.
- Write articles and headlines for a class newsletter.

© International Center for Leadership in Education

A Systemwide Approach to Rigor, Relevance, and Relationships

English Language Arts

Student Activities in the Rigor/Relevance Framework

High School Examples

6

Quadrant C Assimilation

- Compare and contrast literary styles of different authors.
- Relate literature to historical context.
- Discuss role of media in a democracy.
- Research limits of First Amendment freedoms.
- Analyze characters from a novel.
- Create a storyboard.
- Analyze and improve typical student writing.
- Role-play characters from literature in new situations.

5

4

Quadrant D Adaptation

- Write and perform a radio play.
- Simulate a presidential debate.
- Write a legal brief defending a school policy.
- Prepare a demonstration video.
- Review newspaper editorials for a week and write a letter to the editor expressing an opinion in response to one of them.
- Develop guidelines for publishing content on Internet pages.
- Develop a reading list of historical biographies for a middle level social studies course.

3

Quadrant A Acquisition

- Practice SAT vocabulary words.
- Select books and read to younger children.
- Read important works of literature.
- Give an extemporaneous speech.
- Learn several graphic organizers.
- Use word processing outlining and table tools.
- Write an essay on a historical topic.

2

1

Quadrant B Application

- Participate in a debate on a current political issue.
- Write a research report on a national problem.
- Identify and analyze typical body language traits.
- Create a personal or class Website.
- Research a career field.
- Use word processing software to write a business letter.
- Prepare a multimedia presentation.

1   2   3   4   5

Chapter 2: DSEI and the 21st Century 3R's: Rigor, Relevance, and Relationships

Mathematics — Student Activities in the Rigor/Relevance Framework — **Elementary Examples**

Quadrant C Assimilation

- Create a measurement scale (hand span, book, length of string, etc.) and measure objects in classroom.
- Predict and analyze patterns of sides of three-dimensional boxes.
- Use pattern blocks to construct desired shapes.
- Identify next numbers in a sequence.
- Find values in number sentences when represented by unknowns.
- Round off numbers and estimate answers.
- Use a balance to predict and determine equivalent value.
- Create math word problems for younger students.

Quadrant D Adaptation

- Develop formula for determining a large quantity without counting, such as beans in a jar.
- Calculate change of values to double or halve a recipe.
- Discover similar characteristics of different geometric solids.
- Collect data on an event and compare to expected results, such as the number of faulty parts manufactured.
- Evaluate situations when estimates are acceptable and unacceptable, e.g., paying for something vs. making a budget.

Quadrant A Acquisition

- Explore likenesses and differences of objects (color, shape, size).
- Sort and classify objects, such as buttons, blocks, bottle tops.
- Use color counters to solve simple computational problems.
- Divide objects to illustrate whole, half, third, quarter.
- Construct shapes and patterns with craft sticks.
- Memorize multiplication tables.
- Find the lines of symmetry in letters of the alphabet and numerals.
- Use pegboards to discover multiplied values.

Quadrant B Application

- Divide quantities of objects into equal groups.
- Calculate the area of objects.
- Make a graph comparing characteristics of two groups.
- Find patterns outdoors and indoors.
- Collect temperatures at different times of day for several days and make a graph to display recorded data.
- Use rulers to measure objects.
- Sort quantities to discover fractions of the whole.

A Systemwide Approach to Rigor, Relevance, and Relationships

Mathematics

Student Activities in the Rigor/Relevance Framework

Middle Level Examples

6

5

4

Quadrant C Assimilation

- Measure interior angles of polygons and discover the relationship between number of sides and sum of angles.
- Graph the perimeters and areas of squares of different sizes.
- Express probabilities as fractions, percents, or decimals.
- Evaluate equivalency and relationship of decimal and fractions.
- Determine the largest area for a fixed perimeter.
- Fill in missing numbers for ordered pairs for an algebraic function.
- Evaluate objects for similarity and congruence.
- Estimate sums of complex fractions.

Quadrant D Adaptation

- Hold a competition to determine when using a calculator or doing mental math is most efficient.
- Obtain historical data about local weather to estimate amount of snow, rain, or sun during a given season of the current year.
- Use graphing calculators and computer spreadsheets to organize and analyze data.
- Test consumer products, such as absorbency of paper towels, devise a scale, and illustrate data graphically.
- Plan a large school event and calculate resources (food, decorations, etc.) needed and costs.

3

2

1

Quadrant A Acquisition

- Select computational operation to solve word problems
- Calculate volume of regular solids.
- Measure angles with a protractor.
- Find and measure the sides and angles of a right triangle using the Pythagorean theorem and trigonometric ratios.
- Organize and display collected data, using tables, charts, or graphs.
- Use basic properties of equality to solve equations with one variable.
- Plot the coordinates for quadrilaterals on a grid.

Quadrant B Application

- Make a scale drawing of the classroom.
- Calculate percents of daily requirements met through a typical school lunch.
- Calculate potential combinations of a group of variables, such as wardrobe components, and estimate the probability of any one combination being picked at random.
- Calculate percentages of advertising in a newspaper.
- Play a simulated baseball game and calculate statistics.
- Calculate paint needed for a summer business painting houses.

1 2 3 4 5

Chapter 2: DSEI and the 21st Century 3R's: Rigor, Relevance, and Relationships

Mathematics — Student Activities in the Rigor/Relevance Framework — **High School Examples**

Quadrant C Assimilation

- Solve interdisciplinary problems with signed numbers, such as molecules with a charge of protons and electrons.
- Identify congruence of shapes from expressions and truth statements.
- Complete Euclidean proofs in geometry.
- Construct truth tables as a shorthand method for discussing logical sentences.
- Analyze factors in difference between theoretical and empirical probability.
- Select best measures of central tendency to support a particular point of view.
- Solve quadratic equations and linear inequalities.

Quadrant D Adaptation

- Determine types of measurements/calculations involved in designing everyday items.
- Make calculations of electrical load of appliances based on usage in homes in the community.
- Examine the different elements, visual effects, and features found in a computer game and use mathematics to design some of these elements.
- Create formulas to predict changes in stock market values.
- Design support posts of different materials and size to handle stress load in a building.
- Develop a sampling plan for a public opinion poll.
- Design a roller-coaster ride.

Quadrant A Acquisition

- Distinguish rational and irrational numbers
- Simplify, factor, and compute polynomials.
- Solve and graph linear equations.
- Create and solve factorial expressions for permutation problems.
- Construct and solve for unknowns in ratio problems.
- Compute numbers with scientific notation.
- Predict the probability of events using ratios.
- Bisect line segments and angles.
- Provide examples to illustrate properties of real numbers.

Quadrant B Application

- Draw Venn diagrams to represent a set of real conditions, e.g., common characteristics of students in class.
- Find length of line segments without measuring.
- Take measurements using calipers and micrometers.
- Calculate measurement error in real observations.
- Calculate frequency of vibration of various piano strings.
- Calculate medical dosages for different weight animals.
- Calculate mathematical values for an excellent golf swing.
- Plot changes in temperature at different altitudes from a NASA space flight.

© International Center for Leadership in Education

A Systemwide Approach to Rigor, Relevance, and Relationships

Science

Student Activities in the Rigor/Relevance Framework

Elementary Examples

6

5

4

Quadrant C Assimilation

- Write and illustrate biographies of inventors.
- Make diagrams of animal life cycles.
- Classify a group of similar objects to create a dichotomous key.
- Conduct experiments to show photosynthesis.
- Research an endangered species.
- Make observations of similarities and differences of fish heads and predict food sources.
- Research characteristics and habits of insects.
- Write a story describing the movement of water through municipal water systems.

Quadrant D Adaptation

- Design a candy dispenser that works without gravity.
- Invent a musical instrument.
- Design a zoo.
- Study bread chemistry, purpose of ingredients, and how changes affect final product.
- Set up experiments to test life length of batteries.
- Research and write a field guide for identifying local trees.
- Build a simple robotic device with string, tape, and rubber bands.

3

2

1

Quadrant A Acquisition

- Memorize names of planets in solar system.
- Demonstrate phases of the moon.
- Participate in simple hands-on activities that demonstrate Bernoulli's principle of air pressure and air flight.
- Match pictures of insects with their names.
- Illustrate parts of a cell.
- Make a model of the layers of Earth's atmosphere.
- Make daily observations of the life cycle of a selected species.
- Create a mural showing various kinds of creatures that live in the ocean.

Quadrant B Application

- Develop a food list for a space trip.
- Create a class book about the animal and plant life in local rivers.
- Take photographs of insects to describe characteristics and behaviors.
- Study examples of paper airplanes and then create one.
- Keep a field journal about the insects that live near your school.
- Develop an acid test and sample rainwater for acidity.
- Create electric circuits of various materials and determine properties of conductivity and insulation.
- Analyze characteristics of different soil types.

1   2   3   4   5

Chapter 2: DSEI and the 21st Century 3R's: Rigor, Relevance, and Relationships

Science

Middle Level Examples

Student Activities in the Rigor/Relevance Framework

Quadrant C Assimilation

- Design a science project to illustrate a science concept (e.g., photosynthesis).
- Analyze similarities and differences of spiders and insects.
- Research and sequence ages of plant and animal species.
- Discuss the impact of fat and cholesterol in nutrition and health.
- Research and produce news program on earthquakes.
- Research and give presentations on astronomy topics.
- Identify chemicals dissolved in an unknown solution.

Quadrant D Adaptation

- Measure light pollution in the community.
- Collect data and make recommendations to address a community environmental problem.
- Design an air pollution control device.
- Design a device to transport human organs.
- Develop a concept for a new product and research the process for patenting the design.
- Collaborate with other students in collecting data on acid rain pH levels in area lakes.
- Design a model bridge to carry a specific load.
- Research communication innovations and predict innovations in the next 20 years.

Quadrant A Acquisition

- Measure the effect of temperature and concentration on the rate of a reaction, such as Alka-Seltzer in water.
- Observe wave properties of light, especially the phenomenon of interference, using soap bubbles.
- Construct models of molecules using toothpicks, marshmallows, and gumdrops.
- Examine biological rhythms by recording changes in body temperature.
- Use different colored clay/dough to demonstrate tectonic plates.
- Catalog human physical traits to determine inherited genetic traits.
- Illustrate proportion of world's freshwater, ice caps, and saltwater using an aquarium.

Quadrant B Application

- Analyze heat produced from different fuel sources.
- Build a simple electrical circuit to illustrate digital principle of computers.
- Explore the stopping characteristics of a toy car, altering one variable at a time.
- Investigate the importance of interdependency and diversity in a rain forest ecosystem.
- Collect data on dissolved oxygen, hardness, alkalinity, and temperature in a stream.
- Complete an energy audit of heat loss in a home.
- Conduct experiments to measure calories in foods.

© International Center for Leadership in Education

A Systemwide Approach to Rigor, Relevance, and Relationships

Science — Student Activities in the Rigor/Relevance Framework — **High School Examples**

Quadrant C Assimilation

- Solve a hypothetical science-related problem, such as helping dinosaurs to survive.
- Design experiments and collect evidence to describe the movement of light.
- Design a WebQuest on an aspect of chemistry.
- Design observations to demonstrate basic laws of physics.
- Calculate potential and kinetic energy in the movement of a roller coaster.
- Create a digital electronic counter.
- Write test questions to illustrate understanding of empirical gas laws.
- Research the discovery of a chemical element.

Quadrant D Adaptation

- Explore designs of car safety restraints using eggs in model cars.
- Design and construct a robot.
- Conduct debate on genetically modified food (GMF).
- Solve an organic chemistry case study problem in petroleum distillation.
- Select a method to build a tunnel under a real city.
- Discuss the social, ethical, and emotional consequences of genetic testing.
- Participate in an online debate on a science issue, such as acid rain or deformed frogs.
- Research and write a newspaper article on a viral disease, examining economic and societal impacts.

Quadrant A Acquisition

- Conduct laboratory experiments to observe chemical reactions.
- Apply number and computation skills to science, including scientific notation and significant figures.
- Determine latitude and longitude of geographic locations.
- Use a mnemonic system for remembering metric conversions.
- Demonstrate modulation of sound waves using computer animation.
- Conduct experiments to observe properties of acids and bases.
- Memorize elements in Periodic Table.
- Make observations about the visual effects of concave and convex lenses.

Quadrant B Application

- Map a community site by collecting data with GPS device.
- Collect and categorize organisms from a natural stream.
- Apply Laws of Gases to design gas storage containers.
- Make weather forecasts based on data.
- Solve electrical current values using Ohm's law.
- Isolate DNA from unknown plant tissues and compare to sample DNA.
- Participate in an online collaboration to collect scientific data on a global problem.

Chapter 2: DSEI and the 21st Century 3R's: Rigor, Relevance, and Relationships

Student Activities in the Rigor/Relevance Framework

Social Studies — **Elementary Examples**

Quadrant C Assimilation

- Write an essay on some aspect of your family or neighborhood.
- Analyze similarities/differences between current and previous practices, e.g., compare school today to the 19th century.
- Role-play a simulation of the American Revolution to seek resolution of grievances.
- Study African art and folk tales and create art objects and related tales.
- Contrast citizens' roles/responsibilities under different forms of government.
- Speculate on and describe how changes in climate and natural resources will influence various regions of the world.
- Play a simulation game that illustrates supply and demand.

Quadrant D Adaptation

- Create a class business by designing, producing, marketing, and selling a product, such as cookies.
- Explore an online resource on inventions, such as National Geographic Invention Game, and then design an invention to solve a problem.
- Research a location in the U.S. and explain why it is a good place to live.
- Create a school bank simulation to illustrate loans, investments, and interest.
- Read a story about survival and brainstorm strategies for surviving a disaster, e.g., snowstorm, tornado.
- Identify a family buying choice, list benefits and costs, and explain why decision was made.

Quadrant A Acquisition

- Brainstorm meaning of a term such as "citizenship" and read a related book.
- Create a book illustrating and describing landforms using geographic terms.
- Memorize names, locations, and capital cities of U.S. states.
- Read a biography of a Native American.
- Research and celebrate a holiday from another country.
- Read historical novels about the contributions of U.S. women.
- Develop a time line of U.S. history events.
- Visit a historical museum.

Quadrant B Application

- Map a school facility.
- Describe geographic and climatic characteristics of the local community.
- Prepare foods from different countries.
- Trace family histories of the class and map immigration movements and time lines.
- Interview people who have lived elsewhere and develop a list of different community characteristics.
- Observe a local farming enterprise and discuss career and business opportunities.
- Explore buying options and comparison shop for a product.
- Use different map scales (linear, fractional, and word) to measure the distance between two places.

A Systemwide Approach to Rigor, Relevance, and Relationships

Social Studies

Student Activities in the Rigor/Relevance Framework

Middle Level Examples

6

Quadrant C Assimilation

- Complete interdisciplinary research project for a significant historical event.
- Use physical, topographical, political, and economic maps to compare and contrast early American civilizations.
- Research and role-play the first U.S. Constitutional Convention.
- View a historical video and critically evaluate perspective and point of view.
- Play a budget simulation game to analyze results of economic decisions.
- Identify and analyze primary and secondary source documents to understand the usefulness of each.
- Research and compare how economic decisions are made in other countries compared to the U.S.

Quadrant D Adaptation

- Participate in an online discovery adventure exploring historical ruins.
- Analyze and debate the role of advertising in school.
- Solve problems by evaluating, taking, and defending a position on an issue, such as immigration or public transportation policy.
- Create a WebQuest to illustrate the "American Dream."
- Create a Website for the local community.
- Research and present opinions of candidates running for office.
- Find examples of stereotyping in historic and current events.
- Compare the shaping of public opinion in Colonial times to modern times.

5

4

3

Quadrant A Acquisition

- Discover characteristics of society in an earlier decade by reading historical documents, such as wills and letters.
- Read about and discuss personal credit options.
- Research inventions of ancient civilizations.
- Define common terms used in various forms of government.
- View an historical video and answer factual questions.
- Construct a replica of a Native American village.
- Study colonial life through historical fiction.
- Make a map showing the growth of the United States from 1783 to 1914.

Quadrant B Application

- Develop a personal financial plan.
- Compete in a stock market investment simulation or game.
- Locate and catalog community services organizations in the community.
- Research status of specific legislation using Congressional Internet site.
- Research what items cost in other countries and use exchange rates to relate to U.S. prices.
- Explore buying options and comparison shop for products.
- Plan and participate in a community service activity.
- Hold an international festival.

2

1

1 2 3 4 5

Chapter 2: DSEI and the 21st Century 3R's: Rigor, Relevance, and Relationships

Social Studies

Student Activities in the Rigor/Relevance Framework

High School Examples

6

5

4

Quadrant C Assimilation

- Compare/contrast how ancient civilizations valued women, social responsibility, and equality.
- Research and give a presentation on a historical example of nationalism.
- Answer data-based questions using copies of original historical documents.
- Participate in a Socratic seminar on a policy issue, such as privacy.
- Use case studies to investigate how economic systems affect people's incentive for economic gain.
- Analyze decisions leading to major turning points in U.S. history and hypothesize about what might have happened if decisions had been different.

Quadrant D Adaptation

- Conduct a survey and analyze results on First Amendment issues related to Internet use.
- Analyze a local, state, or national issue and prescribe a response that promotes the public interest or general welfare, e.g., a voter registration campaign.
- Research and debate economic issues and public policy related to the Internet, such as sharing of online music.
- Evaluate a common practice or proposed legislation for consistency with the Constitution/Bill of Rights and write your opinion in a letter to an elected official.
- Analyze a school/community problem, suggest a solution, and prepare a plan to solve it.

3

2

1

Quadrant A Acquisition

- Observe local government proceedings.
- Complete interactive mapping activities on European geography.
- Report on a complex historical event.
- Complete an in-depth geographic study of a world region by analyzing demographic data.
- Recognize why international trade takes place and the role of exchange rates in fostering or inhibiting trade.
- Trace the evolution of U.S. values, beliefs, and institutions through a study of their constitutional and institutional development.
- Research key aspects of the state constitution.

Quadrant B Application

- Be a juror on a local youth court.
- Conduct a school/community survey on a social issue and analyze results.
- Write letter of support for a proposed local or state policy.
- Complete an income tax form.
- Draw from memory a map of the world; indicating the relative location of continents, oceans, major river systems, nations in the news, and important cities.
- Locate and interpret current and historical economic data, e.g., GDP, CPI, employment.
- Analyze credit options, calculate purchase costs, and complete a credit application.

1   2   3   4   5

© International Center for Leadership in Education

A Closer Look at "Real World"

The Application Model is based on the premise that the highest level of application is to connect knowledge to situations and problems in the real world. This notion is easy to understand, and it gains strong support from those outside education as the correct course to follow. But how do we define the term *real world*? Is it as simple as stating that everything inside school is "artificial" and that everything outside school is "real world"? If this is the case, and our goal is "real world," then we should tear down the schools and rely solely on work-based learning, community internships, and apprenticeships.

Real-world instruction is defined by the instructional activity, not by the location of the instruction.

Definitions of *real world* are useful in sharing ideas on what types of education meet the test of "real world." One explanation of a real-world application is that it occurs in the same way that adults use it. Moreover, standards of performance are the same as expected in adult roles, the most significant of which are worker, parent, citizen, and lifelong learner.

The following five criteria can be used to examine the real-world nature of instruction as it relates to the use of skills and knowledge in adult roles:

- setting
- tools/resources
- standards
- relationships
- use of time

Setting refers to the environment surrounding the use of skills. In the workplace and home, skills and knowledge are seldom used in isolation, and the problems to be solved are rarely clearly defined. Moreover, workplaces often have challenging working conditions, such as noise, distractions, or extreme weather, which can greatly affect the adequate performance of skills. In many learning situations, a workplace setting can be simulated by replicating the physical environment or providing access to the actual information or people available on the job.

Tools/resources refers to the materials, equipment, and resources with which people work and communicate with one another. In the area of information technology, this includes telephones, fax machines, computers, and, equally important, the same software that is used in the workplace. When students use the same design software that is used by engineers, for example, they are equipped to engage in real-world design tasks. Doing a school research project by using the Internet and libraries all over the world is an example of using real-world resources.

Standards are used to measure the quality of work. In the real world, standards are often set based on the products or services that consumers are willing to purchase. A competitive marketplace drives businesses to reach for higher standards of products and service in order to stay in business. These standards are set by external customers.

In education, standards are often combinations of standardized tests and curriculum standards set by the state, school, or teacher. In nearly every case, the level of performance is determined by the judgment of teachers. For example, the standards of acceptable 5th-grade writing and what score is required to pass 9th-grade algebra are set by individual teachers or schools; in other words, educators within the system determine these standards.

One way to bring the real world into the school setting is to use adults from outside school to set the standards. For example, when a state develops reading comprehension tests, instead of arbitrarily picking 65 as the passing grade, the state would ask employers, parents, or elected officials to designate acceptable or exemplary performance. Likewise, community or business groups can be valuable in reviewing the scoring guides for performance-based assessments. This adds an aspect of external-driven standards in education.

Relationships are an important defining characteristic of the real-world use of skills. Most people work with other people; indeed, our democracy is based on participation. When teachers attempt to plan real-world activities, they should make an effort to create group learning and performance situations in which students must work together.

Time is the final defining characteristic. In the real world, there are often clear timelines that must be met. Usually, there is no delay in getting feedback as to whether something worked. In school, however, a student may get feedback on the quality of an assignment several days later, when the teacher returns it with a grade. Employees tend to have their work evaluated almost instantly; so if teachers want real-world instruction, they need to set real-world deadlines and provide more immediate feedback to students.

Teachers can move toward real-world instruction by focusing on the setting, tools/resources, standards, relationships, and use of time. While not all instruction needs to be "real world," community expectations are clear: Students must be better able to use the knowledge that they acquire in school. Limited resources will inhibit all school instruction from meeting the test of "real world," but working toward these five criteria will move instruction toward that goal.

Review Questions

1. How do you think that asking the seven questions proposed by Tony Wagner might help you implement rigor, relevance, and relationships?
2. In what ways would your curriculum need to be updated to address the "less is more" approach of the Common Core State Standards?
3. In what way do you think your school might address both state testing and the higher, more complex skills that students need to compete in society?
4. Why do you think that the importance of relationships is often overlooked? How might you go about convincing co-educators of their significance?
5. What are some ways in which you might be able to improve student learning by developing relationships?

# Chapter 3

Rigorous and Relevant Instruction

Being able to confidently implement rigorous and relevant instruction requires instructional leaders to have a thorough understanding of how to support use rigor and relevance, including useful interdisciplinary instruction.

Instructional Planning

Instructional planning can be divided into three components: curriculum, instruction, and assessment. Curriculum is *what* students will learn, instruction is *how* students will learn, and assessment is *in what way* and *how well* students are expected to demonstrate what they have learned as a result of the instruction.

Traditionally, these three elements have been approached as three separate steps, one following the other, as shown in the following figure. Many teachers learned to plan their lessons using this linear model: Decide what to teach, design how to teach it, and then decide how to measure student achievement.

Teaching also proceeds in a linear manner. Topics are introduced one after the other, pausing only long enough for a chapter or unit test. Particularly at the secondary level, instructional planning focuses on covering the topics at a uniform rate of speed and tools like district curriculum pacing guides beat out a rapid tempo.

A Systemwide Approach to Rigor, Relevance, and Relationships

Traditional Planning

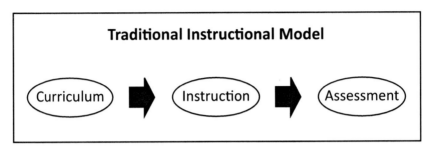

Recent research and innovations in teaching and learning have concluded that curriculum, instruction, and assessment are not separate and linear but interrelated. Good learning takes place when there is a dynamic linkage of instruction and assessment. In a performance planning model, instruction and assessment, in particular, should have significant overlap, as shown in the following figure.

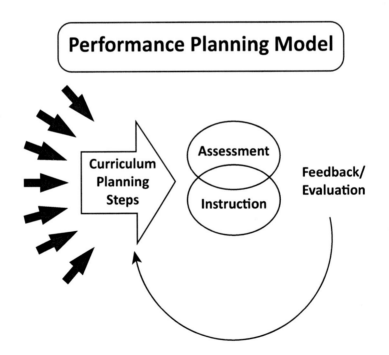

Chapter 3: Rigorous and Relevant Instruction

Planning Curriculum

Improving student learning requires deliberate interventions by teachers and other staff. The Rigor/Relevance Framework is helpful to teachers in facilitating high levels of student learning in the new school design.

Student learning is the result of a combination of facilitated instructional experiences and assessments. (See the Performance Planning Model.) Rigorous and relevant student learning starts with a specific expected student performance, using the Rigor/Relevance Framework. After completing a unit, the teacher can reflect on the actual level of student performance and decide whether it is necessary to modify and attempt to improve the instruction and assessment to attain higher levels of performance.

Good learning takes place when there is a dynamic linkage of all components. In rigorous and relevant learning, instruction and assessment should have significant overlap. Authentic assessment should occur more naturally, embedded as part of the instructional process. The current assessment reform movement seeks to place greater emphasis on student performance rather than on recall of facts. Teachers are better able to plan good instruction and assessment if they abandon the image of linear steps and of having assessment follow instruction.

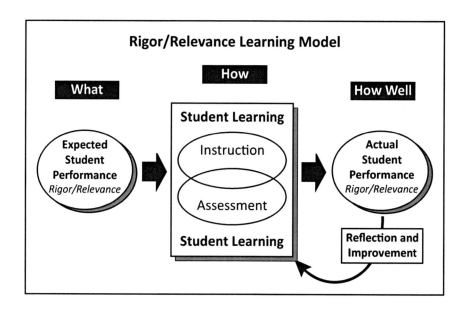

© International Center for Leadership in Education

Curriculum planning does occur prior to instruction and assessment. Without effective planning, there is very little likelihood that students will achieve the expected rigor and relevance. Curriculum planning is a complex process; it is much more than simply picking out a work of literature or a textbook chapter and deciding that it would make a good instructional topic. Teacher experience and data should be considered in order to make thoughtful decisions about instruction and assessment.

When teachers and leaders hear the word *curriculum,* they generally think of unit or lesson plans that describe teacher procedures and/or student activities that would take place in a classroom. It is natural for teachers to think about these plans and immediately jump to imagine what they would look like in their classrooms. Teachers are under constant pressure to present activities that engage students, and there is precious little time to do much planning — such is the structure of the U.S. education system.

While curriculum must lead to unit plans and lesson plans, curriculum planning does not begin with them. Teachers who begin and end their curriculum planning by writing a lesson plan miss important curriculum decisions.

The curriculum is a means to an end: a performance by the student. Teachers typically focus on a particular topic (for example, the volume of three-dimensional figures), use a particular resource (for example, the Periodic Table of Elements), and choose specific instructional methods (for example, problem-based learning) to produce learning that meets a given standard. However, each of these decisions is actually a step in a learning process that should end in a performance by the student. Student activity without an end performance in mind is busywork. Instruction, no matter how engaging or intellectual, is beneficial only if it ends with students demonstrating their knowledge and skills resulting from the learning experience. A performance approach to curriculum planning starts with the specific student performance. Ralph Tyler described the logic of this approach clearly and succinctly more than 50 years ago in *Basic Principles of Curriculum and Instruction.*

A curriculum process that begins with the end in mind is referred to by Wiggins and McTighe in *Understanding by Design* as "backward design." It may seem backward to many teachers who move "forward" with textbooks, favored lessons, and time-honored activities rather than deriving those tools from targeted goals or standards. The *Understanding by Design* model is one of a number of excellent approaches to designing curriculum with the clear goal of student learning as the first step. Regardless of the model selected, teachers should start with the end — the desired results (goals or standards) — and then derive the curriculum from the evidence of learning (performances) called for by the standard and from the teaching needed to equip students to perform.

Backward design may be thought of as purposeful task analysis: Given a task to be accomplished, how do we get there? What kinds of lessons and practices are needed to master key performances? This approach to curriculum design is a logical systems approach, but it runs contrary to conventional habits, whereby teachers think in terms of a series of activities or how best to cover a topic.

This backward approach to curricular design also departs from another common practice: thinking about assessment as something to plan at the end, after teaching is completed. Rather than creating assessments near the conclusion of a unit of study (or relying on the tests provided by textbook publishers, which may not assess state standards completely or appropriately), backward design calls for teachers to think about the work that the student will produce and how it might be assessed as they begin to plan a unit or course. Curriculum planning is a complex process that occurs prior to instruction and assessment. Without effective planning, there is little likelihood that students will achieve the expected rigor and relevance.

Planning Steps

There are four major steps in planning rigorous and relevant instruction:

1. Define the focus of instruction.
2. Create the student performance.
3. Design the assessment.
4. Develop the learning experiences.

A Systemwide Approach to Rigor, Relevance, and Relationships

The four steps are presented in the order in which ideal planning should occur.

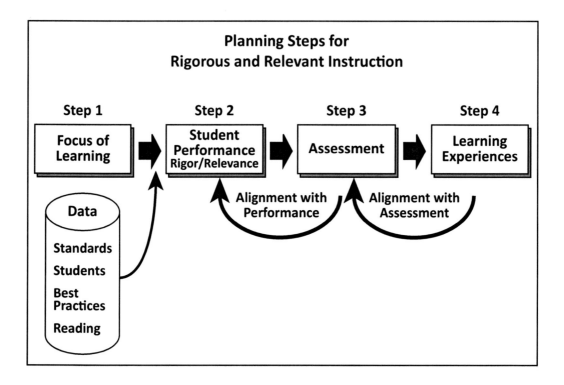

Step 1: Define the Focus of Instruction

This planning step ensures that the design of student work, content, and instructional activities is not random; rather, it is defined by the limits of time, students served, and relationship to other units or courses. Begin by defining the audience and the context.

- For what group of students is this unit (grade level, previous experience)?
- Is there a unifying theme, problem, or project?
- What subject or subjects are included?
- Is there a specific standard on which the unit will focus?
- Is there a specific project students will complete or a problem to be solved?

In defining student performance, teachers should use objective data as well as their experience. In an era of increased accountability, teachers must use data to drive their decisions. Four categories of data are important in defining student performances: standards data, best practices data, student data, and reading data.

Standards Data. Knowing what the standards are in several disciplines is an important piece of data. Teachers should look beyond their own discipline's standards for interdisciplinary connections and opportunities to link performances to standards from other disciplines. This helps to reinforce student learning and to use limited instructional time more efficiently.

One of the issues regarding standards is meeting the high expectations set by the Common Core State Standards, wherein teachers must possess depth of knowledge in order to go deeper into the content. Teachers need to set priorities, and it is important that teachers make these decisions based on data rather than personal preference.

Instructional Practices Data. Teachers acquire effective learning approaches from experience and observations. With so many variables in schools, however, it is often difficult to predict that a certain practice will work in a certain situation. Therefore, emphasis is being placed on selecting instructional practices based on education research. Teachers can expand their repertoire of strategies and student performances through reviewing the research and conducting action research on their own practice. With advancements in technology it is also important to support teachers in trying new strategies. These strategies can be found in the International Center's handbooks *Effective Instructional Strategies — Volume 1*, *Effective Instructional Strategies — Volume 2*, and *Effective Instructional Strategies — Quadrant D Moments*.

Data-Driven Curriculum Checklist

This checklist will help teachers to make curriculum decisions based on objective data related to standards, students, best practices, and reading.

Yes No

Standards

- ☐ ☐ Instruction is based on state standards or Common Core State Standards.
- ☐ ☐ Students and parents are informed at the beginning of the year that the state standards or Common Core State Standards are included in your course.
- ☐ ☐ Instruction is differentiated to adjust to individual student differences in prior experience and learning style.

Students

- ☐ ☐ Students' existing knowledge and skills levels have been determined.
- ☐ ☐ Formative assessments are used to inform instruction.
- ☐ ☐ Student learning styles have been determined.
- ☐ ☐ You ask students about their interests and aspirations.
- ☐ ☐ You make home visits to meet parents and understand students' family situations.

Instructional Practices

- ☐ ☐ Instructional strategies have been researched and evaluated to determine effectiveness.
- ☐ ☐ You analyze the effectiveness of your innovative practices through action research.
- ☐ ☐ You observe other teachers in your subject or grade.
- ☐ ☐ You observe teaching strategies in different settings—for example, watching a special education teacher for ideas on classroom management or a technical teacher conducting a problem-based learning activity.

Reading

- ☐ ☐ Reading levels necessary for competence on assessments have been determined.
- ☐ ☐ Reading levels of students have been determined.
- ☐ ☐ You know the reading levels required for students to be college and career ready.

Student Data. Student performances need to take into consideration the prior experience of students, their interests, and their various learning styles. For example, a teacher could decide to have students engage in independent research to demonstrate knowledge gained in a specific area. If students have had little prior experience in conducting research, it may be disastrous to turn them loose and expect them to achieve the expectations. Some students may need more supervised performance before engaging in an independent activity.

Another area of modifying performances based on student data is competence in prerequisite skills and knowledge. Teachers need to know the existing performance levels of students in order to provide new experiences that build on prior knowledge.

Teachers also need to determine individual learning styles and interests to predict how students will respond to specific learning experiences. Depending on individual interests, students may need more encouragement or support for an activity.

Reading Data. Educators know how important reading is to continued learning. At the secondary level, reading should be the responsibility of teachers in all disciplines. Students improve their reading proficiency when they receive guidance in content areas. Teaching reading in the content area involves knowing and incorporating reading and vocabulary strategies into instruction. In addition, there is reading data that teachers can use in planning instruction. One of the best open source measures of reading is the Lexile Framework for Reading®, which can measure the levels of reading materials and readers.

Teachers should know the reading levels of their students in order to select appropriately challenging text. If the material is at a much lower reading level, then students will become bored. More common is the assignment of reading materials that are far above the reading level of some students, who then fail to grasp the content and become discouraged. The Lexile Framework for Reading® can help teachers identify textbooks and other materials at the appropriate level for students.

An additional type of reading data for teachers to know is the level of reading proficiency that students need to attain in order to succeed in adult life. Knowing this information can help to motivate students to improve their reading to a specified goal. Using Lexile measures, teachers found out the Lexile measure required for proficiency in state examinations and for such adult tasks as reading newspapers and income tax forms. The International Center for Leadership in Education has also analyzed hundreds of employee reading materials in various job clusters. This gives an accurate measure of reading required for working in various careers. This data helps to set expectations for students regarding the specific level of reading they will need beyond school.

An important instructional change that has come about as a result of the Common Core State Standards is a shift toward regular practice with complex text and the related academic vocabulary. The previous approach was to focus on reading and writing skills. However, the standards require texts that are of greater complexity and that have real-world applications. By building complexity gradually, students are ready for college and career demands by the end of high school. In addition to the increasing complexity of the text, words that appear across content areas must also be developed.

Mathematics Data. The Common Core State Standards have led to a similar shift in the area of mathematics. Rather than a cursory presentation of a wide range of topics, teachers can limit the breadth of content but greatly increase its depth. By focusing on the concepts emphasized by the standard, students are able to develop a stronger conceptual understanding and gain the ability to solve mathematical problems both in the classroom and in daily life.

In addition, topics should be linked across grades rather than being taught as disconnected topics. Doing so enables students to build upon foundations built in previous years. Each standard thus becomes an extension of previous knowledge as opposed to an entirely new concept. The mathematical practice areas are intended to be included in every grade level to further deepen learning.

Finally, the Common Core State Standards require students to demonstrate deep conceptual understanding of core math concepts rather than memorization of disconnected procedures. Students must be able to solve conceptual problems, apply math to new situations, and verbally describe their understanding of a concept.

Step 2: Create Rigorous and Relevant Student Performance Tasks

This step has two important purposes. The first purpose is to place emphasis on student learning. By thinking about what students need to know and to be able to do, the curriculum planning process shifts its focus from the teacher to the student. The second purpose is to use the Rigor/Relevance Framework to analyze expected levels of skills and knowledge, using the following tips:

- Make statements that identify the skills and knowledge as specific as possible. Include only one thought in each statement.
- Use verbs that indicate some action to be taken rather than the passive accumulation of knowledge.
- Once the statements are written, examine each statement to determine its level on the Rigor/Relevance Framework. Until a teacher is comfortable with the four quadrants of the Rigor/Relevance Framework, it may be easier to rate each statement according to its level on the Knowledge Taxonomy and on the Application Model separately and then place it in a quadrant.

Many skills and concepts can be taught at several levels of complexity or difficulty. By using the Rigor/Relevance Framework in this planning step, a teacher can develop appropriate levels of instruction more accurately. When an expectation of real-world application is set by designating Quadrants B or D on the Rigor/Relevance Framework, for example, there is a conscious commitment to work toward real-world application. Likewise, designating high rigor in Quadrants C or D will require instruction that supports higher-level thinking skills.

Student Work. Student work is at the heart of learning. Focusing on student work is also an excellent means of measuring the quality of instruction. Teachers can improve learning in their classrooms by concentrating on student work as part of curriculum planning. *Student work* is defined as the observable effort or tangible products produced by a student. Examples of observable efforts are group discussion, research, reading, troubleshooting a process, and brainstorming. Tangible products might include pieces of writing, science experiments, solutions to problems, test questions, and project designs.

Student work provides the most tangible evidence of the learning process. The best way to judge the quality of teaching and learning is by looking at the work that students are producing in the classroom and asking questions such as these:

- Is the work meaningful and challenging?
- Are all students actively engaged?
- Do students have a clear understanding of what constitutes outstanding work?
- Do students show commitment to and enthusiasm for their work?
- Does student work require extensive creativity, originality, design, or adaptation?

The answers to these questions provide rich evidence of the quantity and quality of learning taking place.

Teachers should spend time thinking about what significant pieces of work students will produce and not limit themselves by simply defining the content and objectives for what students will learn. Taking the time to reflect on student work will lead to more application in instruction and assessment.

By defining *student work* early in the planning process, teachers will have an indication of what is appropriate to assess. In most cases, the work should be used to evaluate the students. If this work is some type of performance, teachers should develop objective criteria to judge the quality. If the work involves gathering knowledge or memorizing facts, a multiple-choice or constructed-response test is appropriate. Using student work as the basis for assessment helps to identify clearly for students what they are expected to learn.

The following list of student work is a good reference for defining student work as part of assessment planning.

Advice letter	Film analysis	Poster
Analysis of painting	Geometric analysis	Preparing for a discussion
Analyzing primary sources	Graph	Proposal
Argument analysis	Interview Questions	Proposals and criteria
Article reviews	Journal entry	Questionnaire
Biography analysis	Letter writing	Questions
Blog	Literary analysis	Real-world problem solutions
Cartoon	Logical sequences	Road trip directions
Character analysis	Map	Rules
Chart	Memo	Scale model
Complaint letter	News report	Speech critiques
Data analysis	Oral history	Survey
Debate	Persuasive letter	Taxonomy
E-mail	Planning for a task	Timelines
Error analysis	Poem	Video
Field guide		

Standards and Priorities. This step relates to why this unit is being taught and makes connections to:

- local, state, or Common Core State Standards to which the topic is related (multiple standards if interdisciplinary/thematic unit)
- content tested on state tests
- what the community/public believes is essential for students to know and be able to do

As part of curriculum planning, teachers must prioritize what will be taught and give careful attention to the most important knowledge and skills, such as those which form the basis for further learning. Making these decisions is challenging and complex. Teachers gain some knowledge of priorities through experience. However, with standards-based state assessments, decisions about which standards to teach, how much time to expend, and which instructional strategies to use have consequences beyond the course or grade.

Step 3: Design the Assessment

In the Rigor/Relevance Learning Model, instruction and assessment will often occur together; however, assessment should be considered before planning instruction. There are many types of assessment, and no single type is better than another. The point is to choose an assessment type that matches the student work. If the work involves learning a body of knowledge, a multiple-choice or short-answer test may be fine. If the work is a project or performance, a scoring guide/rubric would be more appropriate.

It is important at this point for us to be clear about the types of assessments used in schools to assess student progress for purposes of accountability and to guide the planning and adjustment of instruction. Let's look at three basic types: summative assessment, benchmark assessment, and formative assessment.

Summative Assessment is the formal testing of what has been learned in order to produce grades, scores, or developmental levels that may be used for reports of various types. It is primarily used for Accountability. It is different from Formative Assessment, in which the emphasis is on ongoing assessments of different types used to adjust instruction to best help pupils learn the concepts or skills.

Summative assessment is an attempt to summarize student learning at some point in time and has a number attached (that is, a grade). It usually occurs at the end of the year/chapter/etc. Most standardized tests are summative assessments. It is not designed to give immediate feedback for assisting in the student learning process. Summative tests, such as state assessments, are for accountability, such as required measures for NCLB.

Benchmarking compares one's own standards with those of others at a local, state, or national level. Benchmark assessments are often used on a regular basis, such as monthly or quarterly. They are used to provide feedback to the instructor so that instruction can be modified. Benchmark assessments are often unpopular with teachers due to the time it takes to administer them.

Formative Assessments are a process, not a test. They happen in the classroom on a daily basis and usually involve conversations between the teacher and student. Formative assessments are informal but are targeted to assist student learning. They often are student-driven and self-reflective. For the most part, in the Rigor/Relevance Learning Model we are talking about using formative assessments.

Some examples of frequently used formative assessments include:

- observations
- questioning
- rubrics
- discussion
- exit/admit slips
- learning/response logs
- peer/self assessments
- practice presentations
- visual representations
- four corners
- constructive quizzes
- think/pair/share

To ensure uniform criteria and understanding of what constitutes quality performance on assessments, common rubrics should be used across the curriculum in the various disciplines. Having a common standard or benchmark, one that all staff follows, provides clear expectations to students and ensures that the staff has a uniform understanding of the various degrees, or levels, of meeting benchmarks. With common rubrics, the performance that constitutes a 1, 2, 3, or 4 rating is similar, regardless of the student's course of study or the student's teacher. Common rubrics are particularly important within the same discipline; for example, science teachers should have the same standards of performance on all lab work.

In small learning communities, common rubrics become even more important in light of the interdisciplinary approach to instruction. Using the same rubric for writing, presentations, homework, and other common areas across disciplines reinforces the core academics and ensures a quality performance that all students, staff, and parents understand.

Many states have developed rubrics for selected academic areas. This is often the case with writing. Where a state rubric exists, it is best to use it across the curriculum so that the standard of performance expected on state assessments is understood and consistent with acceptable performance throughout the school year.

Step 4: Develop the Learning Experiences.

Learning experiences or activities have seven components. The first two components provide additional description of what students will learn.

Content Knowledge. Performance planning emphasizes application of knowledge; however, without content knowledge, students have nothing to apply. One of the strengths of the Rigor/Relevance Framework is that it creates a connection and balance between content knowledge and application. Decisions about curriculum should not be a forced dichotomy between knowledge and application; students must have both. To ensure a strong, direct connection of content knowledge and real-world applications, it is best to start with the end in mind. Develop a clear idea of the real-world application and select content necessary to achieve that goal. Content is not covered in instruction just because teachers know it or the textbook contains it.

Decisions about what content to teach must be based upon how students will use the knowledge; that is, the content knowledge is based on the work in which students will be engaged. Instruction should focus on the body of knowledge necessary for an instructional unit.

Essential Questions. Posing an initial question is an excellent way to introduce an instructional unit. A broad, open-ended question will pique students' curiosity and focus interest on the main concept or concepts to be introduced or expanded upon in the lesson. The question should never have a simple *yes* or *no* answer, nor does it necessarily need to be resolved in the lesson. If a question engages students in learning, then it has done its job.

Launching Activity. It is important to "hook" students into learning when beginning any new learning experience. Give additional thought to the first part of a lesson to try to heighten student interest in the learning. This might be done with a particularly dramatic video clip or demonstration. It might be an observation around the school or something that is important to students. Consider the interests and likes of students and create excitement for learning with an engaging launching activity.

Strategies. Teachers should select and plan a series of varied activities that will enable students to develop and demonstrate the expected skills and knowledge for the instructional unit. As students engage in the activities, their work should be evaluated using specific objective criteria. The activities must be consistent with the levels of knowledge and application as well as closely connected to the identified student work set in Step 2 (student performance).

Most teachers teach from their own experience, replicating the models of good teaching they have experienced. However, this approach does not work for all students. A lesson is only as effective as its reflection in student achievement. In some cases, students do not understand the content because of the manner in which that information is delivered. Teachers must search for strategies that work. Selecting the appropriate strategy for each situation, when coupled with the teacher's expertise, will lead to greater student learning.

The appropriateness of a particular instructional strategy to a given situation depends on matching the characteristics of the strategy, the learner, and what needs to be learned. Teachers should be familiar with many instructional strategies so that they can confidently select the best strategies for each situation.

Learning Steps. A good lesson clearly outlines the steps that you will take as facilitator. It lays out the sequence of steps that you will need to follow. However, it is also important to plan out the learning steps that students will need to take in completing the learning. These student learning steps will help them to sequence the work that they will do and to know when it will be assessed. Learning steps communicate to students their responsibility in the learning process.

Extending Learning. Before ending a lesson and moving on to the next topic, think about how to extend the lesson to make sure that students apply what they have learned and continue to learn. For example, if students learn a safety procedure or writing process, indicate how this will be used and evaluated regularly during the entire course. You might also suggest Web sites or additional reading for students. You can also extend learning by connecting it to other courses or higher levels of courses that students will complete. Show students that learning is connected, not a set of disjointed experiences.

Resources. After deciding on the student work and the strategies to be used, make a list of student and teacher resources that will be needed to carry out the learning experiences. This list is important to effective planning to make sure that all resources are available before instruction begins. It is also a useful point for thinking about needs. If the resources required exceed the realistic capacity of the school or teachers to provide this learning experience, this is the point to go back and revise the student work/strategies to make sure that they require manageable resources.

Student-Centered Learning: The Key to Learner Engagement

As we learned in Chapter 2, the Rigor/Relevance Framework is a tool that enables teachers and school leaders to look at classroom instruction in the context of two important dimensions: the knowledge taxonomy that represents levels of thinking, and the application model, which takes into account the level of application of newly learned knowledge and skills. The four quadrants of the Framework progress from Quadrant A through D.

We discussed how one way to think about the Rigor/Relevance Framework in day-to-day instruction is in terms of the roles that teachers and students take. When instruction and expected student learning is in Quadrant A, the focus is on "teacher work." Teachers expend energy to create and assess learning activities — providing information, creating worksheets, and grading student work. The student is often a passive learner.

When the student expectation moves to Quadrant B, the emphasis is on the student doing real-world work. This student work is often more complicated than Quadrant A work, and it requires more time. Learning in Quadrant B is best described as "student work" because students are doing extensive real-world tasks. When the learning is placed in Quadrant C, it is best described as "student think." In this quadrant, students are expected to think in complex ways — to analyze, compare, create, and evaluate.

The term that best describes Quadrant D activities is "student think and work." Learning in Quadrant D is more demanding, and it requires the student to think and work. Roles shift from the teacher-centered instruction in Quadrant A to student-centered instruction in Quadrants B, C, and D. Teachers still work in Quadrants B, C, and D, but their role is more as a coach or facilitator.

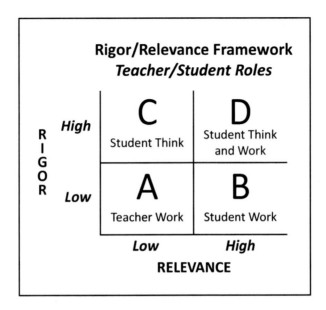

The Rigor/Relevance Framework presents a powerful distinction between teacher-led and student-centered learning. Activities in a student-centered classroom are conducive to maximum student engagement. There are several key characteristics of student-centered learning experiences:

- self-direction
- working with others
- flexible time
- intrinsic rewards
- application

Self-Direction. Students devote more energy to learning when they feel they have some self-determination in what they are doing. The more that students are able to select their own path of learning, the greater will be the level of engagement and interest. Obviously, it is not appropriate to switch to the extreme and give students complete freedom to choose what they want to learn at all levels. Often the student's choice will not involve the learning objective, since it is required of all students, but some self-determination in selection of learning activity is an excellent way to engage students. This is where learning styles come into play. The more that teachers are able to create conditions of self-determination and let students take initiative, the greater will be the students' level of involvement and ultimately their achievement.

Working with Others. While students are expected to develop individual competence in school, one of the characteristics of student-centered learning is to learn together. Working with others allows for sharing of creative ideas, testing of solutions, and feedback as to performance and achievement. The more that teachers are able to structure joint learning activities, the more they will be able to increase the engagement of students. The application of cooperative learning techniques is very useful in increasing the scope of learning in groups.

Flexible Time. One of the most difficult student-centered characteristics to achieve is the flexible use of time. Allowing more time does not mean simply extending tasks for students. Some students need more time; others need less. The challenge for teachers is to find creative ways to allow each student to move at an individual pace. This is difficult in classroom settings, but many teachers have found ways to do this by structuring varied instructional activities, with time devoted to large-group work, small-group work, and individual work. During individual time, some students can review difficult material while others accelerate to more challenging tasks.

Intrinsic Rewards. Schools have long relied on external recognition systems, primarily the use of grades, to quantify student achievement. However, grades are not sufficient to motivate high levels of student learning. Teachers should also work to help students develop the ability to derive satisfaction from doing high-quality work. It is this sense of personal goal setting, commitment, and satisfaction that will drive individuals to continual learning.

Application. The last aspect of student-centered learning is application and practice. Application of knowledge is an objective of student achievement, but it is also a way to practice and reinforce learning. Research consistently supports that practice, and actually using knowledge leads to the greatest retention and learning. In addition, many individuals have a preferred style of learning that involves concrete, practical applications. Instruction that includes a high degree of practice will result in higher levels of achievement. It is no surprise that "if you don't use it, you lose it." Application needs to play an important role in developing student-centered learning.

Linking Curriculum to Common Core State Standards

Schools today face conflicting challenges. The most immediate and well-publicized challenge is for students to meet state testing requirements under *No Child Left Behind* (NCLB). At the same time, schools are being pressured to prepare students more effectively for the world in which they will live and work. School leaders and teachers want to ensure that their students receive a rigorous and relevant education.

A rigorous and relevant curriculum will not be effective for students, however, if it is not linked to standards. Standards can help to raise student achievement. Over the past decade, educators have come to understand that curriculum must be based on standards, just as state assessments are.

In the rigorous and relevant planning model, standards are emphasized as one of the key data elements in setting student performance. The difficulty in effectively linking to standards is that the number of state standards in most subject areas far exceeds the time available for students to learn the content of these standards. As a result, teachers often merely cover the standards through direct instruction by default. This type of instruction is far from rigor or relevance, and actual student learning is minimal. However, teachers feel they have met their obligation to teach the standards.

A far better approach to learning is to prioritize the standards and ensure that these priority standards are taught to high levels of rigor and relevance. This approach is more interesting to students and more rewarding for teachers.

The challenge for teachers is to figure out which standards are priorities. Teachers may feel isolated in trying to make the decision on which standards to teach and which to ignore. Certainly, covering material that will be on the state tests makes sense, but this is not always easy to determine from the testing information provided. Changes in state testing programs do not always reflect the standards. Should teachers ignore the standards and only teach to the test? Possibly, but many essential standards, such as speaking and listening skills, are not tested.

Teachers can reduce their anxiety about making isolated decisions on teaching priorities by using data. Nextpert is a powerful, easy-to-use tool to assist teachers in improving the performance of their students on high-stakes assessments while making sure that students acquire the knowledge and skills they will need to succeed in life.

Chapter 3: Rigorous and Relevant Instruction

Nextpert correlates a state's standards in English language arts and mathematics with (1) the state assessments required by NCLB and (2) the results of the National Essential Skills Survey (NESS), in which 20,000 educators and community members identified the most essential curricular content for high school graduates to have learned. Nextpert indicates which state standards/benchmarks/performance indicators/topics are high priorities based on whether they are tested and whether they were rated highly in the National Essential Skills Survey. With this tool at their fingertips, educators can make informed decisions about whether to place more or less emphasis on a standard, confident in the knowledge that the decisions will help students succeed on tests and are consistent with what educators and the community believe that a high school graduate should know and be able to do.

The following provides a sample page of the search options in Nextpert.

Explore Standards

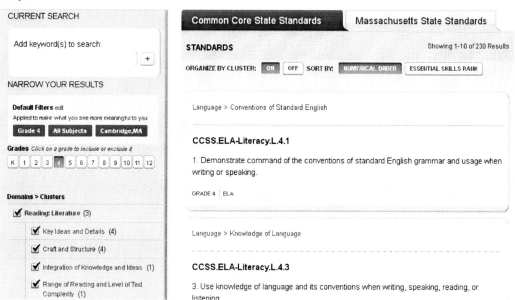

Using the priority data on standards available, teachers can make data-driven decisions about which standards to emphasize. Without such data, teachers must choose between trying to cover all the standards superficially or eliminating some, which runs the risk of leaving students unprepared for the assessments or without the skills considered essential for adult life. With data, however, instructional leaders and teachers can make decisions to inform instruction and to place more or less emphasis on a standard or to skip it completely, confident in the knowledge that the decisions will help students succeed on the assessments and that they are consistent with public expectations. Although teachers may wish to incorporate supplemental criteria in making decisions about emphasizing, adding, or deleting topics, Nextpert provides a clear indication of the impact of such decisions. Additionally, Nextpert includes aligned Common Core State Standards for each state's standards for English language arts and mathematics. Nextpert also includes a library of next generation assessment items and a tool for teachers to create their own.

Chapter 3: Rigorous and Relevant Instruction

Suggested Activities for Curriculum Planning

Curriculum Standards

- Relate lessons and unit plans to the appropriate state standards.
- Inform students and parents at the beginning of the year which state standards are included in your course or grade level.
- Volunteer for any state or local curriculum groups that will be working with standards. These firsthand experiences will expand your knowledge.

Content Knowledge

- Subscribe to professional journals in your subject.
- Collect potentially useful content articles in organized electronic or paper files so you can locate them in the future.
- Join and participate in regional and state professional organizations and conferences.

Community Expectations

- Develop questions that you routinely ask all parents to get their opinions on topics.
- Read local editorials regularly.
- Participate in a community service organization.
- Listen to nonteachers in your social groups to learn about their perceptions of the schools.

Student Knowledge

- Use a learning style assessment with your students.
- Ask students about their interests and aspirations.
- Make home visits to meet parents and understand students' family situations.

Teacher Self-knowledge

- Continue to try new strategies and to measure your comfort level with these teaching activities.
- Look for opportunities to team teach and ask for feedback from colleagues.
- Mentor student teachers or beginning teachers; you also will learn a great deal about yourself and your teaching philosophy and style.

Assessment Practices

- Try new assessment techniques.
- Participate in the scoring of state tests.
- Volunteer for projects to develop state assessments.

Effective Instructional Strategies

- Try something new each time you repeat a lesson.
- Observe other teachers in your subject or grade.
- Observe teaching strategies in different settings. For example, observe a special education teacher for ideas on classroom management or watch a technical teacher conduct a problem-based learning activity.
- Volunteer to present at local staff development workshops.
- Experiment with instructional technology.

Reading in Content Areas

Teachers have always understood the fundamental importance of reading to student success. Elementary teachers introduce young students to the basics of phonemic awareness, vocabulary, and sentence structure. In the higher grades, science and social studies teachers, for example, understand that the reading ability of their students plays a critical role in their ability to grasp content in those subjects. Likewise, teachers of career and technical education help their students decipher technical materials in repair manuals and other workplace documents. Every teacher must support the continued development of reading skills in order to help students fully master the course content.

In planning instruction, teachers often are frustrated in trying to choose reading matter that matches the reading levels of their students. When planning and facilitating instruction, teachers must know the reading levels of their students so that they can select texts that will be appropriately challenging: not too difficult to turn students off and not too simple to bore them. Of course, teachers must also know the reading level of the materials they assign. There is a tool and a data bank to help teachers in this decision-making.

Since 1984, MetaMetrics, Inc., an independent research and development firm, has focused on developing a tool to improve the students' overall learning, specifically reading comprehension, by placing both student and text on the same scale. The research on reading and psychometric theory culminated in the development of the Lexile Framework for Reading®. Today, this tool is recognized as the most accurate way to match readers with reading materials. Many current textbooks and thousands of works of literature have been rated by the Lexile Analyzer and given a number between 200 and 1700 on the Lexile Framework scale.

A reader's Lexile measure can be determined by a variety of informal and formal methods. Informal methods include a read-aloud conducted by the teacher using text with a known Lexile measure. Formal methods include standardized reading assessments. Teachers can then use this information to monitor, evaluate, and enhance a student's reading comprehension ability through targeted instruction. Information on Lexile and MetaMetrics can be obtained at www.lexile.com.

The Lexile Framework is composed of tools and resources that educators can use to plan instruction that correctly targets students' reading levels. It does not replace existing reading programs or prescribe a pedagogy; rather, it is a means to quantify the difficulty of reading materials compared with the ability levels of students, much the same as experienced teachers already do when they are familiar with the materials and know the students well.

The Lexile Framework can be used in instructional planning by teachers of all subjects to do the following:

- monitor student progress in reading by giving formal and informal assessments and charting results to the Lexile scale
- communicate with parents about expectations for reading in the course and about the progress of their children in meeting those goals
- help students set learning goals for reading based on the Lexile measure required for curriculum content
- select instructional materials that are at an appropriately challenging level for a student's Lexile level
- develop assessments that are consistent with the reading level of students
- communicate with other teachers by evaluating the Lexile level required to master content in the various curricula
- make instructional decisions earlier in the planning process even if they are not familiar with the reading material
- identify reading intervention services required for individual students more precisely based on Lexile level

See the International Center's handbook, *Effective Instructional Strategies for Content Area Reading 7–12*, for more information.

Real-World Relevance Demands Interdisciplinary Instruction

It is often difficult to comprehend how interrelated the world around us is. A small change in a law or policy, the invention of a new tool, or the extinction of some insignificant-seeming plant or animal can have far-reaching consequences of an unexpected nature and magnitude.

Education should increase students' understanding of the interconnectedness of the world. Unfortunately, the traditional subjects and courses taught in U.S. schools are separate and disconnected. As students move from class to class and grade to grade, they are exposed to bits and pieces of knowledge, but they are not taught how what they learn in one class is related to another.

Although the real world uses knowledge in an integrated form, the U.S. education system has broken it apart into specialized studies. This fragmented approach is not an effective way to prepare students for the world:

- It ignores some extremely important knowledge.
- It fails to show students the integrated nature of the world.
- It disregards basic principles of learning.
- It has no built-in mechanism to adapt to change.
- It emphasizes information absorption rather than construction.
- It lacks criteria for determining the relative significance of content.

Integrating subjects costs little — no new textbooks, no additional equipment, and no bureaucratic reorganization or retraining of teachers. Often, all that is required is a change of attitude and the willingness to restructure education so that it prepares students for life, not just for more school. With a little vision of how skills are used outside the educational establishment, a vastly superior interdisciplinary curriculum can be put in place.

The ultimate objective of education must be to provide students with foundation knowledge for dealing with the real world, skills to succeed in their various adult roles, and the ability to continue to learn. An interdisciplinary curriculum is more natural than the present curriculum. Unfortunately, that does not mean it is easily understood, especially by those whose perceptions of the world have been structured by traditional schooling.

The problem is not that an interdisciplinary curriculum requires more effort to plan but that it is different. It demands a paradigm shift in thinking. Consider how long it took to gain acceptance for the idea that sunrise was a consequence of the Earth's rotation rather than the sun's movement or how long it took to "discover" gravity. When change in the familiar is threatened, people often resist because they are greatly attached to their perceptions of reality.

While the development of interdisciplinary learning experiences is important, teachers often find it difficult to plan such experiences because they have neither the information nor the planning time. Textbooks and teachers' guides rarely show relationships among subject areas. Although teachers cannot change the content of textbooks rapidly or directly, they can use a planning process that encourages the incorporation of cross-disciplinary ideas and activities in instructional strategies.

Most teachers have a particular subject-matter expertise, but they have also accumulated knowledge and developed interests in other areas. What is more, they have access to other teachers with different subject-matter concentrations. With these resources at hand, teachers can construct lessons that help students understand important and interesting relationships among the disciplines.

Giving students opportunities to explore interconnections among the subjects that they are studying has many advantages. Interdisciplinary instruction adds meaning and relevancy to learning, as students discover applications between disciplines. New perspectives are developed to help students construct a more integrated web of knowledge. This integrated knowledge structure not only facilitates learning new information; it also helps students appreciate the wealth of information and ideas they already possess.

Nextpert: A Tool That Supports Standards-Based Curriculum Integration

The national focus has been on the shift to the Common Core State Standards, which build on the standards developed by the states to provide a consistent, clear understanding of what students are expected to learn. The larger challenge, however, will be increasing the rigor and relevance of instruction to prepare students for success on the Next Generation Assessments (NGA), which will be fundamentally different from current state tests.

NGA will be performance-based assessment: Students will need to demonstrate their ability to think in complex ways and apply their skills and knowledge when confronted with complicated problems.

Nextpert will help instructional leaders and teachers plan the kind of instruction that will prepare students for these more challenging requirements. This resource shows similarities and disparities among state standards, essential skills, and Common Core State Standards. It illustrates the differences between current state tests and NGAs with hundreds of exemplary performance tasks that mirror the rigor of the new assessment. Nextpert also encourages reflective practice by showing the higher expectations of the new standards and assessments.

Each item available in Nextpert provides a task for students to complete, the time required for that task, the work the student must produce, and the criteria by which the student work will be assessed. Along with the task, the item lists the Common Core State Standards and the state standards associated with the task. Several samples follow.

A Systemwide Approach to Rigor, Relevance, and Relationships

Sample Next Generation Assessment: A Political Cartoon

Subjects: Social Studies and English Language Arts	Grade Level: 4

Primary Common Core State Standards (no more than 3):

Reading — Integration of Knowledge and Ideas (ELA Anchor — Grades K–12)

7. Integrate and evaluate content presented in diverse media and formats, including visually and quantitatively, as well as in words.

Writing — Text Types and Purposes (ELA Anchor — Grades K–12)

2. Write informative/explanatory texts to examine and convey complex ideas and information clearly and accurately through the effective selection, organization, and analysis of content.

Writing — Research to Build and Present Knowledge (ELA Anchor — Grades K–12)

9. Draw evidence from literary or informational texts to support analysis, reflection, and research.

Other Related Common Core State Standards:

Reading — Informational Text — Integration of Knowledge and Ideas (ELA — Grade 4)

7. Interpret information presented visually, orally, or quantitatively (e.g., in charts, graphs, diagrams, time lines, animations, or interactive elements on Web pages) and explain how the information contributes to an understanding of the text in which it appears.

Writing — Text Types and Purposes (ELA — Grade 4)

2. Write informative/explanatory texts to examine a topic and convey ideas and information clearly.

Writing — Production and Distribution of Writing (ELA Anchor — Grades K–12)

4. Produce clear and coherent writing in which the development, organization, and style are appropriate to task, purpose, and audience.

Performance Task

Look closely at this 1869 political cartoon by Thomas Nast, "Uncle Sam's Thanksgiving Dinner": http://cartoons.osu.edu/nast/images/unlce_sam_thanksgiving100.jpg. Remember that political cartoons encourage viewers to develop an opinion about something, often a subject in the news. Determine what this political cartoon is saying to the viewer. Write a paragraph analyzing the photo and decide on its meaning by answering these questions:

1. What do the different figures around the table represent?
2. What is the artist saying about the United States?
3. What parts of the cartoon would be different if it were drawn today? Why?

During class discussion, compare, contrast and defend your interpretation of the cartoon.

Sample Next Generation Assessment:
A Political Cartoon (Continued)

Length: • about 15 minutes
Student Work: • Analysis of painting
Criteria for Student Learning: • Analyzes the figures in the cartoon. • Explains the meaning of the cartoon. • Proposes ways to adapt the cartoon to the present day. • Participates in class discussion.
Resources students will be provided: • Device with internet access

Scoring Guide
Checklist

Criteria for student learning (add rows as needed)	Yes/complete	In part/almost	Not yet
Analyzes the figures in the cartoon.			
Explains the meaning of the cartoon.			
Proposes ways to adapt the cartoon to the present day.			
Participates in class discussion.			

A Systemwide Approach to Rigor, Relevance, and Relationships

Sample Next Generation Assessment: Art Supply Stock

Content Areas: Art, English Language Arts, Math	Grade Level: 10

Primary Common Core State Standards (no more than 3):

<u>Writing — Text Types and Purposes</u> (ELA — Grades 9–10)

2. Write informative/explanatory texts to examine and convey complex ideas, concepts, and information clearly and accurately through the effective selection, organization, and analysis of content.

<u>Writing — Production and Distribution of Writing</u> (ELA — Grades 9–10)

4. Produce clear and coherent writing in which the development, organization, and style are appropriate to task, purpose, and audience.

<u>Statistics and Probability: Using Probability to Make Decisions</u> — Use probability to evaluate outcomes of decisions (Math — High School)

5. (+) Weigh the possible outcomes of a decision by assigning probabilities to payoff values and finding expected values.

Other Related Common Core State Standards:

<u>Language — Conventions of Standard English</u> (ELA — Grades 9–10)

1. Demonstrate command of the conventions of standard English grammar and usage when writing or speaking.

<u>Language — Conventions of Standard English</u> (ELA — Grades 9–10)

2. Demonstrate command of the conventions of standard English capitalization, punctuation, and spelling when writing.

Performance Task

You work as a manager at an art supply store. The owner has given you the task to decide whether to stock the 10-piece Daniel Green brush set or the 4-piece John Howard Sanden brush set in your store. You have a feeling that the Sanden set will sell better because of its lower price, but you're not sure if consumers might opt for the variety and quality of the Green set instead. To decide, you calculate the possible outcomes of sales dollars for each set, assigning a probability that each outcome will occur. You calculate that sales for the Green set are likely to be (in thousands of dollars) 6, 5, 2, or 1, with probabilities of 25%, 25%, 40%, and 10%, respectively. You estimate that sales for the smaller Sanden set are likely to be (in thousands of dollars) 4, 3, 2, or 1, with probabilities of 60%, 20%, 10%, and 10%, respectively. Based on the expected value of each outcome, which product should you choose to stock in your store? Write a short memo to the owner justifying your decision.

Sample Next Generation Assessment:
Art Supply Stock (Continued)

Length: • less than 15 minutes	
Student Work: • Memo	
Criteria for Student Learning: 1. Student correctly calculates expected profits. 2. Student makes a reasonable decision based on calculations. 3. Student develops and organizes memo according to purpose, task, and audience. 4. Student demonstrates command of conventions of grammar, usage, and mechanics.	
Resources students will be provided or will have to acquire: • Computer with word processing program	

Scoring Guide

Checklist

Criteria for student learning (add rows as needed)	Yes/complete	In part/almost	Not yet
Student correctly calculates expected profits.			
Student makes a reasonable decision based on calculations.			
Student develops and organizes memo according to purpose, task, and audience.			
Student demonstrates command of conventions of grammar, usage, and mechanics.			

A Process for Creating Interdisciplinary Instruction

Formulate a goal statement that indicates the principle(s) or concept(s) to be understood at the completion of the lesson. What are the primary pieces of information or the concepts that you want students to understand? Often, interdisciplinary lessons do not concentrate on the mastery of specific skills. By their very nature, these lessons usually focus on the application of skills and knowledge in new contexts. For this reason, the goals of interdisciplinary lessons will usually involve helping students understand how the skills and knowledge they possess can be combined to accomplish a task, discover a solution, or explain a situation.

Select the content that will serve as the basis for instruction. Often, the content base is determined by the text. There are times, however, when the goal necessitates the use of ancillary materials. In either case, determine the primary vehicle that will drive the instruction (for example, a work of art or literature, a scientific or mathematical principle, an event or era in history).

Identify events, discoveries, and writings within other disciplines that relate to the primary content base in a meaningful way. Through talking with colleagues and brainstorming on your own, consider information in other disciplines that seems to relate to the primary content. At this point, you may find it helpful to look at the table of contents in any textbook you may be using. However, do not discount your own expertise, films or plays you have seen, books or magazine articles you have read, and your life experience.

Determine the key points of intersection among disciplines that correspond to the established terminal goal of instruction. As you investigate each cross-disciplinary idea in more depth, keep your goal well in mind. It is easy to become enthralled with the idea itself and to lose sight of the major instructional intent. Some ideas will probably need to be discarded, either because they are too complex or because they do not fully address the goal. Other ideas may be so compelling and enlightening that you may want to revise the terminal goal to reflect new insights you have gained.

Identify the prerequisite skills and knowledge that students must possess in each discipline area. Interdisciplinary instruction can fail if students lack knowledge of key concepts within each discipline. Carefully consider the skills students must have before they can successfully accomplish the objectives you have set forth. Sometimes, missing skills or pieces of information can be taught rather quickly. However, when this is not the case, it will be necessary to revise the interdisciplinary content.

Formulate instructional strategies that will compel students to combine their knowledge from several disciplines. Students are not used to activating their knowledge in one discipline while studying another. For this reason, it is important to develop activities that cross the boundaries of traditional disciplines in a purposeful way. Conceptual mapping, in-class debates, group projects, and a variety of discovery techniques are examples of ways to accomplish this goal. As in all instruction, the critical component of interdisciplinary lessons is active and invested participation by students.

Identify Opportunities for Interdisciplinary Instruction

The following examples can stimulate thinking about areas for interdisciplinary instruction.

- Develop thematic units that involve study of a variety of aspects in different disciplines.

    Example: World War II — economics, literature, different cultures, geography, aerospace technology

- Parallel teach, having two teachers cover related topics at the same time in separate classrooms.

    Example: wave theory in physics and communication systems in technology

- Take students on a field trip (live or virtual), where learning is rarely limited to one discipline.

- Team teach a unit in which each teacher brings particular expertise.

    Example: culture of the 1960s — music, politics, literature

- Have students create projects that include elements of mathematics, science, and technology.

    Example: bridge design

- Use a standard scoring guide across all subjects.

    Example: a scoring guide used by teachers in all subjects to evaluate student writing with the same criteria

- Have students complete a community service project.

    Example: restoring a town park or playground

- Bring in outside speakers to talk about their jobs.

  Example: a journalist who covers current events in social studies might also discuss the use of language and editing skills

- Have academic teachers and career and technical education teachers work together to infuse more academics in technical courses and to add real-world projects in academic courses.

Use the following checklist to evaluate your school's readiness for developing interdisciplinary instruction to address Common Core State Standards and Next Generation Assessments.

Chapter 3: Rigorous and Relevant Instruction

Readiness for Interdisciplinary Instruction Checklist

YES	NO	
		Getting Ready
☐	☐	Teachers have a short list of priorities for instruction.
☐	☐	Everyone knows the priority needs of the community.
☐	☐	Staff members know key areas of state/standardized assessments.
☐	☐	The district has local curriculum standards and student competencies.
☐	☐	Career and technical education and arts courses have been analyzed to identify content that supports academic standards.
☐	☐	Career and technical education and arts teachers have a priority to reinforce academic standards.
☐	☐	Teachers use a consistent process to develop instructional plans.
		Getting Started
☐	☐	Teachers have access to curriculum resources.
☐	☐	Teachers have access to resources to help develop instructional plans.
☐	☐	Local assessments that are consistent with district and school priorities are developed.
☐	☐	Teachers have access to resources to develop local assessments.
☐	☐	Teachers offer a variety of instructional activities and methods.
		Implementing Interdisciplinary Instruction
☐	☐	Applied academic courses are developed and offered.
☐	☐	Professional development on integrating academics, career and technical education, and the arts is provided.
☐	☐	Team teaching of career and technical education/arts and academic teachers is practiced in school.
☐	☐	A balance is achieved between recall assessments and performance measures.
☐	☐	Parents are fully informed of options for students and referrals.
☐	☐	Teachers facilitate instruction that supports the standards.
☐	☐	Instruction is motivating to students, and they are actively engaged.
☐	☐	Teachers exhibit interest in continual improvement.
☐	☐	Teachers have common planning time to meet with interdisciplinary teams.

© International Center for Leadership in Education

Review Questions

1. How is the performance planning model an improvement over traditional planning methods?
2. What are the four major steps in planning rigorous and relevant instruction?
3. How might the Lexile Framework be used in instructional planning?
4. What facets of Nextpert assist with instructional planning?
5. How do the characteristics of Next Generation Assesments provide educators with opportunities for addressing the Common Core State Standards?
6. What are the benefits of having interdisciplinary teams?

 Chapter 4

Rigorous and Relevant Learning in the Digital Age

Teaching Digital Natives

As we discussed in previous chapters, our students have changed radically in the last decade. They are no longer the people our educational system was designed to teach.

Marc Prensky is an internationally acclaimed thought leader, speaker, writer, consultant, and game designer. In his thoughtful work on the impact of technology on student learning, "Digital Natives, Digital Immigrants" (2001), he lays out the challenge this way:

> Today's students have not just changed incrementally from those of the past, nor simply changed their slang, clothes, body adornments, or styles, as has happened between generations previously. A really big discontinuity has taken place. One might even call it a "singularity" — an event which changes things so fundamentally that there is absolutely no going back. This so-called "singularity" is the arrival and rapid dissemination of digital technology in the last decades of the 20th century.

Prensky points out that today's students — K–16 — are the first generation to grow up with the new technology. They've spent their entire lives using computers, video games, digital music players, videocams, cell phones, and all of the toys and tools of the digital age. Average college grads have spent fewer than 5,000 hours of their lives reading, but more than 10,000 hours playing video games and 20,000 hours watching TV. Computer games, e-mail, the Internet, cell phones, and instant messaging are integral parts of their lives.

Prensky refers to today's students as "Digital Natives": They are "native speakers" of the digital language of computers, video games, and the Internet. He refers respectfully to the rest of us who were not born into the digital world but have, at some later point in our lives, become fascinated by and adopted many or most aspects of the new technology, as "Digital Immigrants." He believes that the single biggest problem facing education today is that our Digital Immigrant teachers, who speak an outdated language (that of the pre-digital age), are struggling to teach a population that speaks an entirely new language.

Jim Warford, Senior Consultant for the International Center for Leadership in Education, goes a little further to make the point that today's students really ARE wired differently. He asks the question "How do you think today's students feel about our schools?" He provides this illustration as his response: "They feel like I feel when I board an airplane and hear the flight attendant tell the passengers to power off all electronic devices so we can listen to a syntillating presentation about the plane's safety features."

Thomas Friedman offers a powerful insight on how we must face this dilemma in his 2006 visionary work, *The World Is Flat*: "How we educate our children in the future will be more important than how much we educate them." Jim Warford adds, "We must close the 'engagement gap' before we can close the 'achievement gap'!"

The Tools of Technology as Tools of Rigor, Relevance, and Learner Engagement

Computers, the Internet, mobile devices, and apps are changing education as we know it. Embracing technology and learning to use it effectively are among a teacher's many challenges today.

The focus of this chapter is to consider the digital tools and applications used to plan and deliver instruction. Administrative applications of technology are also helpful in improving student performance. For example, technology can improve timely decision-making through the efficient use of "just in time" individual student achievement data and knowledge of what the student has already learned. Technology enhances communication, as e-mail, Web sites, electronic bulletin boards, homework hotlines, and voicemail give teachers the chance to share information conveniently with colleagues, parents, and students. Online testing, once we work out some of the start-up bugs, offers great potential for testing students when they are ready and at multiple points in the school year.

Technology can produce a positive impact on achieving rigor and relevance in several ways, including:

- equalizing learning access.
- increasing learning effectiveness and efficiency.
- creating new learning opportunities.

One of the lofty goals of public education in the United States is **equalizing learning access**. Technology offers great potential to make the same information available to all students, regardless of their location or the size of the school library. The responsibility falls to teachers to expand student learning beyond the classroom walls and to advocate for the technology infrastructure and access to materials and activities that will expose students to high-quality learning experiences. Teachers must find ways to integrate these explorations into their subject or grade through technology. To enhance rigor, especially for those students who conquer materials faster than other students do, teachers can turn to the Internet for a large number of online courses and enrichment activities. For relevance, there is no better way to apply communication or research skills than to interact with scientists, government officials, or international students via the Internet.

Teachers always want to be **increasing learning effectiveness and efficiency**. With many applications of technology, the learning objectives remain the same; students just have tools to accomplish the objectives more quickly or to a higher performance level. As the carpenter today uses technology in the form of air-powered hammers to shingle a roof, so the student writer uses word processing technology to write. Technology allows the carpenter to finish the job faster while fastening the shingles more consistently than is possible by hand. Likewise, word processing allows the student to make edits more easily, check spelling, and create more a polished document.

One traditional student objective that is accomplished more effectively with technology is student research. Of course, students still need to learn how to document sources and cite references in a virtual space in which plagiarism is temptingly easy. The online student researcher also requires enhanced skills to know how to distinguish credible sources from opinion or propaganda in the virtual world, where an editorial may look very similar to an encyclopedia entry.

Another way to increase learning effectiveness is to have students enhance their presentations and data analyses with graphics, charts, and images. The students of tomorrow will be communicating ideas in visual form with audio background because it is so easy to edit multimedia material. The means that teachers use to have students submit work and demonstrate competence can be greatly expanded with technological tools.

Some Digital Learning Opportunities

The most exciting aspect of technology is the chance for **creating new learning opportunities**. Technology opens up possibilities for students to acquire skills and knowledge not possible without the technology. Many of these skills and knowledge extend student learning into Quadrants B, C, and D on the Rigor/Relevance Framework. Once students have mastered foundation skills, technology-based projects offer opportunities to build knowledge with other students.

ThinkQuest and WebQuest projects involve students in designing Web pages with video and animation to create new learning environments and activities. Each year, the projects become more sophisticated as students build upon the previous work of others. It is similar to the work of research scientists, who push the frontiers of discovery by building upon the work of colleagues. These are exciting and relevant projects for students, not only because they use technology but also because students can see the real application of their knowledge.

Student collaboration is not new, but the ease of communication on the Internet means that students can collaborate across time and continents. The International Education and Resource Network's iEARN projects have thousands of participating students in more than 100 countries involved in joint student collaboration. Animation graphics and the ability to create branching controls by the user lead to creation of discovery activities, which the student can gradually explore and discover based upon his or her interest.

The Exploratorium in San Francisco (see www.exploratorium.edu) has created a virtual "hands-on" discovery center for students to learn about science concepts.

Another science-oriented initiative is Project Jason (see www.Jason.org), which takes students along on scientific expeditions to explore the ocean depths or the rainforests of South America without leaving their classrooms.

Technology and the Rigor/Relevance Framework

The degree to which technology is beneficial to learning depends on the way that it is applied in the classroom and beyond. When used effectively, technology offers great possibilities for expanding learning beyond what schools previously have taught. Technology puts vast amounts of knowledge at students' fingertips. Databases on every subject imaginable are available for study in all curriculum areas. Encyclopedias and complete collections of literary works reside on compact discs. Telecommunication satellite links expand the walls of classrooms to encompass the world.

The digital tools of technology offer students a chance to delve deeply into a topic. Greater accessibility to information gives students the opportunity to gather data easily and to analyze and synthesize the data in new ways. Students can manipulate data to identify the portions that are relevant to their needs. They can use data from one subject area in another area, integrating the information to enhance their understanding and giving them greater control over their learning.

Technology provides teachers with a tool to create their own teaching materials, to go beyond what is in the textbook and use alternate resources, and to organize information in new ways. Technology can be very helpful to teachers because it accommodates various learning styles and can enhance instructional strategies in many ways.

The way in which technology is used can be linked to the quadrants of the Rigor/Relevance Framework. The following chart lists a few ways that students can use technology for learning in each quadrant.

Transforming the Way We Teach Digital Natives

So how can we (must we) change teaching and learning in our schools if we are to connect with the current generation of digital natives? Marc Prensky, in his look at digital natives taught by digital immigrants, explains how they learn. He refers to these "nomadic grazing patterns of digital natives":

- Digital Natives are used to receiving information very quickly.
- They like to parallel process and multitask.
- They prefer their graphics before their text rather than the opposite.
- They prefer random access (like hypertext).

- They function best when networked.
- They thrive on instant gratification and frequent rewards.
- They prefer games to "serious" work.

Prensky offers a helpful tool for digital immigrants, those of us who are adapting to digital technologies but need a little help. He suggests that all teachers must at least understand the language and communication style of their students. This doesn't mean changing the meaning of what is important, or of good thinking skills. He points to a web site that, with a light approach, can help teachers translate the language and ideas of the digital generation students in their classroom: http://transl8it.com.

In his 2006 work, *Confronting the Challenges of Participatory Culture: Media Education for the 21st Century*, Henry Jenkins describes the "new literacies" that teachers must see as the pathways to rigorous, relevant student learning. He includes the following:

- play — the capacity to experiment with one's surroundings as a form of problem solving
- performance — the ability to adopt alternative identities for the purpose of improvisation and discovery
- simulation — the ability to interpret and construct dynamic models of real-world processes
- appropriation — the ability to meaningfully sample and remix media content
- multitasking — the ability to scan one's environment and shift focus as needed to salient details
- distributed cognition — the ability to interact meaningfully with tools that expand mental capacities
- collective intelligence — the ability to pool knowledge and compare notes with others toward a common goal
- judgment — the ability to evaluate the reliability and credibility of different information sources
- transmedia navigation — the ability to follow the flow of stories and information across multiple modalities
- networking — the ability to search for, synthesize, and disseminate information
- negotiation — the ability to travel across diverse communities, discerning and respecting multiple perspectives, and grasping and following alternative norms

Technology Applications for Rigorous and Relevant Learning

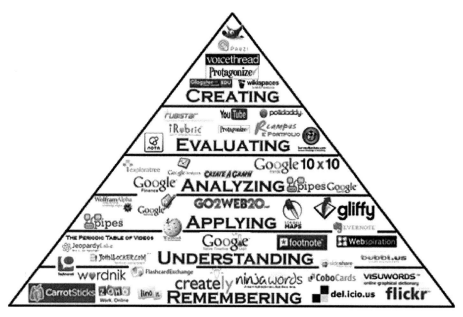

(For a list of apps aligned to Bloom's Taxonomy visit: https://sites.google.com/site/bloomsapps/home)

The Impact of Technology on Teaching and Learning

Technology has been impacting teaching and learning for more than 20 years. However, it must be said that it is never about the technology alone but about attaining higher student achievement through the coupling of technology with sound pedagogical practices, all while facing tighter and tighter budgets.

To understand how technology can lead to higher student achievement, one should become aware of three major trends or developments taking place today. These developments do not just impact education; they also will affect business and society in general. The first two trends described will have an influence on the mechanics of learning — connectivity and devices. The third trend impacts the instructional methodologies used that can support embedded literacy and can engage teachers and students in real-world applications for learning.

The three impacting societal trends are:

- widespread wireless connectivity, creating a hyperconnected world.
- a boom of inexpensive devices in the form of tablets, smartphones, and laptops.
- extensive developments in cloud-based learning applications.

Widespread Wireless Connectivity

As some will remember, part of the stimulus package used during the last economic downfall was earmarked to help our nation achieve a higher level of connectivity. Widespread connectivity, resulting in what is now called a "hyperconnected world," was the outcome of that stimulus investment. Connectivity today is offered through multiple providers and at costs affordable to many in our society, including students. This connectivity will challenge the traditional model of schooling. Schools are used to having complete control over the network and end devices, but that will change, as we will discuss in the next section. Schools will need to develop policies and procedures that will accommodate a world in which students will BYOD — that is, Bring Your Own Devices to school. The recent Speak Up survey, the largest survey conducted in public education today, states that 67% of the parents surveyed would purchase their son or daughter a laptop or tablet so long as schools will allow their children to use them at school. It will not be whether or not schools adopt a BYOD policy, but *when* it will happen. Those who argue against this development will find themselves on the wrong side of history as inexpensive connectivity, coupled with the inexpensive devices described below, will drive that change — and, ultimately, higher student achievement if correctly incorporated into the learning process.

Inexpensive Devices

When the annual Consumer Electronics Show draws to a close in Las Vegas, few will make the connection between the events at that show and what goes on in the classroom. Many of the products showcased at the CES this year were inexpensive computing devices that can access the Internet through the ever-increasing wireless networks, as discussed above. School leaders will need to understand (some willingly, some not) that schools will not be in a position to provide all the technology needed for students to get a quality education in the future. As we learned in the Speak Up survey, parents are willing to purchase devices for their children to take and utilize in instruction at school. They will feel strongly that these devices be used to help in the education of their children. For those unable to afford their own devices, schools can use their limited resources to provide devices to those students. Smartphones, which are carried by many in schools today, will also play more of a role in the instructional process. (Please visit http://www.studyblue.com/projects/infographic-mobile-studying-online-flashcards-on-smartphones/ for some interesting statistics on cell phone use with students.) The end result is that all schools should start planning for a 1 to 1 learning environment, complete with personalized learning plans for all students.

Cloud-based Learning Applications

Delivering a personal learning plan for all students has always been a long-term goal in education. In the 1970's it was called, "individualized instruction." It was impossible then; but with the advent of the "Cloud," it is totally doable and affordable today. As mentioned above, the first two trends provide for new teaching and learning environments to form in our schools. However, the third and most important category impacts how instruction can be delivered and customized to the individual learner, increasing relevance. The *Horizon Report* is one of the most respected sources for researching and documenting coming trends in education. The categories sited in this year's report as being the most important and closest to widespread adoption are cloud computing, mobile devices, electronic books, and collaborative environments.

It is made clear that the most important trend named in the *2011 Horizon Report* is that of cloud computing. In the past, several states tried to implement a 1 to 1 learning environment but found the resulting impact on student achievement to be less than convincing, and in some cases almost embarrassing when decision makers looked at the ROI. This failure was not due to lack of planning or hard work on the part of many 1 to 1 administrators, but actually due to initiatives that were somewhat ahead of their time. At their initial implementation, we did not have the ability to deliver compelling software through the Internet to the individual learner. The result then was that student computing devices (mostly laptop computers) sat unused or vastly underused for their potential in participating classrooms. In successful implementations today, that is not the case! Many Web 2.0 tools have evolved to deliver a robust learning environment, greatly impacting the outcome of 1 to 1 programs and the promise that they hold for innovative teaching and learning scenarios. However, it must be said that without proper teacher training, all three of the trends described in this document will have little impact on instruction. Only when teachers are properly trained can dramatic student achievement be realized.

When educators are properly trained and use the power of these three trends to their advantage, dramatic advancements can be realized. Through a concept called the Flipped Classroom, early results on student achievement have been quite impressive. The Flipped Classroom comes from incorporating the new capabilities provided by cloud computing into the instructional model. It is a result of knowing how to use the cloud and how it can deliver on the long-sought-after goal of personalized learning for students. (For more on the Flipped Classroom, see http://kuglinlive.wikispaces.com/The+Flipped+Classroom.)

Of course, other recent new developments in technology, such as iBooks, will have an impact on teaching and learning. However, one should exercise caution when referring to what is an electronic textbook. Don't fall into the trap that some companies have set by describing their products as being the textbook of the future. New models for delivering curriculum called "Custom Curriculum Publishing" hold tremendous potential regarding the way in which content may be aggregated and delivered in the future. Change is coming and is inevitable, especially given the latest data from the Speak Up survey. Students in the future will demand more from their schools. In a hyperconnected world, students have the ability to force change on those wishing to keep the status quo or who fear making the necessary changes. In a hyperconnected world, think about the power that a 22-year-old girl had when using the Internet and social media to bring about change. Yes, it was a 22-year-old girl who forced the Bank of America to change its policy for charging account holders a $5.00 monthly fee to access their own money. That same 22-year-old took on Verizon Wireless as it attempted to charge its subscribers an extra fee, and her work caused that company to reverse its policy as well. Now, consider 14-year-olds sitting in one of your classrooms, tired of not being able to reach content that they find valuable to them on the Internet; or not being able to use their phone in an instructional way in class; or feeling discouraged by countless policies, restrictions, and teachers who feel insecure with technology — all described as key obstacles to learning in this year's Speak Up survey results. Now, think about your district's being the next to change its policies and/or procedures when one of your students finds his or her new power, just like that 22-year-old girl did, and brings about change in your district using the same channels. It is a hyperconnected world and a different playing field for us now. Use these trends to help bring the change to your district and to reach those goals of higher academic achievement for all students.

Internet Resources

The following are some excellent sources of lesson plans on the Internet, drawn from Kathy Schrock's Guide for Educators (http://school.discoveryeducation.com/schrock-guide/index.html).

Technology Infusion Lesson Links

Adobe Education Exchange (http://edexchange.adobe.com/pages/home)
A searchable database of teacher-created lessons, tips, and tricks for the infusion of technology across the curriculum

Best Practices of Technology Integration (http://www.remc11.k12.mi.us/bstpract/)
Lessons created by Michigan teachers that demonstrate how technology can be used as a valuable tool in the classroom

Integrating the Internet in Your Curriculum
(http://www.kathimitchell.com/integrate.html)
A well-done tutorial to give educators ideas and a foundation for Internet use in the classroom

School Projects That Connect with the Internet
(http://mercury.siec.k12.in.us/west/proj/index.html)
Samples of Internet lessons for grades K–3

Teach Using Technology as a Tool
(http://web.archive.org/web/20050204112731/http://pd.l2l.org/tch_classroom.html)
Classroom activities which provide a framework and strategy for implementing a lesson that integrates the Internet and other technology tools into the classroom

TrackStar
(http://trackstar.4teachers.org/trackstar/;jsessionid=691D8697EB31053520927D6A2A80EAD7)
An awesome series of Internet integration curriculum "tracks"; use one of these or create your own

WebQuest Page (http://www.webquest.org/)
A site which provides descriptions and examples of how to use this great model of Internet integration in the classroom

General Lesson Plan Links

AskERIC Search (http://www.eric.ed.gov/)
The premier reference site for educational research and lesson plans information

Big Six Skills (http://edweb.sdsu.edu/courses/edtec670/cardboard/board/b/big6/)
A lesson devoted to this systematic approach to information problem solving that relies on critical thinking skills

Curriculum Mapping
(http://www.curriculummapping101.com/curriculum-mapping-resources)
Resources and practical ideas to support mapping of the curriculum

Designing Performance Assessments (http://www.pgcps.org/~elc/developingtasks.html)
A wealth of information and templates for designing performance assessment tasks for your students

edHelper.com Lesson Plans (http://www.edhelper.com/)
A compilation of over 5500 lesson plans that are subject categorized

EDinformatics Lesson Plan Page (http://edinformatics.com/lessons/lessons.htm)
A page with the collected search tools from many of the major lesson plan databases

GEM: The Gateway to Educational Materials (http://www.thegateway.org/)
A searchable (keyword and subject) database of quality curriculum support lesson plans

K–12 Lesson Plans (http://teams.lacoe.edu/teachers/index.asp)
An exemplary and updated list of lesson plan links

Lesson Plans Page (http://www.lessonplanspage.com/)
Sponsored by Scholastic, this page contains hundreds of teacher-submitted lesson plans

Smithsonian Education: Educators
Lesson plans and links to hundreds of resources in the arts, social studies, science/technology, and language arts utilizing the vast collections of the Smithsonian; searchable by grade level, subject, and state standard

Project/Challenge Based Learning Links

Project-Based Education for the 21st Century (http://www.bie.org/)
A collection of videos, links to resources, research studies, and much more dealing with PBL in the classroom

Project-Based Learning (http://pbl-online.org/default.htm)
A instructional resource site with material to help teachers develop and design PBL projects for middle and high school students

Project-Based Learning from Edutopia (http://www.edutopia.org/project-based-learning)
A project learning site with an overview of the process, videos illustrating what it looks like, and an extensive library of links

Project-Based Learning Space (http://college.cengage.com/education/pbl/index.html)
Originally a textbook support site, this resource provides an overview of PBL, sample social studies projects, and teaching concepts to support this method of instruction

Understanding by Design Exchange (www.ubdexchange.org/)
This database of lessons was created using the process developed by Grant Wiggins and Jay McTighe

Review Questions

1. How might you use technology to make a positive impact on achieving rigor and relevance?
2. What are some ways that technology can be used to create new learning opportunities?
3. How can technology tools be used to support teachers' improvement efforts?
4. How might your school use the "new literacies" as vehicles to meaningfully engage students in rigorous and relevant learning?

Chapter 5

Relationships Make Learning Possible

At a gathering of several hundred principals from the School District of Philadelphia, International Center for Leadership in Education Chairman and Founder, Willard R. Daggett, was sharing a story about Jack, his 6-year-old grandson in North Carolina. To Daggett's surprise, Jack had recruited his grandfather to play touch football. Once in the huddle, Daggett couldn't believe what he was hearing. Jack, the team quarterback, called the play, with instructions for his receiver. "Go out 20 feet and cut 25 degrees to the left," Jack said. Right away, Daggett realized his grandson had made a slight mistake — he should have told his friend to cut 90 degrees. But what really stunned him was the fact that these 1st-graders were using percents at all, since they're generally considered to be a 6th or 7th grade math concept.

"Where'd you learn that?" Daggett asked afterward. "From our 1st-grade teacher," Jack replied. Intrigued, Daggett met Jack's teacher, who told him that — after learning Jack and his friends loved football — she invited the local high school football coach to teach her students pass plays.

The anecdote about Jack's football game provided perfect example of the larger point that Daggett was making to the room full of school principals. Relationships make learning possible. Jack's teacher knew enough about the boys' interests that she realized a visit from a football coach would engage and focus their minds. "Until you have a relationship with kids," Daggett pointed out, "you can't tell what's relevant for them, and it is relevance that makes rigor possible." This powerful truth about the connection between relationships, relevance, and academic rigor helps explain, as much as anything else, why the International Center's Rigor/Relevance Framework has become a cornerstone of many school reform efforts throughout the country.

Strong relationships are critical to completing rigorous and relevant work successfully. Building strong relationships with students is a critical element of the teaching segment of the DSEI. Students are more likely to make a personal commitment to engage in rigorous learning when they know that teachers, parents, and other students actually care about how well they do. They are willing to continue making the investment when they are encouraged, supported, and assisted, much in the same way that a personal trainer might work with an athlete who lacks the will or confidence to continue.

Relationships involving the student as learner are important, but so are relationships among staff. In model schools, it is clearly evident that staff members support each other and learn from one another. In these schools, teachers enjoy their work and perform as a team, sharing the challenge of effective teaching. Again, it is the quality of relationships that is apparent in these effective schools.

Four dimensions of relationships are important in schools:

- **Learning Relationships:** These are the relationships with students that are essential for support in the learning process. They are formed from a combination of relationships with parents, peers, and teachers.
- **Staff Relationships:** These are the relationships among teachers, administrators, and support staff that influence teaching and that support functions, staff retention and development, and school decision-making and problem solving.
- **Professional Relationships:** These are the relationships that each educator creates and maintains to learn and develop in the profession. It includes individual mentors and groups from whom an educator learns and those who provide a supportive environment in the profession. This group often extends beyond the school or district in which an educator is employed.
- **Community Relationships:** These are the relationships of the school as an organization with parents and business and community leaders.

The Critical Importance of Teacher-Student Relationships in Learning

Research supports what most of us see as common sense: what goes on between the teacher and each student is central to high-level learning. Effective teaching is not the end goal, but it *is* the means to an end: student achievement.

Several significant research studies have particularly informed the DSEI. One is John Hattie's *Visible Learning: A Synthesis of Over 800 Meta-Analyses Relating to Achievement*. In this comprehensive study, Hattie analyzed 200,000 "effect sizes" (that is, the relative impact of one factor compared to other factors) from 52,637 studies involving more than 50 million students and covering an exhaustive number of factors relevant to learning.

Hattie's approach relies on the notion that effect sizes are the best way to identify what has the greatest influence on student learning. The calculations behind his work are complex, but — to simplify — an "effect-size" of 1.0 (defined as an increase of one standard deviation) is typically associated with the equivalent of approximately two years of growth in one year.

Hattie's analysis shows that most variables in schools have an effect size of around +0.3 or +0.4, what Hattie calls his "hinge point." Any factor below +0.4 is of lower value. Factors below 0.0 have negative effects. Some factors can be directly affected by an education organization; others cannot. Some noteworthy effect sizes from his research include:

- Formative Evaluation: +0.90 (~ 1.7 years of growth)
- Providing feedback: +0.73 (~ 1.44 years of growth)
- Student-Teacher Relationships: +0.72 (~ 1.44 years of growth)
- Prior Achievement: +0.67 (~ 1.34 years of growth)
- Professional Development: +0.62 (~ 1.24 years of growth)
- Socioeconomic Status: +0.57 (~1.14 years of growth)
- Peer Tutoring: +0.55 (~1.13 years of growth)
- Teaching Test-taking: +0.22
- Reducing Class Size: +0.21

The point is clear — student-teacher relationships are very important. But whatever steps a school takes to improve growth, every one of them — including the factors listed above — are much more effective when they are effectively supported. For instruction to improve and student growth to increase, schools and districts require a supportive and aligned system. Stated another way, effective teaching is essential, but it will not — on its own — maximize achievement for all students. This understanding of the need for an organization-wide commitment to success lies at the heart of the DSEI.

The DSEI's comprehensive approach leverages more than the teacher in the classroom. It emphasizes the entire educational organization. More specifically, it emphasizes vertical alignment — with organizational systems and structures and with instructional leadership — and horizontal alignment — with teaching colleagues and classroom resources — as keys to success. Because teachers are the most powerful influence on instruction, the entire system needs to be focused on making teachers effective. Therefore, the DSEI provides a coherent focus across an entire education system: Organizational Leadership, Instructional Leadership, and Teaching.

Relationship Framework

Good leaders inspire others and, in the process, develop positive relationships among staff. Likewise, good teachers break down student isolation and facilitate learning that provides a strong supportive environment for students. Positive relationships occur in many schools. The question is whether, in the process of school improvement, we can elevate relationships from a characteristic that we observe to a dimension of schools that we measure, set goals around, plan for, and systematically improve.

Perhaps what is needed to bring relationships into a viable aspect of school improvement is the development of a Relationship Framework. Such a taxonomy will enable quantifying relationships. More than 50 years ago, Benjamin Bloom and others developed the Knowledge Taxonomy that has become universally accepted as a way to designate levels of cognitive thinking. Teachers set and improve levels of student thinking in their classrooms using this knowledge framework. Bill Daggett and the International Center for Leadership in Education created the Application Model to describe a taxonomy of learning along higher degrees of application. In the same way that the Knowledge Taxonomy and the Application Model have helped define knowledge and application, a clear taxonomy for relationships can help us understand the continuum

Chapter 5: Relationships Make Learning Possible

of personal relationships as it functions in dynamic, real-world conditions. This sort of taxonomy can also help us maximize the positive impact of these important connections as they relate to learning.

The Relationship Framework describes seven levels of relationships:

- **Level 0 is Isolation.** This is the lack of any positive relationships. The individual feels alone and isolated from social relationships that would enhance learning.
- **Level 1 is Known.** A person must know someone before a relationship is formed. When teachers seek to develop positive relationships with students, the first step is getting to know them — their families, likes, dislikes, aspirations, and learning styles.
- **Level 2 is Receptive.** Often a learning relationship is described in terms of providing the assistance and support that a student needs. However, a preliminary step is showing that you are interested and genuinely care about developing a relationship. This comes from frequent contact in multiple settings and taking an active interest.
- **Level 3 is Reactive.** In this case, one person receives guidance or support from another. This relationship yields emotional support or cognitive information.
- **Level 4 is Proactive.** At this level, the partners have made a proactive commitment to do more than assist when needed and take an active interest in supporting the other person.
- **Level 5 is Sustained.** Positive support is balanced from all family members, peers, and teachers. It is a relationship that will endure over a long period of time. This is the level of relationship that effective parents have with their children.
- **Level 6 is Mutually Beneficial.** This level occurs rarely in education, for at this point, both parties contribute support to one another for an extended period of time.

When the Relationship Framework is applied to learning, it refers to the support that is provided to students from teachers, parents, peers, and the community. The following chart describes the degrees of student support at each level of the framework.

	Relationship Framework	Learning Relationships Support for Students
0	Isolated	Students feel significant isolation from teachers, peers, or even parents. Students lack any emotional, social connection to peers and teachers.
1	Known	Students are known by others and frequently are called by name. Teachers know students and their families, interests, aspirations, and challenges. Students are known by peers with whom they interact at school.
2	Receptive	Students have contact with peers, parents, and teachers in multiple settings. Teachers exhibit positive behaviors of "being there" that show genuine interest and concern.
3	Reactive	Teachers, parents, and peers provide help to students when requested, but support may be sporadic and inconsistent among support groups.
4	Proactive	Others take an active interest in students' success. Teachers take initiative to show interest and provide support. Students and others express verbal commitment for ongoing support and validate this commitment with their actions.
5	Sustained	There is extensive, ongoing, pervasive, and balanced support from teachers, parents, and peers that is consistent and sustained over time.
6	Mutually Beneficial	Positive relationships are everywhere and commonplace among the way that students, teachers, and parents interact and support students as learners.

How the Relationship Framework Helps Teachers

Once teachers make relationships important, they can begin to reflect on current practices and discuss how to improve relationships. Relationships are not simply good or bad; they exist on a continuum. Furthermore, relationships can change over time.

The Relationship Framework is useful because it first helps teachers understand that there are degrees of relationships. When they think about their relationships with students, teachers can use the framework to apply a qualitative measure to the relationships that they establish. This qualitative measure helps teachers reflect on their current levels and allows them to decide whether they wish to make changes to improve relationships. When relationships are categorized as a simple dichotomy of "good" or "poor," teachers are not likely to reflect on practice or make self-directed changes. If relationships are "good," there is no need for change. If relationships are "poor," it is easier to become defensive, to blame the other party, or simply to accept things as they are. When a leveled framework is used for describing relationships, it has a different effect on teachers. Even if relationships are poor, there are at least some positive aspects on which to build. This makes teachers less defensive.

At the other end of the scale, relationships categorized as generally "good" are usually never as good as they could be; there is the potential for growth and further improvement. This motivates even the best teachers to continue to work on improving relationships and strive to reach higher levels. In this case, all teachers need to work on improving relationships, regardless of the current level of success.

The various levels in the Relationship Framework help to identify the changes that need to be made to improve relationships. If a teacher observes that a student is "isolated," the first step is to engage in interventions to get the student "known." The teacher can get to know the student and facilitate activities among peers to expand what they know about one another. Just because students "hang out" together does not mean that they really know much about each other. Sometimes a student in a group can be just as isolated as a student who sits alone in a school cafeteria.

If a teacher observes that current student relationships are at the "known" level, relationship interventions can focus on frequency of contact and exhibiting behaviors of receptivity. The next level moves to behaviors that provide support to students.

The various levels of the Relationship Framework provide guidance to teachers on how gradually to move to higher levels of learning relationships. Again, relationships are not a dichotomy of "good" or "bad"; rather, there are degrees of relationships, and teachers can work on behaviors that will improve learning relationships.

Classroom Management Versus Learning Relationships

The teacher's responsibility in teaching and learning in the classroom is often divided into instruction and classroom management. Instruction refers to the content and pedagogy of what is learned. Classroom management refers to the processes and techniques that teachers use to set the climate for learning. The term *classroom management* creates the impression that the classroom is an industrial process rather than a collaboration among people. It suggests that the teacher applies certain management techniques, without any emotion, to make sure that the classroom runs smoothly and efficiently. The term originates in the industrial model of education, the same model that gives us a rigid bell schedule, differentiation of labor, and large schoolhouses.

School leaders are now questioning many of these industrial model characteristics. Perhaps one of the changes that schools should make is to abandon the term *classroom management* and replace it with *relationship building*. Teachers do need to create a climate for learning in the classroom, but this is not a process to be managed. The classroom is made up of a group of students who desire and deserve high-quality personal relationships with adults and peers. It is the quality of these relationships that drives their behavior and leads to learning. The following table describes some differences in looking at the climate of instruction as relationship building rather than as classroom management.

	Classroom Management	**Relationship Building**
Classroom Rules	Mandated	Negotiated
Power	Without question	Power with respect
Observation of Effectiveness	Students sitting passively and quietly	Students actively engaged
Risk-Taking	Discouraged	Encouraged
Control Mechanism	Negative punishments	Positive reinforcement
Primary Teacher Role	Absolute attention	Source of encouragement

Staff Relationships

When the Relationship Framework is applied to staff, it refers to the level of respect, communication, and collaboration that exists among all staff in a school. The following chart provides additional descriptions of staff relationships at each level of the framework.

Relationship Framework		Learning Relationships Support for Staff
0	Isolated	Staff members perform their work but feel significant isolation from other staff or lack frequent feedback from school leaders and others.
1	Known	Staff members know each other personally, including their interests, aspirations, and challenges.
2	Receptive	Teachers, support staff, and leaders have frequent contact and respect each other's contributions to the school environment. All exhibit behaviors of interest in others.
3	Reactive	There are many examples of teachers or support staff working together, and staff members consistently and eagerly help when requested.
4	Proactive	Strong levels of collaboration exist, and there is obvious ongoing commitment in team teaching, mentoring new teachers, and professional development.
5	Sustained	There is demonstrated ongoing collaboration from all staff over a significant period of time. New staff members are incorporated into the school culture of collaboration.
6	Mutually Beneficial	Staff members work as a total community committed to each other and to school goals.

Professional Relationships

The Relationship Framework is applied to educators beyond their work with colleagues employed at the same school or district. Professional educators learn their craft by working with mentors and other educators at universities, other school districts, and in professional organizations. Educators often rely on national, state, or regional professional organizations for ideas and encouragement in their specific profession. The dozens of professional organizations for educators testify to the importance of professional relationships in education. Educators often rely on formal mentors for guidance throughout their career. The term *professional relationships*, then, refers to the ongoing collaboration that exists among all educators outside of the school or district where they work. The following chart provides additional descriptions of professional relationships at each level of the framework.

A Systemwide Approach to Rigor, Relevance, and Relationships

Relationship Framework		Learning Relationships Support for Educators
0	Isolated	Educators work with little interaction with others in the profession.
1	Known	Educators know many educators within their profession. They attend regional or state professional meetings.
2	Receptive	Educators make frequent contact via telephone or e-mail with like professionals beyond formal meetings. They exhibit a willingness to actively participate, share ideas, and answer questions.
3	Reactive	Educators offer and seek help from others in the profession. Also, they may present programs, write articles, or simply meet one-on-one with another educator.
4	Proactive	Educators have formal agreements with other educators to serve as mentors, providing ongoing advice and feedback.
5	Sustained	There is ongoing collaborative and active involvement in professional organizations.
6	Mutually Beneficial	Educators are recognized as making significant contributions to their profession. Professional relationships are essential rewards in personal satisfaction in the educators' work.

Community Relationships

When the Relationship Framework is applied to the community, it describes the level of respect, support, involvement, and communication that exists among various community groups and the school as a whole. The following chart describes examples of community relationships at each level of the framework.

	Relationship Framework	Learning Relationships Support for Community
0	Isolated	The school may be strong or weak, but it functions independently from the community at large.
1	Known	School staff knows families, community organizations, and community leaders. Staff members are knowledgeable about major local businesses.
2	Receptive	Staff and administration exhibit openness to parents and community. Parents feel welcome in the school.
3	Reactive	Parent requests for information are responded to promptly. School activities include community service. There are many active parents involved in a variety of school activities and instruction.
4	Proactive	Active partnerships exist with community and business organizations. There are community groups that formally support various school functions.
5	Sustained	A long tradition of parent involvement and community partnerships exists. The school attributes a large share of its success to community partnerships.
6	Mutually Beneficial	Relationships at this level are mature and committed. They benefit both the school and the community.

How to Build Relationships

Building relationships is determined by the way that teachers create either a respectful and positive relationship that elevates the level of learning or a negative relationship that stands as an obstacle to learning. Relationships are carefully constructed, one conversation or action at a time. It takes many interactions to create a positive relationship — but only one careless comment or action to destroy it. The development of a teacher-student relationship can be compared to a large display of dominoes. After tedious and careful construction, the builder steps back to see the beautiful result. However, one misplaced domino can destroy the display before it is completed, and the builder will have to start all over again. Such is the case with building relationships: One negative comment or conversation can ruin a relationship between a teacher and a student, forcing them to rebuild what they created together. In building relationships, teachers must be patient, for relationships take time to build. They also must be cautious in what they say and do.

Actions That Value Others

Sandra Harris, in her book *Bravo, Teacher! Building Relationships with Actions That Value Others*, offers practical suggestions and moving stories about building relationships. (Harris has written a similar book about the teacher-administrator relationship; see the Appendix.) Actions that help to build relationships include the following:

Actions That Uphold High Standards
- Search Your Soul
- Accept Responsibility
- Create a Culture of Achievement

Actions That Are Empowering
- Build Leadership Capacity
- Encourage Authentic Learning
- Demonstrate Democratic Principles

Actions That Demonstrate Respect for All
- Be Fair
- Be Caring

Actions That Support All Students
- Communicate Effectively
- Encourage

Actions That Challenge the Imagination
- Be Open to Change
- Solve Problems Creatively

Actions That Demonstrate Culturally Responsive Teaching
- Confront Your Own Personal Biases
- Confront Biases in the Classroom
- Acknowledge and Affirm Cultural Diversity
- Be Careful About Crossing Bridges

Actions That Are Courageous
- Advocate for Others
- Abound in Hope

One education initiative that has relationships as a primary focus is the Tripod Project, introduced in Chapter 2. The purpose of the Tripod Project is to increase communication and build knowledge among teachers about ways of achieving success in the classroom. It focuses on three legs of the instructional tripod — content, pedagogy, and relationships — with the aim of helping all students, especially African-American and Hispanic students, to achieve at higher levels.

The project encourages teachers to attend more carefully to how each leg of the tripod interacts with five key tasks of social and intellectual engagement in their own classrooms. These five key tasks are:

- **Task One: Trust and Interest vs. Mistrust and Disinterest.** Introductory class sessions provide a good start to the semester by fostering positive feelings about the class.
- **Task Two: Balanced vs. Imbalanced Teacher Control and Student Autonomy.** Teacher and students seek and find an appropriate balance of teacher control and student autonomy.
- **Task Three: Ambitiousness vs. Ambivalence.** Each student collaborates with the teacher to commit to ambitious learning goals and to overcome ambivalence by either party.
- **Task Four: Industriousness vs. Disengagement or Discouragement.** Teacher and students work industriously to achieve goals for learning and to recover from any disengagement or discouragement due to setbacks.
- **Task Five: Consolidation vs. Irresolution and Disconnection.** Teacher helps students to consolidate what they have learned and to connect goals to future classes and life experiences, where what they have learned will be applicable.

Communication That Signals Caring

Timely Talking

The first component of effective communication is the decision to even talk at all. Sometimes the decision to engage in a conversation has more impact on building positive relationships than the actual conversation does. For a school leader, one of the important concepts to instill in teachers is making good decisions about when to engage in conversation. For example, seeing a negative behavior is best corrected with an immediate direct response; for if a teacher fails to speak and acknowledge this inappropriate behavior, then students will quickly assume it is acceptable. A teacher must act quickly when a student obviously exhibits frustration, shows lack of interest, or feels isolated. By asking a question, giving a compliment, or even making a personal greeting, a conversation can start that will continue to build positive relationships with students. Teachers need feedback both from school leaders and peers about the timely decisions of talking and engaging in conversations. Too much talk can create negative feelings in students. All teachers should be constantly aware of the timeliness of their conversations so that they can take advantage of opportunities to build positive relationships, show interest, and assist students in engaging learning situations.

Tactful Honesty

The second component of effective communication is honesty. Students observe much more than we frequently give them credit for. A poor communication practice occurs whenever teachers provide inaccurate information, try to cover up negative events, or share only part of "the story" with students. Often this is done to try to protect students, but students usually will get the full story at a later time. This lack of full honesty acts as a roadblock to the building of high-quality learning relationships. Students often indicate that they value teachers and administrators who are open and honest with them, sharing both good news and bad.

Being honest is often a significant burden. Full disclosure can create strong emotions and can even be brutal to students. So while it is important to be fully honest in talking with students, it is also important for teachers to use some measure of tact in sharing information with students. One way to improve tactfulness in conversations is for teachers to be very precise in their observations. For example, when a teacher observes that a student frequently is late to class, the teacher really has no idea of the reason or motivation for the tardiness. If the teacher makes a comment that the student is lazy or unorganized, that assumption may be wrong and may lead to additional confrontation. It is far more tactful to say to the student, privately, "You've been late four times this week. That negatively affects the rest of the students in this class." This latter comment is still accurate, but it is less judgmental. An instructional leader working to improve student relationships recognizes the importance of providing feedback to teachers regarding the use of tactful honesty in improving conversations.

Active Listening

The third component of communication for building relationships is active listening. Active listening is intentionally focusing on the person with whom you are having a conversation, whether it is in a group or one-on-one, in order to understand what he or she is saying. Teachers wanting to use good communication skills to build relationships must practice focusing on students one on one and engaging in the conversation. Looking directly at the other person, turning toward the subject, and removing other distractions help the teacher to be more aware of the student's nonverbal cues and show a greater interest in the conversation as well as the individual.

Active listening may also require suppressing emotional involvement with the conversation. It is hard to truly listen if the teacher is yelling at students. Active listening requires both hearing and observing. Verbal clues and other observations help to decode a student's message. Give each student time to complete his or her message. Express appreciation for sharing information and encourage him or her to engage in future conversations. It also may be helpful to ask questions and restate key points to affirm your understanding. Finally, avoid making snap judgments; reflect on what has been said and then respond appropriately.

Consistent Body Language

Body language is the unspoken communication that occurs in nearly every human encounter. We all have many innate and learned physical characteristics that reveal a great deal about our unspoken thoughts and emotions. Having the ability to read and understand body language can make a significant difference in good communication between teachers and students. Teachers should learn to read students' body language and recognize the important characteristics that indicate students' feelings. In addition, teachers should reflect on their own posture, mannerisms, and gestures that might convey hidden meanings to students. Following are several tips to keep in mind when it comes to knowing how to use one's body effectively in conversations.

- Eye contact is one of the most important aspects. While there are cultural exceptions, good conversation generally requires making eye contact. Eye contact is essential for conveying interest in a conversation.
- Posture also conveys a great deal about emotions. Walking around with slumping shoulders or with head down conveys a lack of confidence or interest and a generally weak attitude. Students are not likely to approach teachers who exhibit such negative posture.
- Head position is also an important indication of confidence. When we are confident, we keep our heads level both horizontally and vertically. To appear more authoritative, keep the head straight and level. To appear friendly and receptive, tilt the head just a little to one side or the other.
- Hand gestures and arm movements also give clues. In general, the more outgoing people are, the more they tend to use big arm motions in conversations; the quieter they are, the less they will move their arms away from the body. Try to strike a balance of arm movements so that you convey both friendliness and enthusiasm.
- Distance from others is crucial for giving off the right signals. Standing too close will label a person as "pushy" or "in your face"; standing too far away will suggest a person's lack of interest.

Relationships in school can always be improved. Schools engage in specific practices to improve the quality of relationships that influence student learning and the operation of a school. In regard to student learning relationships, school practices fall into three categories:

1. **Supportive Behaviors:** ways that teachers act and interact with students to support positive learning and good relationships
2. **Supportive Initiatives:** school initiatives that contribute to positive learning and good relationships
3. **Supportive Structures:** major organizational changes that contribute to learning and good relationships

Supportive Behaviors

Following are examples of adult and peer behaviors that influence learning relationships in a positive manner.

- showing respect
- "being there" for students, with frequent contact
- active listening
- one-on-one communication
- encouraging students to express opinions
- avoiding "put-downs"
- writing encouraging notes
- praise of students by their peers
- displaying students' work
- identifying unique talents and strengths
- exhibiting enthusiasm
- using positive humor
- serving as a role model
- celebrating accomplishments

Showing Respect

Showing students respect can be as simple as calling students by their names. When an adult shows interest in what a student has to say and allows all ideas to be expressed, respect is present. The tone of voice that a teacher uses in recognizing or responding to students makes a difference in the students' interpretations of the teacher's respect for them. A learning environment characterized by order, focused on learning, and free of disruptions signals respect to the students. Behavior and activities that encourage diversity and demonstrate the acceptance of different cultures also illustrate respect. Rules about acceptable behavior among students, such as an intolerance of bullying, also provide evidence of respect for students.

"Being There" for Students, with Frequent Contact

Educators project an interest in their students by their presence at and participation in school functions. When students notice that teachers are there, they recognize the sense of value that the teachers place on the students and their activities. Some examples of school events and activities that teachers can observe or participate in to demonstrate their interest include advising extracurricular and cocurricular activities; coaching sports; judging school competitions; chaperoning school events; and attending music programs, theatrical productions, and art shows.

The presence of teachers in their classrooms before and after school sends a message to students: Teachers "are there" for students. Giving students exact times when a teacher might be available for extra assistance tells students that the teacher is willing to give extra academic help and is available to do so. Some teachers provide e-mail addresses and telephone numbers so that students may contact them if necessary. Participation in after-school, Saturday, and summer academic assistance programs is another example of "being there" for students. In some districts, teachers visit students in their homes, or the district might sponsor a door-to-door community outreach to let parents, students, and community members know that the school values working with youth in the community.

A simple yet highly effective example of "being there" and having contact with students occurs at the beginning of the school day and during the change of classes. A teacher who stands in a hallway to greet students creates a strong contact with students and sends an indirect, subtle message of caring.

Active Listening, One-on-One Communication, Encouraging Students to Express Opinions

Adults can show that they are interested through active listening and by using words of encouragement, regardless of the situation. Raising questions on what is being shared and agreeing or disagreeing with thoughts let the students know that the adult is paying attention and desires to continue the dialogue.

One-on-one communication can be very powerful in assisting students to express their ideas. Often, students are afraid to speak their mind because of how others might perceive their ideas. Teenagers do not want to be unaccepted or unpopular.

Avoiding "Put-downs," Writing Encouraging Notes, Praise of Students by Their Peers

Students are not unlike adults in their need for recognition and encouragement. They want to be praised, they want their accomplishments to be noticed, and they want to be validated and recognized for their achievements. "Put-downs" should not be tolerated. Sarcasm at the expense of another becomes a form of cruel humor that brings down a student's self-esteem. Learning is supported by words of encouragement. Showing students how their work has improved and citing specific examples of growth encourage students to continue to improve.

In one school, teachers write each student a note every month. The note, personal to the student, outlines accomplishments as well as areas that the student needs to continue to work on in order to improve. The tone and words of the note are encouraging, giving the student a sense of "Hey, I've done this much, and now I can do more."

Peer review is an effective means to have students praise one another, to develop an understanding of what constitutes quality work, and to interpret exemplars and rubrics. Praise from fellow students is as valuable as praise from adults to encourage continued learning and improved performance.

Displaying Students' Work

Hanging up students' work for others to see validates their effort and performance. Such a display also sends an indirect message to others within the school. The work shown on bulletin boards or in display cases serves as an example for others, and it states that academic performance is valued. Academics are the first order of business in the school. In some schools, sports trophies in the entryway have been replaced with student work. While it is true that athletics and sports are important to the school and to the lives of the students, trophies for performance in these areas are found near the gym.

Identifying Unique Talents and Strengths

One student may create well-organized and attention-getting digital slideshow presentations, another may be able to solve complex mathematical equations, and yet another may compose beautiful song lyrics. Recognizing individual talents and academic strengths are not enough. Teachers must also find ways for students to demonstrate, practice, and "shine with" their unique capabilities. These strategies will further strengthen students' personal sense of potential and nurture continued growth in the recognized area of accomplishment.

Exhibiting Enthusiasm, Using Positive Humor, Serving as a Role Model

Students pick up on everything that the adults in the school community say or do — or that they do not say or do. Enthusiasm breeds enthusiasm; positive humor brings laughter and creates an "okay" environment. Whether adults realize it or not, they set the tone and atmosphere of a school; their enthusiasm, humor, ideas, attitude, and behavior are what create the culture of the school. Adults within the school community are the role models for the development of future adults and lifelong learners. "Imitation is the greatest form of flattery" rings true, for students do "imitate" the roles of the adults they interact with on a daily basis within the school community. The adult role models set the norms.

Celebrating Accomplishments

All school communities enjoy celebrations. Celebrations are important in building close relationships among students and staff members. These occasions can be especially meaningful to developing a sense of community. Celebrations such as graduation ceremonies are held for the school at large. Students in a small learning community also participate in special events, such as the opening night for an arts academy performance.

Celebrations in schools take a variety of forms. Some honor outstanding students. There are also assemblies to give public recognition to high-performing students, award ceremonies, or special dinners. Business and community members and advisory councils may hold celebrations to honor various students and programs.

Supportive Initiatives

The following supportive initiatives can influence learning relationships in a positive way.

- social activities to start the year
- team building
- mentoring

- rewards, recognition, incentives
- student advocacy
- advisory programs

Social Activities to Start the Year

At the beginning of the school year, schools hold a variety of activities to welcome new and returning students, as well as their parents. Some of the activities include orientation sessions led by student leaders. These events help familiarize students with the school facilities, policies, and procedures. Typically, the student handbook is reviewed. Similarly, there might be a dinner meeting for families, where staff members review policies and opportunities for students. Other introductory activities may include picnics, pep rallies, welcoming assemblies, skits, and dances. To introduce students to extracurricular and co-curricular activities, a "club rush" allows representatives to explain the purpose and activities of each organization.

Team Building

In academic teaming, teachers are organized across departments into groups called teams. Each team shares the same students and is responsible for the curriculum, instruction, evaluation, and sometimes even the scheduling of their students. The team has common planning time and usually teaches in the same physical location within the school. Teaming adds to the personalization of the learning community. Together the team focuses on each student's progress. With teaming, it is easier to focus on the "whole" student.

Mentoring

Mentoring consists of one-to-one relationships between young people and interested, caring adults who can provide assistance academically, personally, socially, or professionally. Some mentoring relationships develop naturally — for example, the connections that form between students and older friends or relatives. Others are planned — for example, a student may be matched with a mentor through a structured program that has a specific purpose.

Mentoring programs typically have an educational, career, or personal development focus. Academic mentoring assists students in raising their academic achievement, improving attendance, or preventing dropouts. Mentors tutor students and help with homework and other assignments; they also spend time with students, encouraging them and taking an interest in their lives. The goal is to improve the students' attitudes toward school and to help them identify and reach personal goals, as well as raise grades.

Career mentors help students understand particular careers and develop related skills and competencies. The student is paired with an adult who works in the student's field of interest. The mentor offers information, support, and opportunities for the student to better understand what is involved in the career and whether it is a good match to the student's interests and talents.

Personal development mentoring provides support and guidance for students in areas of personal need. These programs may focus on building self-esteem, drug and alcohol abuse, dealing with the death of a parent, gang involvement, and so forth. Programs can be designed for any group of students with specific needs, such as gifted students, minority students, low-performing students, and English language learners.

Researchers note a number of benefits of mentoring programs for students, mentors, and schools. Benefits for students include:

- improved academic performance
- career awareness
- positive attitudes about school
- reduced likelihood of dropping out
- improved relationships and communication with parents and teachers
- heightened self-esteem and self-confidence
- higher academic aspirations and goals

Benefits for mentors include:

- the opportunity to contribute to the community
- contact with and better understanding of young people
- the development of new skills

Benefits for schools include:

- higher academic achievement
- increased community support
- lower dropout rates
- higher engagement levels of students
- partnerships with business and community representatives

Key to implementing an effective mentoring program is giving attention to developing goals, addressing liability issues, determining staffing (possibly including the use of volunteers) to coordinate and facilitate the program, identifying logistics, and securing funding. Once the program's goals have been determined, a plan for recruitment of mentors and their orientation, training, and pairing with mentees needs to be designed. Ongoing management and supervision of the program will ensure its sustainability and success.

Rewards, Recognition, Incentives

Student achievement, engagement, participation, and positive behavior are improved through rewards, recognition, and incentives. The recognition of academic success and positive behavior motivates students to continue to strive toward higher degrees of engagement and academic achievement. Typical incentives used to motivate students to learn and demonstrate new academic content include grading systems, verbal praise and attention, and various tokens and prizes (stars, coupons, stickers, movie theater passes, discounts at local retail stores, raffle tickets for drawings of special prizes, and so forth). There is no question that these are effective means for improving academic performance and behavior, for most students respond favorably to the "prize" for their efforts and accomplishments.

If these incentives are to be effective, rewards must be known, and the criteria for receiving them must be clearly understood. Explicit procedures for incentives ensure that they are awarded fairly and objectively. Specific standards form the rationale for the reward. Individual student success in meeting the criteria determines whether a reward is given, and rewards should not be based on one student's performance as compared to another's. The rewards are selected because of their appeal to students and must correlate to specific student successes. For example, students may receive a special award each month for perfect attendance.

Rewards are based on the attainment of a specific standard of performance. They should not be given for merely completing a task. The rationale for rewards, incentives, and recognition needs to be established and described to students. Students need to understand exactly what they must do to obtain the reward. Students who do not receive an award have not failed; their performance simply has not met the standard tied to the incentive. This distinction is important for students, particularly those in elementary and middle school, to understand. The system for rewards and incentives should not in any way breed unmotivated, discouraged students.

Recognition or praise is also an effective strategy to support student learning. Educators need to develop rationales for the kinds of recognition they will give students. As with rewards and incentives, students need to know when recognition can be expected; it must relate to performance at a particular degree of proficiency for a specific task.

In *Classroom Instruction That Works*, Marzano and others refer to the use of the "pause, prompt, and praise" technique to recognize students who are having difficulty completing a task. When the student looks to the teacher for help with a challenging task, the teacher pauses to give the student more time to identify, correct, solve, or express the academic difficulty. Following the pause, the teacher provides a prompt or suggestion for the student to correct an error or to solve the academic difficulty. Finally, after the student has corrected the error and improved performance, the teacher provides praise for the specific demonstrated achievement.

Student recognition must be prompt and provided on an individual student basis. Receiving accolades weeks after the successful performance is somewhat meaningless to the student, who has long forgotten the completed task. Likewise, general recognition to the entire class for successful student performance does not provide individual students with feedback about their particular attainment of knowledge or demonstrated abilities.

At Kennesaw Mountain High School in Kennesaw, Georgia, the school works very hard to create high expectations, and it expects students to work hard to meet these goals. The school has a faculty member who serves as student leadership coordinator. This person is also responsible for Vision Quest, an awards program for academic success. To motivate students with some additional external symbols of excellence and continuous improvement, the school has created numerous awards, including medallions, medals, certificates, and a wide variety of school-related clothing that can only be earned by achieving specific goals. Students proudly exhibit their accomplishments by wearing shirts and medals that say such things as "Scholar Athlete," "Academic Excellence," and "Academic Success." Kennesaw Mountain has created the same degree of excitement and recognition for academics that many schools have only for athletics.

Celebrations and rituals are inherent to a school's culture. These celebrations vary from school to school. One held in common by most schools is graduation. The pomp and circumstance, the ritual of caps and gowns, and the role the teacher plays in this special event provide great satisfaction, pride, and evidence of support to the teacher.

Celebrations are formal, public evidences of success. When these involve staff members and their accomplishments, they become a means of renewing staff enthusiasm and commitment to the profession. Celebrations are an excellent means of supporting staff and creating positive, collaborative relationships.

Student Advocacy

Advocacy involves teachers or volunteer community members and students in a relationship that provides students with caring, attentive adults. Teacher/community members become student advocates, assisting students in developing self-understanding, planning and goal setting, and reviewing academic progress and achievement. Students may gain a better understanding of themselves and their ability to connect to their academic studies through various activities with their advocates, such as dialogue; interpretation of various questionnaires; and recognition of learning styles, academic strengths and weaknesses, and career interests. Advocates help students set academic and career goals and help determine short-term goals and expectations to meet long-term plans. Advocates meet periodically with students to develop and maintain a relationship of trust and support. During meetings, considerable time is given to reviewing and evaluating student progress and challenges.

As an advocate, the teacher/community member provides not only support but also services. The advocate intervenes on a student's behalf, monitors participation in programs, and may even negotiate for additional services for the student. This adult lends proactive support for the whole student so that the student can be successful. The advocate never gives up on the student — an essential measure of a student advocacy program's success.

Research indicates that advocates can have some positive influence on student outcomes. Typically, a student advocacy program will help students develop more positive attitudes about school and improve student attendance and academic performance. Continuing contacts result in a more successful advocacy relationship and more students' success in meeting defined goals. Student advocacy programs sometimes fall under the description of mentoring, tutoring, and homeroom advisory programs.

Advisory Programs

Various forms of advisement programs have been in place in middle schools and high schools for many years. Some variations, although called advisory periods, are really homerooms. Homerooms exist only for the purpose of taking attendance and making announcements; advisories have the objectives of getting staff to know students, identify academic needs, and provide advice. Advisories feature a professional development initiative, whereby teachers receive significant training in how to be an adult advisor. Some advisory periods meet on a daily basis, others once per week, and still others less often. Frequently, students stay with the same advisor for all four years of high school.

The common characteristic of successful advisor/advisee programs is adults' commitment to establish a personal, caring relationship with assigned students. There is also a curriculum or agenda to be followed.

The publication *The Power of Advisories* offers five key dimensions of an effective advisory program. The following discussion is adapted, with permission, from *Changing Systems to Personalize Learning: The Power of Advisories* (Osofsky, Sinner and Wolk, 2003). (For more information, visit http://www.alliance.brown.edu/pubs/changing_systems/power_of_advisories).

Key Dimension #1: Purpose

The program's purpose is clearly defined and is supported by the community.

Which of the following purposes makes the most sense for your school?

- to advise students about academic decisions and monitor academic achievement
- to provide developmental guidance (both formal and informal)
- to foster communication between the home and the school and among members of the school community
- to encourage supportive peer relationships and practice conflict resolution
- to promote an awareness of diversity and tolerance
- to undertake community service both within and outside the school
- to facilitate community governance and conversations
- to prepare students for life transitions, including career development and post-secondary opportunities

- to promote character development and explore moral dilemmas
- to explore the process of group development and have fun

Key Dimension #2: Organization

The program is organized to fulfill the purpose and to ensure personalization.

The Education Alliance at Brown University offers the following guiding questions as you discuss how your advisory program should be organized.

People and Size

- How many advisees will each adviser have?
- Which adults in the school building will serve as advisers? What characteristics should they possess?
- If some teachers do not serve as advisers, what supportive roles can they take on? Will any advisories be cofacilitated, (that is, a first-year teacher with a veteran teacher)?
- By what criteria will students be sorted into advisories (for example, by age, grade level, gender, race/ethnicity)?
- By what criteria will individual advisees be assigned to individual advisers (for example, advise only students you teach, common interests, previous relationship, self-selection, at random)?
- Will advisers and advisees be paired for one year or for multiple years?
- What will be the specific roles and responsibilities of advisers and advisees?
- How will parents be involved in the advisory program?
- How will community members outside the school be involved in the advisory program?

Time and Space

- How often will advisories meet (for example, once daily, twice daily, twice weekly)?
- How long will advisory meetings be (for example, brief check-ins, longer activity periods)?
- Will there be time for individual meetings as well as group meetings?
- How will this time fit into the master schedule?

- Where will advisories meet?
- How will advisories be able to personalize their space?
- Will each advisory have its own space?

Professional Development and Support
- How do we create regularly scheduled time for advisers to meet (time for training, curriculum development, sharing successes, having kid talk)?
- In what types of configurations can advisers meet for training and support (for example, in clusters, teams, full faculty, pairs)?
- How will we identify the types of training and support that advisers need (such as group process and development, communicating with parents, listening skills, knowing when to refer advisees to others, academic advising)?
- How will initial and ongoing training be conducted, and by whom?
- What resources do advisers need (for example, a program coordinator, curriculum, parent volunteers, counselors, petty cash)?
- What additional support will be given to advisers who are new to advising?
- What additional support will be given to advisers who are struggling?
- How will advisers be observed and assessed?
- How will advisory responsibilities be dealt with in the master contract?
- What type of budget will be required for the program?

Student Ownership
- What role will students take in creating/overseeing the advisory program?
- How can advisories serve as a vehicle for empowering students (for example, through school governance, through student-led groups, by taking on a community responsibility)?
- How can students in upper-grade advisories mentor students in lower-grade advisories?

Key Dimension #3: Advisory Program Content

Program content is based on the purposes to be achieved, on the nature of the school, and on individual advisers. Content may:

- be organized around essential questions, themes, or skills.
- be consistent across advisories or vary based on an adviser's knowledge of his or her advisees.
- follow a common curriculum, be chosen from an advisory handbook, or be activities organized by advisers to personalize their own advisory experience.

Key Dimension #4: Assessment

Program assessments should determine whether the purposes of the program are being met and whether participants are meeting expectations.

Assessment should be done at several levels:

- individual students/advisees
- individual advisers
- advisory groups as a whole
- overall advisory program
- school and program leadership

Key Dimension #5: Leadership

The program requires strong leadership by an individual or team charged with designing, implementing, overseeing, supporting, and assessing the program.

Essential leadership duties include creating buy-in among community members and ensuring that advisers have adequate training, resources, and support. Questions to be answered include:

- Who will take primary leadership of your advisory program?
- What specific barriers do you foresee in the planning, implementation, and maintenance of your program? How do you plan to avoid and/or overcome these barriers?
- What processes can be put in place to build support for your advisory program among all school community members, including consideration of the master contract? How will you ensure that consensus is achieved around the state purposes?

Example of an Advisory Program

At Brockport High School in Brockport, New York, the advisement period is central to the school's schedule. This period is scheduled every other day, permitting students to seek extra help from teachers or to participate in club activities during the school day. Each teacher is assigned 15 students to advance the goal of personalizing the school. There are no scheduled classes during the advisement period, so that all teachers are available to provide extra help to students. For the first 15 minutes, students stay with their assigned adviser. They can then "travel" to other teachers with whom they have made an appointment. If a student does not require academic assistance, the time can be used for club or activity meetings. If a student is in need of academic assistance, no travel is permitted to extracurricular events. The advisement period contributes to an incredible sense of school spirit, ownership, and participation at Brockport.

Peer Mediation

Peer mediation is a process that enables trained student mediators to reconcile disputes between students or small groups of students. Those engaged in a dispute enter the mediation process voluntarily. Students who act as mediators are trained in conflict resolution skills; they must be totally objective and act in an impartial, nonjudgmental manner. Student mediators also must recognize when a situation under dispute is beyond their power or area of expertise to resolve, in which case the situation is referred to a more knowledgeable peer mediator or an adult in the school community. In all instances, all parties involved in the mediation agree to keep confidential the matter under dispute. Mediators, however, need to recognize when some areas of the dispute are serious enough to warrant the involvement of a member of the school staff.

Peer mediation allows students an opportunity to engage in dialogue and seek joint solutions to disputes. Through mediation, students learn to manage conflict and develop speaking, listening, critical thinking, and negotiating skills. Teamwork is encouraged, and problem solving is the strategy used to resolve the dispute. The assistance that students bring to other students through this process nurtures a sense of belonging, concern, and care within the school community.

Examples of the types of problems that may be resolved through peer mediation include rumors and gossip, cheating and stealing, relationship difficulties, racial confrontations, and vandalism. Serious problems such as drug use, sexual abuse, and weapon possession require referrals to appropriate professional staff members within the school. The goal of mediation sessions is to reach an acceptable solution to all parties involved in the dispute.

Prior to mediation sessions, all parties become familiar with the ground rules and commit to follow them. Students in the dispute meet with mediators to ensure that they are objective and have no conflict of interest. The mediators explain exceptions to the confidentiality rules and explain the mediator's role. During the session, each disgruntled party tells the mediator its version of the situation. The mediator summarizes the facts on both sides and facilitates a discussion of the issues. Next, suggestions for resolution are sought and acknowledged, and solutions are discussed, particularly those on which both parties can agree. Then each party involved in the dispute selects the best possible solution. The mediator obtains verbal and written agreement among all parties, and a monitoring process is developed to ensure that the solution is carried out.

Students as Teachers

Learning is best remembered when one has the opportunity to teach another. With tutoring, students can succeed at their own level and pace without being publicly compared to proficient learners. The extra attention and support given while a student is being tutored may fill a gap left by the lack of support from adults outside the school. Research has demonstrated that when students are provided with appropriate training, they can successfully tutor other students.

The tutor offers a positive role model for learning and brings enthusiasm to exploring new topics. The goal is to help raise the academic achievement of the student being tutored. A variety of programs in schools enable students to serve as teachers or tutors for other students. These teaching opportunities may occur informally in a classroom setting with a student who needs academic assistance or has been absent.

In cooperative learning activities, the group "sinks or swims together" as group members work interdependently. Many teaching moments occur this way among students. In these positive interdependence activities, students feel that they need one another in order to succeed. Each member of the group is essential in helping to complete the task. When students perceive that their achievement is correlated with that of other students, a sense of positive interdependence develops. Students recognize that each member functions as a part of a team and that the success of the whole group depends on the contributions of each member. This relationship fosters peer tutoring, support, and encouragement.

Some cooperative learning strategies are designed so that students teach other students. In Lineup, team members divide and learn new information. Then they teach each other their particular part/topic. In Jigsaw, academic material is broken down into sections. Each student is responsible for a part of the information and must learn it and teach it to his teammates. Cooperative learning strategies create a learning environment in which students are willing to help one another, give and receive feedback, respect others' ideas, and validate their own ideas.

One-on-one instruction has been recognized as superior to group instruction. Student tutoring programs have many benefits, both to the students doing the tutoring and to those receiving the assistance. Peer tutoring occurs when the tutor and the person tutored are the same age. Cross-age tutoring has an older student assisting a younger one. Student tutors may assist with class projects, provide direct instruction, lend support in lab work, help with homework, assist with in-class assignments, discuss ideas with students, and so on.

The perceived roles of the tutor include adviser, facilitator, mentor, motivator, friend, peer, team member, communicator, mentor, and role model. The tutors benefit by improving communication and interpersonal skills, reinforcing knowledge of the subject being tutored, enhancing reflection, increasing self-confidence, and gaining insight into the teaching profession. The students being tutored are given a positive role model, receive individual attention and thus have opportunities to learn more, and obtain assistance in areas of academic deficiency.

Structured student tutoring programs involve volunteer students or students who are fulfilling a service learning requirement. For a program to be successful, specific and measurable goals need to be identified and evaluated; procedures for selecting and matching tutors and students to be tutored must be established; tutor training and supervision need to be provided; and teachers and administrators must support the tutoring program. Well-planned, well-implemented student tutoring programs can improve student achievement, enrich students' self-confidence and self-esteem, and add to a positive school environment that is focused on high expectations and learning.

In some schools, mentors from the upper classes remain with students through 9th and 10th grade and help monitor and celebrate academic success. In other instances, volunteer junior and senior students are assigned to the freshmen who are most at risk of failing. At Kenwood Academy High School in Chicago, mentors from the upper classes make connections with their mentees in 8th grade and play a significant role in the orientation activities during the summer before 9th grade begins. At Roswell High School in Roswell, New Mexico, volunteer juniors and seniors who speak both Spanish and English are part of a formal organization to serve as ELL (English language learners) tutors for freshmen with language deficiencies. They are also on call by teachers to serve as classroom assistants and to interpret for parents with limited English skills during parent conferences and other parent programs. At Kennesaw Mountain High School in Kennesaw, Georgia, high school students mentor and tutor elementary students as part of their student leadership activities. Students travel to four elementary schools to assist teachers by providing one-to-one instruction to readers who need additional assistance under the Reading Is Succeeding Everyday (RISE) program.

Student Behavior

Another approach to increasing academic success is by focusing on positive student behavior. There are numerous ways to go about achieving this goal, as in these suggestions:

- Develop community support for and involvement in the character education initiative.
- Make parents partners in the initiative.
- Determine the community's key guiding principles.
- Provide staff development so that all staff can develop proficiency in character-centered teaching skills.
- Establish and communicate clear expectations for positive and appropriate behavior.
- Cultivate a caring school environment that focuses on positive relationships and respect between students and faculty.
- Hold students accountable for inappropriate behavior.
- Find alternative educational settings for students who persistently disrupt the learning environment.

Parent Partnerships

Despite uncertainties about many matters related to education, the research about the value of parent involvement in schools is clear. Unquestionably, involving parents of high school students is not an easy task. Yet, a plethora of studies, including action research by the International Center for Leadership in Education, has found that parent involvement is a key factor in supporting and promoting student academic success. For more information on parent involvement, see the handbooks *Engaging Parents in Student Learning — Grades K–6* and *Engaging Parents in Student Learning — Grades 7–12*. High schools with limited parent involvement historically are finding that a special 9th-grade initiative can lay the foundation for continuing parent partnerships throughout the high school years.

Making connections with a student's family usually strengthens the support a student receives for learning and gives the teacher support for instructional activities, classroom rules and policies, grading systems, and so forth. Teachers and instructional leaders need to reach out to parents to engage them in their student's program.

School administrators often remark, "But I have an open-door policy for parents. Why aren't more parents involved in our school?" Principals at successful high schools have learned that an open-door policy is somewhat irrelevant. The real issue is an "open heart." Parents can sense a lack of sincerity from a mile away. If schools truly want parents involved, they will find that parents respond best to "hands-on" principals who are actively involved with the parents. Here are some tips for school leaders from successful schools.

- Get to know parents on a first-name basis and encourage them to address you by your first name.
- Occasionally sacrifice the administrative business suit for more informal dress, if that is consistent with the parents you serve.
- Work hard to demonstrate to parents that they are equal to you as human beings; you just have different roles.
- Remember that a liberal use of humor breaks down barriers. Accept good-natured teasing from parents and enjoy a good laugh together.
- Demonstrate active listening. Seek first to understand and then to be understood.
- Be aware of your nonverbal behavior. Realize that this communication says more than the actual words you speak.
- Practice truth-telling with parents. Be candid about the school's challenges and adopt this philosophy: "In this school, we tell the truth. Our problems are opportunities. What makes us different is that by recognizing these 'probletunities,' we have the chance to improve conditions for our children."
- If you practice authenticity with parents, you will be able to anticipate and prepare for the types of questions and concerns that parents will present.
- One of the most important personal attributes for any school leader is visibility. When parents perceive that you are everywhere — at sporting events, concerts,

performances — they conclude that you care about their children. This type of visibility takes a great deal of time, but the dividends pay capital gains.

- When parents sense that you care, they will open up and ask questions. In addition, the authentic leader is available to work with parents on a one-to-one basis.
- In engaging parents in partnerships, always focus on the children, not on the attributes or behaviors of the parents. Experience has taught many successful administrators that when parents trust you and realize that you care about their children, their behavior changes unobtrusively.
- Recognize that in order to develop trust among parents, you must exhibit trustworthiness. Always be true to your word.
- Always remember that you and your staff work for the parents; they pay the taxes and elect the school board members who employ you.

When true parent-school partnerships are established, the word gets out that the principal and his or her leadership team can be trusted. When the inevitable school difficulties occur, this trust will pay dividends in terms of a large core of parents who will support the administration. The bottom line is that authentic parent partnerships will contribute to 9th-graders' being more successful in their academic endeavors.

How We Communicate with Parents

Effective schools recognize that there are multiple strategies for communicating with and involving parents. Although necessary, the least effective communication vehicle is often the written word: newsletters, newspaper articles, and letters.

When school leaders make a commitment to authentic, long-term, and frequent partnerships with a significant core group of parents, experience indicates that one trusted parent might communicate with 10–20 others. In other words, a core group of 25 involved parents can easily serve as effective communicators for an additional 400–500 parents who interact with the core group through various means in the community.

Ways to communicate with parents include the following:

- daily updates from students
- person-to-person interactions at school events and community gatherings
- incentives for students to bring their parents to school programs

- the media, including cable television and radio
- churches and other community organizations
- electronic means, such as e-mail and school websites
- classroom parent networks
- telephone calls
- interactions with trusted community leaders, who are encouraged to communicate with school leaders about issues or concerns that come to their attention
- formal parent leadership organizations: PTA, parent councils, parent advisory organizations
- newsletters, both all-school and one specifically intended for 9th-grade parents
- newspaper articles, pictures, and letters to the editor
- social events such as family outings, picnics, and "get to know your school" nights
- volunteer tutoring or chaperone programs
- dinner events that include a brief program focusing on one of the priority instructional areas or explaining an assessment program
- presentations through the guidance department about college admissions and scholarship opportunities and financial assistance programs
- meetings to explain specific programs
- student-led conferences
- parent-teacher organizations
- school visits

Finally, one of the most vital yet most frequently overlooked ways to communicate is through the inviting nature of a school's practices and policies. Sometimes called the five P's of invitational education — people, programs, places, policies, and processes – the most successful schools conduct an audit related to them. How do we answer the telephone? How are parents greeted when they visit our school? Are our policies user-friendly and easily understood? How is the appearance of the outside of our school? Are our classrooms inviting places in which students truly want to learn? Is the school clean, are washrooms safe, and is graffiti removed immediately? In general, do we have a philosophy that our school should be the most inviting place in town?

Another way of communicating with parents that a number of schools have found successful is using the concept of student-led parent/teacher conferences. In this approach, the student conducts the conference and explains his or her academic progress (or lack thereof). David Douglas High School in Portland, Oregon, has experienced 95% parent participation at the 9th- and 10th-grade levels in student-led conferences at the conclusion of the year. Of course, schools must provide teachers with professional development to understand thoroughly how these conferences should be conducted. Students must also be briefed on their responsibilities.

Meaningful Parent Involvement

For all high school parents, involvement must be meaningful. If parent involvement is not meaningful, parents will "turn off" and may not return. The following ideas can help make this involvement valued:

- Hold in-depth discussions on the curriculum offerings available to 9th-grade students and the learning expectations of teachers.
- Share instructional strategies.
- Give frequent updates on student rules and regulations; solicit parent involvement in suggesting changes.
- Always emphasize that by being involved on a regular basis, parents will be the most knowledgeable and the first to know about school challenges, successes, and planning.
- Remember that meaningful parent involvement means easy access to the principal, other administrators, and often one or more school board members.
- Encourage parents to visit during the school day, sit in on classes, volunteer to chaperone field trips or serve as tutors, and so forth.
- Sponsor programs for parents on how to make the transition to high school easier, such as creating a "survival kit" for parents of 9th-graders.
- Facilitate discussions to help parents understand that they are all in this together. Many parents of 9th-graders believe that the challenges they face with their child are unique when, in fact, they are the norm. Be sure to inject humor into the discussions.

- Encourage parents to develop parent mini-networks whereby they have easy access to the telephone numbers of other parents; develop a common set of expectations for their students; and are comfortable communicating with each other in order to know where their children are, whom they are with, and what they are doing.
- Limit or avoid fundraising. By the time their children get to high school, most parents are tired of helping to raise money.
- Above all, make meaningful parent involvement fun and inviting. Involve food when appropriate. When people truly feel welcome, they will return.

Schools That Say "Welcome"

Relationships in schools are very intangible and hard to quantify. Yet, it is very easy to get a sense of the relationship atmosphere when you first walk into the school. Staff can begin to identify the level of relationships by thinking about what school appears to be to visitors.

Use the following checklist to reflect on the characteristics of your school toward visitors.

Schools That Say "Welcome" Checklist

Use this checklist to evaluate your school's relationship with visitors and parents. Does your school say "Welcome" in every aspect of the school culture?

Yes	No	
☐	☐	Office staff greets visitors in a friendly, courteous way.
☐	☐	Parents who pass staff in the hallways are greeted warmly.
☐	☐	Staff members offer assistance if anyone appears lost or is new to the school.
☐	☐	Teachers, staff, and students answer the telephone in a friendly, professional way.
☐	☐	A welcome sign (in all common languages of the community) and school map are displayed near the entrance.
☐	☐	There is an area where visitors can easily find information about the school and its curriculum.
☐	☐	The school holds regular social occasions or events at which parents and school staff can get to know each other.
☐	☐	An orientation program is provided for new families in the district.

Review Questions

1. How might the levels of the relationship framework be significant in your role?
2. How might you utilize an example of an action that helps build relationships?
3. In what ways do you think you can use a supportive initiative to influence learning relationships in a positive way?
4. How can you make advisement programs more effective?
5. What might you do to improve parent involvement?

Chapter 6

Supportive Structures and Strategies for Building Rigor, Relevance, and Relationships

If schools — and, more specifically, teachers and school leaders — hope to provide all students with a rigorous and relevant education, an education that adequately prepares them for success in the 21st century, they will need to take advantage of new tools, strategies, and organizational structures.

If meeting that challenge is now still merely a hope, there is good reason to believe that this hope can become a reality. That reality is supported by a great deal of current research, most significantly by the Harvard Graduate School of Education's 2011 study, *Pathways to Prosperity: Meeting the Challenge of Preparing Your Americans for the 21st Century*. This report examines the reasons why we too often have failed to prepare so many young people for success in adult life and advances a vision for how the United States might regain its role as a leader in educational achievement. The report advocates the development of new structures and new points of emphasis in order to transform the way young people learn. As schools and districts collaborate to meet the new Common Core State Standards, they would do well, the report suggests, to emphasize three essential elements:

1. Meaningful alternative pathways to help young people successfully navigate from adolescence to adulthood that offer additional approaches to a traditional bachelor's degree.
2. Employer support in providing more opportunities for young adults to participate in work-based learning and actual jobs related to their programs of study.
3. Ensuring that, by the time they reach their mid-20s, every individual will be equipped with the education and experience needed for success in life as an adult.

By emphasizing such elements, more and more schools, with courageous leadership, are developing new models and structures to bring the traditional school "out of the box." That box, for a long time, supported learning. More recently, however, it has placed stifling constraints on the possibilities for active, student-centered learning. With new strategies and structures in hand, schools will be equipped to provide students with an education that is relevant to their lives, and none too soon, as students prepare to shape a world that is changing at warp-speed.

These kinds of exciting, broad changes in education will only happen if we the harness the best lessons available on effective leadership. Accordingly, the DSEI underscores the fact that empowered leadership at all levels — the classroom (teaching), the school (instructional leadership), and the district (organizational Leadership) — is crucial for the success of schools. Under the DSEI, leadership starts and is modeled by the traditional school principal but is not reserved for a single individual. We can see the wisdom of this notion of leadership when we look more closely at the countless model schools and districts that employ models of distributed and shared leadership. In nearly every case, it takes many leaders in various roles to make a successful school. This does not mean, though, that a school has many independent decision makers, with each leading a school toward his or her own unique vision of learning. Shared leadership is successful only when a common vision exists for the school community and individual teachers and when groups of teachers make incremental decisions that are consistent with that vision.

The models and structures described in this chapter exemplify bold leadership, the kind of leadership that transforms both the setting and circumstances of education in ways that empower powerful student and professional learning.

Chapter 6: Supportive Structures and Strategies for Building Rigor, Relevance, and Relationships

Small Learning Communities

Numerous studies and successful models in middle schools and high schools substantiate the value of small-scale schooling. Academic and social benefits include improved attendance and graduation rates. Students achieve higher test scores in small schools and are more likely to pass their coursework, graduate, and attain a higher level of education than students attending larger schools. Smaller class sizes and integrated curricula enhance and encourage the growth of teacher-student relationships. The opportunity for personalization in a small learning community also enables the teacher to be more cognizant of a student's performance and thus increases student accountability. Administrators and teachers can more easily reform curricula, teaching methodologies, instructional strategies, and assessment systems in small schools. Small schools also do better than large schools in closing the achievement gap between students in different ethnic and socioeconomic groups. For a more detailed approach on how to create small learning communities, see the International Center's handbook *Increasing Student Achievement through Small Learning Communities.*

Students feel valued and cared for in the personalized environment offered by a small school. They feel better about themselves and their academic future. Students' attitudes are more positive in a small school community.

Small learning communities capitalize on their downsized environment by implementing strategies that enable teachers to know all students well. Teachers can become knowledgeable about students' strengths and weaknesses, build relationships with students, and respond to individual needs of students more easily in a small school setting.

Students and teachers experience a strong sense of belonging in a more personalized environment. Interpersonal relationships are fostered. Students feel less alienated and have more opportunities to participate in school activities because there is less competition for selection on athletic teams and in membership for extracurricular and youth leadership organizations. This is significant because involvement in extracurricular activities is often related to positive attitudes, high self-esteem, and appropriate social behavior.

Students in smaller schools have better attendance rates than those in larger schools. This is particularly true for minority and low socioeconomic status students. Dropout rates are lower, and graduation rates are higher than in large schools.

Disciplinary problems are reduced in small learning communities, which can be attributed to the strong teacher and other adult relationships students have, as well as the personalization of the environment. Students are suspended less often and use drugs less often than their counterparts in larger schools. Also, there are fewer instances of vandalism, assault, gang participation, theft, and aggressive behavior. Students feel safer in small schools because of their connections with adults. Moreover, parents are more likely to be involved in small schools.

Larger schools, with bureaucracies to manage their large number of students, have a tendency to spend more than small schools do to support their efforts. Small schools may save money by doing away with some of the specialized staffing that is common in large schools.

Organizational Options for Small Learning Communities

Several different kinds of small learning communities are being established in schools, particularly high schools. With research overwhelmingly supporting the fact that students are more successful when they attend small schools, educational communities are turning to new organizational structures to support learning in this type of environment. Belief in the success of small learning communities is further evidenced by the financial support provided by public and private agencies to develop this new approach to learning.

Small learning communities may differ in size and structure, but they usually:

- are established with a small body of students who are taught by the same group of teachers
- share a designated physical space
- have an instructional theme

Most of the small school structures emerge from a larger organization within a building; however, some small learning communities are designed initially to be just that — small. These dedicated small schools have facilities that are deliberately structured to house smaller numbers of students.

The most common types of small learning community structures are magnet schools, academies, schools-within-schools, and house plans. In these configurations, the small learning community arrangement occupies its own space within a school or in a separate building. Under the house plan, students with varying abilities and backgrounds are grouped together. A house may consist of a single grade level, such as freshmen houses;

or it may consist of a 9–12 grade grouping, in which students stay with house members and teachers throughout their high school careers.

In the magnet schools and theme academies, students are clustered around a special focus area of interest. A magnet may consist of integrated academic disciplines, such as a mathematics, science, and technology magnet; it may focus on one academic area, such as a science magnet or performing arts magnet.

In academies, the special focus is generally a career. Some types of career academies include business and leadership, information technology, health services, engineering and design, and arts and communications. Students in magnet and career academy programs stay with the same teachers and group of students.

Schools-Within-Schools

A school-within-a-school is a small autonomous program situated within a larger school physical plant. One school building may have several autonomous small schools within it. Students take all their classes within this school, and teachers teach all their classes within this structure. Students who are not in the school-within-a-school do not participate in any of those classes.

The school-within-a-school model allows for a high degree of personalization and student support because it encourages the development of sustained and continuous relationships between students and teachers. Sufficient time for collaborative planning is usually a characteristic of the school-within-a-school. This enhances the development of a strong community with a small professional learning community within that focuses on a common vision of high expectations, quality of teaching, and student achievement.

A school-within-a-school is responsible to the district, not to the administrative leadership of the larger school that houses it. This type of organizational structure provides the small learning community with the opportunity to develop its own culture and program of studies. The school-within-a-school is self-governing, with its own leadership. Scheduling, budgeting, personnel issues, and professional development are controlled by the leadership and staff of the school-within-a-school. The school-within-a-school has its own dedicated physical space in which to hold classes, and students and teachers are scheduled together and meet in this common area. A school-within-a-school may or may not have a curricular theme or set combination of courses for students.

House Plans

Under the house plan option, students in a large school are divided into smaller groups of students in the same grade or across grades. Students take all or most of their courses within the house, and teachers teach all or most of their classes within the house. Specific space may or may not be dedicated to the house.

The house structure allows for a high degree of personalization since students stay with house members and teachers. Students and teachers identify with the house and have an opportunity to build relationships within the smaller organization.

The impact of this design on curriculum and instruction is limited. The typical methods and levels of instruction take place. Students may also take coursework outside the house.

Vertical house plans refer to houses that serve students in grades 9–12 or grades 10–12. Typically, a school of 1,000 or more students is divided into groups (houses) of several hundred students each. At grade 9, house plans are similar to the vertical model but consist only of 9th-grade students.

The house is under the administrative leadership of the school principal; it does not have autonomy from the larger school. Staff assigned to the house has limited control over the house's program and budget. The larger school determines the schedule and makes decisions about staffing, resources, finances, and student makeup. Since the house falls under the jurisdiction of the larger school, most collaborative efforts are limited. Teachers do not necessarily have common planning time, and professional development is designed on a schoolwide basis rather than by the house alone.

Freshman Academy/House

A small learning community that is growing in popularity is the freshman academy or house. Organized like a typical house, the freshman house provides a place and structure for "newcomers" to transition to the school. Freshmen are kept together in their own physical setting. They share the same staff, whose members frequently team teach in the core academic areas. In this structure, freshmen find additional support and attention from staff and begin to recognize and value their high school experience as a pathway to higher education and careers. The freshmen house is an "adjustment place" that enables students to learn and experience gradually the additional responsibilities of a high school program.

Academies

Academies are generally schools-within-schools that are designed around occupational themes or the arts. Students experience many real-world applications of learning and participate in work-based learning programs. School-to-work elements are immersed in the academic programs of students in academies. The academy consists of a group of students who stay with the same teachers for 2–4 years, resulting in a personalized and supportive learning environment. The course of study provides high academic standards that are integrated within career-technical education (CTE) or arts education areas of study.

In the arts, for example, there are a variety of career focus areas. These may include audiovisual technology and communications, visual communications art, commercial photography, graphic communications, telecommunications, journalism, multimedia production, and performing arts. Some typical examples of CTE academies are business and leadership, information technology, health services, engineering and design, and finance.

Within the academy focus area, students prepare for all levels of jobs. An academy should not limit a student's career or job options any more than taking a traditional high school program does. All students have the necessary courses to enter colleges. Student may choose to enter the workforce or to continue their education.

Business partnerships are a key component of the academy model. Business partnerships may provide related career shadowing, internships, work-study programs, student financial aid, equipment, and occupational information.

Each academy has a business advisory board, which works with educators to determine and update curricular offerings and provide advice on academy options. The focus of the academy is often determined by student interest, but local businesses and industries can play an important part in the implementation of a particular career academy, since related internship/apprenticeship programs and potential jobs are important aspects of the academy's offerings. Members of the advisory board or their respective businesses may teach, mentor, and/or tutor at the academy.

Students take the majority of their courses within the academy but may also take some classes outside. Within this structure, teachers usually teach most of their classes in the academy and have collaborative planning time, as well as time for academy-related professional development. The staff has some control over the program design. However, the academy coordinator or administrator usually reports to the larger school's principal. The academy's budget, schedule, and staff are determined by the larger school. Physical space may or may not be separate from the larger school context.

Comparison of Small Learning Community Options

School Characteristics	School-Within-a-School	House Plan	Freshman Academy	Career/Theme Academy
Changes Affect Entire School	No	Yes	No	Optional
Scheduling Changes	Significant	Significant	Minor	Significant
Creates Autonomous School	Yes	No	No	Optional
Requires Change in Curriculum	No	No	No	Yes
Curriculum Taught in Context	Optional	Optional	Optional	Yes
Adviser/Advisee Program	Optional	Optional	Yes	Optional
Internships/Job Shadowing/Community Experience	No	No	No	Yes
Increases Number of Administrators	Yes	No	No	No

Alternative Scheduling

Many schools implement various scheduling techniques that allow teachers to better meet student learning needs and to provide longer instructional blocks of time. Extended class time enables teachers to cover content in depth, to provide real-world applications, and to incorporate time-consuming strategies (such as project-based learning and work-based learning) into instruction. Alternative scheduling permits community and business representatives to support learning during the school day; it also makes it easier to provide tutoring and to allow some students additional time in areas needing improvement, while other students devote time to in-depth learning. The schedule does not control teaching and learning; the needs of the learner determine the schedule.

Highly successful schools emphasize how personalizing learning and enabling all students to succeed begin with creating master schedules around the needs of students. Other schools develop a master schedule around the convenience of adults and often cite the difficulty of changing a master schedule to meet student needs.

Extended learning time describes scheduling configurations that provide for class periods that are longer than the traditional 45-minute period. The extended learning periods translate into more time for students to spend on learning without interruptions and more time for teachers to develop in-depth instruction and more real-world applications of subject matter. The additional time also gives teachers more time to use a variety of instructional strategies to reach the diverse learning styles and needs of students. These larger blocks of time give teachers flexibility to provide a diversity of instructional activities.

Changing the schedule involves a major restructuring effort. The entire school community needs time to examine the research and successful practice, to assess the need for such a program, to collaborate with all the stakeholders, to ensure compliance with federal and state laws and regulations and employee contracts, to gain awareness and support, and to analyze the fiscal impact. Scheduling modifications usually mean more instructional and learning time. Thus, major professional development support is needed to assist teachers in relying less on the standard lecture and seatwork approach to learning and more on individualized learner approaches and creative teaching strategies.

Block scheduling is the most frequently implemented form of alternative scheduling. *Block* defines any schedule format that has fewer but longer class periods than the traditional schedule, which has 6–8 periods each day of no more than 45 minutes each. A variety of configurations and possibilities are possible in the design of a block schedule. When choosing a particular method, educators must consider the number of semesters; the length of the school year, school day, and class period; the choice of single or double class periods; and the frequency of class meetings (daily or alternate days). The most common models of block scheduling are described below.

Block or 4 x 4 Block Schedule

Under this plan, students attend four classes per day for a semester. Classes are 85–100 minutes in length. At the end of the semester, students have completed four full courses; in the traditional schedule plan, it would have required one full year to complete them. In the second semester, students take four different courses. Some exceptions exist, such as for Advanced Placement and music classes; full-year courses are maintained for these classes.

A/B Block

Using this method, students take eight classes for the entire school year divided into an A group and a B group. Each group consists of four classes that meet for approximately 90 minutes every other day. Thus, in this alternate-day schedule, students and teacher meet every other day for extended time periods.

With the A/B block, there is increased instructional time on a daily basis. Students have fewer classes and assignments per day. The day off between classes allows for "distancing time" in classes that are experiencing disciplinary or other problems.

Modified Block

This method combines some of the 4 x 4 block approach and the traditional 8-period schedule day. The schedule may provide a 4 x 4 block on four days during the week and a regular 8-period day on one day. Another version has students in two blocked classes each day along with three traditional shorter-period classes.

Flexible Schedule

In this plan, students follow a combination of the 4 x 4 block and the A/B block schedules. Class time varies from day to day. One example would be having students attend 90-minute classes three days per week; on the other two days, students would take these classes for 75 minutes and have an additional advisement or resource period of 60 minutes.

The advantage of flexible scheduling is that more time is available for students to complete work, engage in short-term enrichment programs, and obtain additional assistance during the resource period.

Trimester Plan

With the trimester schedule, students take two or three courses for 60 days and earn six or nine credits per year. Variations within this plan include two long classes and one short class per day, two long classes and two short classes per day, and others.

The advantages of the trimester plan are that students focus on only a few courses per trimester, students and teachers prepare for fewer courses per trimester, teachers have a smaller student load per trimester, and fewer textbooks and instructional resources are required.

Advantages of Block Scheduling

Some of the frequently mentioned benefits of block scheduling include the following:

For Students

- Develop stronger interpersonal relationships with teachers and other students
- Spend more time on tasks
- Study in greater depth
- Learn time management skills
- Experience more active learning rather than passive learning
- Have fewer competing teacher expectations
- Have more one-on-one time with teachers
- Engage in more opportunities to apply knowledge to contextual and real-world situations
- Have more time to prepare for classes
- Experience less stress
- Are less likely to fail
- Have better attendance rates and fewer tardies, suspensions, and dropouts
- May obtain better academic results
- Have more opportunities to engage in writing skill development
- Develop higher-order thinking skills and problem-solving skills
- Are better known by their teachers
- Experience more personalized learning
- Are better able to focus on learning
- Master and retain subject matter more easily

A Systemwide Approach to Rigor, Relevance, and Relationships

For Teachers
- Experience less fragmented instructional time
- Spend more time on task
- Complete and evaluate instruction and instructional techniques
- Implement a variety of instructional strategies to address different learning styles and diverse student needs
- Are able to focus on fewer subject areas
- Explore subject areas in greater depth
- Provide more opportunities for real-world applications of learning
- Reduce amount of lecturing
- Have opportunities for more one-on-one contact with students
- Have fewer classes to prepare for on a daily basis
- Gain opportunities for extensive personal interaction with students
- Know students well enough to adapt lessons to their learning styles, abilities, and interests
- Experience greater teacher communication and collaboration
- Appreciate opportunities for student projects and other instructional strategies requiring extended time
- Face fewer disciplinary problems
- Are better able to address discipline problems because of personal relationships with students and have more time in class to attend to these issues
- Can team teach more effectively
- Have greater opportunities for interdisciplinary/integrated learning
- Provide early interventions for students in need
- Teach students who are more engaged, motivated, and successful
- Have time for authentic assessment
- Possess a manageable workload
- Have more time to communicate with parents
- Find more opportunities for peer observations

Chapter 6: Supportive Structures and Strategies for Building Rigor, Relevance, and Relationships

Teaching Continuity

Teachers may stay with their students for multiple years of instruction. Doing so gives the teacher a better understanding of a learner's strengths and weaknesses, allowing the teacher to develop more personalized learning experiences. In some settings, teams of teachers remain with the same students over time. With the team approach (discussed earlier), students are assured that they will be known by more than one adult, and both students and teachers are more likely to respect and support one another.

Other programs that ensure continuity of teacher and student are the advisement program and advocacy programs (also discussed earlier). Mentoring programs also develop a sense of teacher continuity for the student.

Looping Opportunities

Looping brings teachers and students together for longer periods of time, providing the opportunity for teachers and students to get to know one another better. With looping, the teacher moves to the next grade with students, keeping students and teacher together for more than one school year. The number of years that students and teacher are kept together varies with the school's program; typically, looped groups stay together 2–5 years.

Looping includes benefits such as the following:

- Teachers have more time for instruction; in the second year, students are already known, and class policies and procedures are already understood.
- Teachers better understand students' academic strengths and weaknesses.
- Students have less apprehension starting a new school year; they know what to expect.
- Students get to know one another well and thus develop stronger socialization and group skills.
- Students feel a stronger sense of belonging, which encourages student involvement.
- Job satisfaction improves.
- Student achievement improves.

A growing number of schools with successful 9th-grade initiatives are finding creative ways to schedule teachers and counselors in order to personalize education for students. Although not common, looping of counselors and teachers is a practice worth noting.

Some schools loop the counselor from grade 8 to grade 9 and then back to grade 8 to start a new cycle. This system ensures that there is at least one adult in the high school who knows the 9th-graders. Some schools loop 8th-grade and 9th-grade teachers in such subject areas as English language arts or mathematics. The obvious advantage is that the academic program can begin early in the year because teachers already know the abilities of the students. These programs are also successful with special education students when inclusion specialists loop between grades 8 and 9.

Another, more common model is for 9th-grade and 10th-grade teachers to loop. The personalization factor continues, and students begin 10th grade with a greater chance for success.

Multiage Grouping

Multiage grouping is another organizational strategy that ensures continuity of teaching. This type of group involves putting students with different ages or from different classes and with different learning abilities together in the same classroom or group. Lessons and learning activities and tasks are developed to meet the different learning abilities within the multiage class.

The philosophy behind multiage grouping is that all students can learn and that they learn at different rates. Student work is designed to match the developmental levels of the learners. The goal of a multiage grouping structure is to have students of different ages and learning abilities progress at their own rate, rather than to simply move along with a whole class. In multiage grouping, students are expected to do their individual best. Learning is more personalized. Teachers focus on the individual student's needs and strengths, creating a much richer relationship between teacher and student.

Building a Team to Support Rigor, Relevance, and Strong Relationships

Showing Respect

Respect is one of the most often cited essential behaviors. In any school community, there are multiple roles for staff. Sometimes there exists a hierarchy of teachers based on the perceived importance of what they teach. There are certain courses — such as gifted programs, Advanced Placement courses, or college-level courses — that carry prestige because they are serving elite students. Often, teachers compete to be selected to teach in these programs. All teachers should be respected equally, whether it is the AP Calculus teacher or the resource mathematics teacher who works with struggling English language learners. You, as school leader, should pay close attention to the way you treat each teacher and every staff person in the school. Likewise, it is important to call attention to any behavior by staff that shows disrespect. Disagreements are natural and can lead to improvement, but the members of an effective staff are able to disagree and still respect one another.

"Being There," Frequent Contact, Active Listening

Another key set of behaviors is "being there," frequent contact, and active listening. "Being there" means giving full attention to each and every person, regardless of how busy you are or how trivial his or her question seems. "Being there" requires full attention in each personal contact. School leaders are always busy and have incredible demands on their time. In spite of this burden, it is important to give each person his or her full attention. By encouraging this behavior in others, you will build the foundation for improved staff relationships.

A large part of respecting and supporting staff members is communication. Frequent contact, whether verbal or written, is essential for collaboration. How a staff communicates is established through the administration. Consider how memoranda, meetings, and e-mails can enhance relationships within the school walls. Finally, remember that active listening — the rephrasing of what you hear as a question or opinion to ensure that you understand the other person's point of view — is an excellent way to show respect and to communicate.

Enthusiasm, Positive Humor, Avoiding "Put-downs"

Enthusiasm and positive humor make the hard work of school less burdensome. Enthusiasm is contagious: When staff members observe a colleague's smiles, energy, and excitement, they find their own feelings of frustration and fatigue diminishing. Be passionate and look for opportunities to exhibit positive humor. Take your work seriously, but do not take yourself too seriously. Look for opportunities to poke fun at your personality and your role as school leader. When seeking humor, be sure to avoid "put-downs." When a staff is frequently complimented and encouraged, the occasional joke is taken as good humor. However, if the only feedback from others or the leader is humor, it is perceived as a "put-down," and the result can be devastating.

Encouragement, Identifying Talents and Strengths

Effective leaders need to make a special effort to encourage others. Ask staff to take on new responsibilities, try new things, or attempt to accomplish something again in hope of greater success. Write encouraging notes or work to identify unique talents or strengths.

Celebrating Accomplishments, Praising Peers, Being a Role Model

When staff members make extra efforts or significant progress, celebrate accomplishments and encourage peers to praise each other. Leaders need to model these behaviors.

One-to-One Communication, Encouraging Staff to Express Opinions/Ideas

Leaders are perceived as the organization members who are most likely to stand up and speak in front of the whole group. While this may be true, some of the most important (albeit least visible) work is one-to-one communication. Large-group meetings may be useful for reinforcing the vision, but it is one-to-one communication that is essential for building staff relationships. These conversations are opportunities to provide personalized encouragement, coaching, and feedback on negative behaviors. When trying to get volunteers to take on a new challenge, staff may be reluctant to volunteer in a group meeting. However, a one-to-one conversation can create a more comfortable setting for a staff member to take on something new. These conversations are also important in encouraging staff to express ideas and opinions.

Social Activities

Developing shared visions and goals for the school community and encouraging collaboration are enhanced by opportunities for teachers to meet, socialize, and get to know each other as "people." This is particularly important at the start of a school year. Unlike the situation in most jobs, teachers have four, six, or eight weeks of separation from their fellow employees during summer vacation. At the beginning of a new school year, there is some trepidation and uncertainty as staff reconvenes to begin another year. Welcoming luncheons, picnics, and breakfasts that may be sponsored by the administrative leadership or the parent organization are ways of developing and rekindling friendly, supportive relationships. These beginning-of-the-school-year activities are especially significant for new teachers, providing a setting for new staff introductions. New staff members and student teachers gain support when they are invited to go to lunch, when they are introduced by a staff member to others, when they are offered assistance in locating classrooms or supplies, and so forth. These small yet significant activities send a message of collaboration and build trust.

Throughout the school year, other social activities — for example, retirement celebrations, holiday parties, end-of-the-year picnics, golf leagues, sports teams, and birthday recognitions — enhance collaborative, supportive staff relationships.

Team Building

Authentic relationships are fostered by shared work and shared responsibilities. Providing opportunities for staff to work together and to participate in team-building strategies and training sessions supports collaboration. Team building may be integrated into the school's framework by having groups of students taught by a particular interdisciplinary group of teachers and when the school is organized in small learning communities. These teams usually share the same physical space and have common planning time. The most significant aspects of team teaching are sharing the same students and the opportunity to personalize learning for students. Together, the team can more easily focus on the needs of the student.

Before individuals can be expected to contribute well in team teaching, they need to develop a friendly relationship and build trust. Instructional leadership can use team-building strategies, such as trust walks and ropes courses, to foster trust among staff. These professional development programs create a sense of interdependence: Team members "sink or swim" together. The interdependence realized through these types of activities can carry over to the collaborative, collective capacity and creativity of the teaching team.

Instructional leadership needs to cultivate an awareness of unity for all team members. Each team member must recognize that there is an opportunity to contribute to the team, to learn from others, and to work with them to achieve common goals. Leadership empowers the team to act together to reach a joint objective. These team characteristics enable the team to function effectively in a participative leadership manner. All members of the team feel responsible for the team's success; all members of the team have a common purpose and share a sense of ownership in the work of the team; and communications within the team create a climate of trust and openness.

Mentoring

Mentoring brings together the "experienced" educator and the "new" teacher. This type of support helps the new teacher learn the school rules and policies, understand expectations, perceive existing staff relationships, and become familiar with the physical locations of particular aspects of the building. The most worthwhile aspect of a mentoring program is the supportive relationships that the mentor provides the mentee. The mentee has someone to consult with and question when he or she is uncertain about any aspect of the school community — its people, places, events, and the like.

The mentor also assists the mentee with improving instructional practice. Typically, new teachers attend training sessions, as well as have the expertise and guidance of a mentor for their first year in the district. The training might focus on district expectations, curriculum, lesson design, instructional strategies, classroom management styles, and assessment. The mentor teacher observes the new teacher's classroom and assists with instruction, management, classroom systems and procedures, and opportunities for professional growth. The mentor might also model or demonstrate effective teaching strategies for the mentee. The trust and honesty developed through a meaningful mentoring program establish space for classroom observations and demonstrations, both by the mentor for the mentee and by the mentee for the mentor.

The mentor assists the mentee in strengthening pedagogy, best instructional practices, and relationships with students. The mentor may refine and further develop instructional strategies, new skills, and ways to help students be more successful. Sometimes, the mentor may be surprised by the professional and personal growth realized through this supportive activity. Eventually, the mentoring experience redefines the relationship between the new teacher and mentor as colleagues, peers, and friends.

Instructional Coaching

Instructional coaches act as on-site professional developers who assist teachers in implementing proven instructional practices. The instructional coach and the individual teacher (or team of teachers) form a partnership to analyze the teacher's (or team's) needs and to discuss research-based ideas and solutions. They also work together to find ways to meet those needs. Knowledge is gained "on the job." The coach and the teacher mutually address areas needing improvement. Often, the coach models the instructional practice for the teacher and then observes as the teacher engages in the same practice. Action research is frequently carried out as the mentor and mentee share ideas, identify problems, create solutions, and "try out" research-based practices.

The mutual, supportive relationship created by the coaching model enriches not only the professional learning but also the collegiality, friendship, and collaborative spirit of the coach and teacher. The coach analyzes the teacher's needs, observes classes, suggests proven practices and interventions, models the suggested modifications in instruction, and observes and provides feedback. As a result, a form of professional learning community develops that becomes the means to deliver more effective instruction to improve both teaching and learning.

Peer Review

Although the format of the peer review process differs from school to school, the objective is always the same: to help teachers improve instruction. Peer observation involves using one's peers to examine aspects of teaching and learning. It is an opportunity for staff to reflect on strengths and weaknesses and to work together to improve. The overall goal is to establish a culture of self-study that stimulates continuous inquiry, reflection, information sharing, and success. Just as educators provide teacher-to-student support, peer observation provides teacher-to-teacher support.

To make the peer observation process more valuable, conferencing before and after instruction needs to take place. The quality of student work is also a valuable part of the peer review process.

Rewards, Recognition, Incentives

Everyone likes to be recognized and/or to receive some type of reward for work well done. Educators are no exception. Rewards, recognition, and incentives motivate teachers to participate in the school community. Rewards must be known, and the criteria for receiving them need to be clearly defined for teachers. It is important to recognize an instructional success; the attainment of a degree or completion of a particular professional development activity; or the development of a curriculum, curricular map, or pacing guide. The work of those engaged in the creation and implementation of these initiatives are a few examples of teacher contributions that should receive some sort of public validation.

As with learners, teachers respond positively to recognition and are motivated to continue to develop activities and initiatives that improve teaching and learning. Typical incentives for educators are financial honoraria, time allotted during the school day to engage in the development of various initiatives, and the opportunity to assume a leadership capacity. Just as some schools have a "Student of the Month," some schools have a "Teacher/Employee of the Month." A teacher might be awarded a temporary, special parking place near the building for a school contribution. Inclusion of teacher accomplishments in the school newsletter to parents or in the student newspaper are other common ways to provide teachers with recognition. Summer scholarships for additional study in the teacher's discipline or area of expertise are an excellent incentive for some educators. Candidates for this type of an incentive usually have to apply and indicate why they deserve this award. Another type of summer program is an internship in a local business organization. Again, application is usually required.

Whatever the prize, teachers will respond to this form of recognition and support. With teacher recognition, the value and esteem of the profession is affirmed, and indirect gratitude is expressed for the contributions of the individual educator.

Demonstration Classrooms

In a demonstration classroom, teachers visit sites (demonstration classrooms) that provide teacher-to-teacher observations and collaborative teaching. Typically, the demonstration classroom in-service program consists of the following:

- Before visiting the demonstration classroom, teachers participate in an in-service that focuses on the curricular objective of the demonstration classroom and on the successful instructional strategies used to implement the curricular objective. For example, elementary teachers may want to learn how to establish learning centers in their classrooms. Demonstration teachers would first instruct the participants on such matters as the definition, value, and impact on student achievement and engagement and the aspects of successful instruction to implement the learning centers. Challenges and successes of the implementation of learning centers would also be discussed.

- Teachers are asked to think about and eventually implement learning centers in their classrooms.
- Interested teachers visit demonstration classrooms to observe students and teachers within the learning center model. Visiting teachers observe student and teacher behavior and discuss their observations with the demonstration teacher and fellow visiting teachers.
- A follow-up session for the participants in the visitation and the teachers who facilitate the demonstration classes is held.
- Participants implement learning centers in their classrooms.
- Teachers of the demonstration classes visit the participants' classes.
- A post-visitation conference is held; there, teachers and participants reflect upon and discuss the value and success of the learning center model.

The demonstration classroom provides multiple opportunities for teachers to engage in professional discourse and to better understand their own practice. This approach gives teachers confidence in implementing a new form of instructional strategy and builds teacher-to-teacher dialogue and support.

Conflict Resolution

Conflict occurs when individuals or groups do not obtain what they want or what they believe is right. Since life requires dealing with other people's lives, jobs, children, egos, and senses of mission, conflicts appear inevitable. However, conflict may be minimized or resolved. Conflicts frequently occur when the organization or group has poor communication, when someone seeks power at the expense of others, when there is dissatisfaction with the current leadership, when leadership is weak, when there is a lack of openness and honesty, and sometimes when there is a change in leadership.

Conflict may be either destructive or constructive. It is destructive when it polarizes people and decreases collaboration and cooperation. Sometimes, conflict may cause attention to be diverted to areas that are not significant. In some instances, conflict may lead to irresponsible behavior. Conflict is constructive, however, when it helps to relieve anxiety and stress. As people learn more about each other in a conflict situation, cooperation, support, and understanding become more natural responses. Conflict may result in providing solutions to the problems facing the group.

Recognizing the cause of conflict is necessary for a resolution of a problem. Causes of conflict include the following:

- Needs or wants are not being met.
- Knowledge is limited.
- Values are not the same.
- Expectations are unrealistic.
- Assumptions are made and translated into fact.
- Perceptions and values are questioned.
- Differences in personality, values, race, or gender become evident.

Groups experiencing conflict must collaborate to reach some sort of consensus or general agreement. When group members collaborate, each individual receives respect and support. All members are permitted to express their opinions, whether they agree or disagree. Holding different points of view is commonplace and healthy for a group, but the group eventually must reach a point of acceptance and some form of consensus.

Throughout the conflict resolution process, staff members experience and demonstrate respect for one another. A consensus is not reached until everyone has an opportunity to share ideas and willingly agrees to the compromise.

Professional Development

Central to the development of relationships is a common understanding and ownership of the school's mission, vision, and core values. Thus, it is essential for staff to have professional development opportunities to engage in activities and discussions that enrich the school community. As aligned to DSEI, providing opportunities for focused professional collaboration and growth is essential task for an effective instructional leader. Trust and support are rooted in common agreement over what students should know and be able to do, what effective instruction looks like, what successful practices and research-based strategies are most effective in improving instruction and student achievement, and what behavior is acceptable between teachers and students (and between teachers and teachers). Staff members must not only know and agree on these essential components of the school community; they also must realize that their daily actions and decisions need to be consistent with these beliefs.

Building supportive relationships may become a priority of professional development. Measuring the teachers' trust in each other, the instructional leadership, and the school in general may reveal significant areas for staff to focus on in professional development. Conversations may reveal a staff's strengths and areas of concern. These findings may be used to determine next steps and goals for the entire staff.

Certain professional development models encourage building and strengthening relationships. Peer coaching, mentoring, team teaching, peer reviews, and professional learning communities are models that support teachers and make relationships stronger. Instructional leaders need to consider these when designing professional development activities. Individuals are brought together through these professional development models to work together on areas of mutual interest. In some schools, an individual is hired to provide professional development on an ongoing, daily basis. This individual may be the instructional coach, mentor, facilitator of a professional development learning activity, or observer of a new instructional technique; this on-site professional developer provides in-service that meets the needs of staff.

Providing and strengthening networks and communication systems also support staff relationships. It may be necessary to train school staff on effective communication skills or to conduct workshops to revitalize strategies that are already in place. Utilizing available technology to improve communication among staff members might take the form of a faculty chat room or Web site where ideas, concerns, questions, and successes may be shared.

Travel

When teachers are given the opportunity to travel together to attend professional conferences and workshops or to chaperone students on field trips, the travel experience sets up an opportunity for relationships to form and grow. If staff members attend a conference together, then conversation about the value of the ideas learned and the relevance of those ideas to their own school community undoubtedly will occur. Perhaps out of this travel experience, a core group of individuals may initiate dialogue about a new program, curriculum, assessment instrument, and so forth.

Another form of travel is teacher travel exchanges. There are a number of programs available for teachers to explore. Typically, a teacher might exchange positions with someone in his or her own discipline; with someone living in a country where the language that the teacher teaches is spoken; or with someone who is living in a culture about which the teacher teaches.

Some school districts offer teachers an opportunity to take a sabbatical. Often, the teacher may use the sabbatical to travel and enrich his or her knowledge of subjects that he or she teaches. International experiential education opportunities allow teachers to learn unique pedagogical approaches found in different parts of the world. Other study abroad programs may focus on countries where students live in poverty and face daily challenges that are unlike any that students in our country face. In these situations, the teacher usually meets with members of the business community and other leaders to gain a deeper understanding of the culture and its impact on education.

Internships, exchange programs, and scholarship and grant programs help many teachers expand their understanding of countries around the world. Districts that provide any of these travel programs are supporting the continuing professional growth of their staff.

Clustered Classroom Buildings

The most frequent way to design elementary schools is to have a common grade level in one wing of the school. This setup makes it easier for students of a particular age to be together and for teachers teaching a common grade to collaborate. However, at the secondary school level, it is traditional to group teachers by subject area, making it easy for teachers in this common subject area to collaborate. As a result, students move frequently and over long distances in school. This setup makes it hard for teachers who have the same students to collaborate. It also gives precedence to the needs of the content over the needs of the students.

Many schools are attempting to address this challenge by clustering classrooms of the teachers who need to collaborate about groups of students. This more student-centered collaboration can be facilitated by classroom assignment and building construction. For example, a recently constructed building to serve 1,300 high school 9th-graders (an enormous educational challenge) was designed with clusters of five classrooms as a "pod" off intersecting corridors of the school. Near the cluster of classrooms, a new teacher workstation was created. As a result of this design, the school saw a significant increase in staff collaboration and intervention to improve student achievement.

In existing secondary schools, some schools reassign classrooms to cluster 9th-grade and/or 10th-grade classrooms in one wing of the school. This setup makes it easier for teachers to collaborate and discuss common students and their needs. Another variation is to cluster together classes that might team teach or share students. For example, a history classroom and an English classroom for 9th-grade students might be clustered next to each other. This setup allows teachers to meet often and even to group students for team teaching around common themes.

Team Teaching

In the small learning community option, classrooms were positioned near each other to facilitate collaboration for instruction of a common group of students. One form of team teaching takes this collaboration to the next level and places these students and a pair or more of teachers in the same large classroom. These team teaching situations make it easy to draw on the strengths of each teacher to develop enhanced learning experiences for students. For example, a school might create a humanities block by combining traditional English and social studies classes. Teachers from each of these disciplines form a team and work with students in a double block of class time. They lead students through a variety of literature, history, reading, writing, and reflection activities that make connections between language and history. In another example, three teachers from the disciplines of mathematics, science, and technology might create a triple period, project-based curriculum to help students develop required math and science concepts through applied activities. In addition to formal joint teaching assignments, team teaching can also be *ad hoc*, with teachers coming together for a specific lesson. In this case, a mathematics teacher in a Health Academy might bring in a health teacher for a lesson illustrating how mathematics is applied in the real world of medical research. Even this *ad hoc* can be supported to become a common practice if school leaders recognize creative ideas and provide procedures for other staff to cover classrooms when necessary.

Another team teaching structure organizes teachers from the core academic areas into a team to collectively teach a group of students. All the teachers on the team share the same students. The commonality of teaching assignments brings teachers together to plan instruction and to meet the needs of the students under their responsibility. Working in the team structure, staff members have opportunities to reflect on instructional practices that are most effective in raising student achievement. In some instances, team members may focus on improving their practice through peer observations and collaborative scoring. Action research frequently takes place among the team members, who explore, discuss, practice, and evaluate methods of improving teaching and learning. Through the team teaching approach, individual members find support in one another and sense shared accountability for the success of the students and the team.

Teams may be given responsibility to decide on resources to be purchased, student expectations, curricula, assessments, and professional development opportunities. They might even be given responsibility for determining professional and student placements. Working together on these and other initiatives strengthens the collaboration of the team; a sense of interdependence motivates individual team members to assist and support others for the success of the team as a whole.

Team teaching is the exception to the way that most teachers have taught and learned. It requires patience, which enables teachers to compromise and share responsibilities. However, the rewards are significant: Teachers learn from one another and create better instruction. This form of staff collaboration is important in improving the quality of teaching and learning through the combined strengths of educators.

Grade-Level Teams

Probably the most rapidly growing example of staff collaboration is grade-level teams. These types of teams have been more common in elementary schools, where teachers at a particular grade level meet to compare curriculum plans and ensure that instruction is similar across classrooms. These types of teams are an essential part of staff collaboration. It is a strategy for sharing teaching ideas and discussing students who are not succeeding. In secondary schools, grade-level teams traditionally have been less common, and teachers most often have met as departments to share ideas within a subject.

Grade-level teams developed differently at the secondary school level. As concerns rose about lack of student achievement, particularly in 9th grade, teachers were asked to meet as a grade-level team. This is more easily accomplished when a team of teachers is scheduled with a common group of students. This collaboration allows teachers to examine student success (or failure) across all subjects. If there is an inconsistent pattern of failure, the conversation may lead to ideas about what type of intervention would be successful for a particular student. Even if there is no obvious solution, the group of teachers is likely to be more creative in identifying a solution. Also, the group can commit to making changes in all of the classrooms, rather than having each teacher experiment and try to intervene on his or her own. This type of group collaboration is an important avenue to early and effective intervention and to helping make students more successful.

When it comes to allocating time for teams to meet at the secondary level, assigning grade-level team meeting time often provides greater benefit to students. Teachers will naturally find time to meet and discuss ideas with teachers of the same subject, but it often requires a "push" of common meeting time to provide for a grade-level team meeting.

Professional Learning Communities

A staff that functions as a professional learning community comes together for learning within a supportive community. Participants interact, test their ideas, challenge one another's ideas and interpretations, and process new information gleaned from one another. Typically, teachers come together to focus on topics of their choice that are related to instruction, student achievement, and assessment. The professional learning community is characterized by supportive and shared leadership, shared values and vision, collective learning and application of learning, and supportive conditions that enable the group to meet regularly and solve problems and make decisions.

The results of professional learning communities for teachers include the following:

- a decreased sense of isolation
- an increased commitment to the mission and goals of the school
- a sense of collaborative responsibility toward student achievement and school success
- a renewed motivation to teach
- lower rates of absenteeism
- increased knowledge about students' needs and successful teaching practices

Review Questions

1. What aspects of small learning communities would help improve student and professional learning in your school?
2. What schedule configuration would provide the faculty and staff at your school the greatest opportunities for meaningful collaboration?
3. Which specific professional development models and strategies described in this chapter would be most likely to result in teacher collaboration and professional growth at your school? What changes and support would it take to implement these models and strategies?

 Chapter 7

Community Partnerships

Schools have much to gain through partnerships with the business community, especially if the school has a small learning community with a career theme. This clear focus makes it easier to establish partnerships with businesses, to create a business advisory committee, and to solicit advice from business leaders and other professionals. With the transformation of the U.S. economy, the demand for workers with particular skill development has led business, industry, and labor to partner with schools to assist in preparing tomorrow's workforce. Schools should pursue business-community partnerships that are mutually satisfactory to students, teachers, educational programs, businesses, and community economic growth.

Benefits of Business-Community Partnerships

Having a community or business partner may bring many benefits to a school, classroom, and teacher. Teachers gain advice in curricular areas — especially in career and technical education programs or career academies, where members of the business community serve as advisers. It is difficult for an educator to stay current in some of the business practices within some career clusters. Businesses may offer teachers an opportunity to do an internship or to work over the summer vacation. Such experiences can provide teachers with valuable insight into the expectations and requirements of a particular workplace and field. Businesses may also donate up-to-date equipment to the school or allow students and teachers to access their equipment.

Community and/or business representatives can also support teachers by providing an award for an exceptional teacher performance or a program that is possible through the collaboration of the business and the teacher representative.

Among the many benefits of having a business partner are the following:

- **Schools** have more motivated students with better attendance, behavior, and achievement, all of which contribute to school improvement and image.
- **Students** gain an enriched curriculum; identify with successful role models; possess opportunities for significant work experience; gain knowledge, skills, and understanding; are recognized for achievement; have higher self-esteem; and possess a heightened sense of community.
- **Teachers** gain assistance in specific curriculum areas, opportunities for professional development, recognition for achievement, and access to technological advances and equipment.
- **Businesses** ensure a better prepared work force and employees who are more satisfied with their jobs, more committed to their employers, and more productive at work. They also demonstrate their sense of civic responsibility and gain a level of consumer respect and loyalty that conventional marketing cannot generate.
- **Communities** enhance their local business climate and the vitality of their residential areas, both of which can aid in meeting the challenges of the future and ensuring long-term economic growth.

Partnering Activities for Students

A variety of opportunities for students can be provided to enhance learning and prepare them for the world beyond school. These include the following:

- visits to a company/organization
- classroom visits/talks by company/organization representatives
- mentoring of students by business employees
- opportunities for students to shadow in the workplace

- career education and guidance
- providing a congratulatory letter from a business leader to each student who makes the honor roll
- developing student internships and job placement opportunities

Partnering Activities for Teachers

A business partnership supports teachers by keeping them up to date on current industry and business practices and by assisting them in providing a relevant, meaningful curriculum. In return, the company's profile and reputation are enhanced. Partnering activities include the following:

- offering externships in business for teachers
- making business contributions to support instruction
- having employers serve as consultants to teachers
- rewarding exceptional teaching performance
- sharing in the company's training programs, stress workshops, time management seminars, and so forth

Materials and Equipment

Supporting a school with materials or money can help it move forward with lasting effects on student achievement and ultimately on career success. Businesses often have a wealth of resources to share, such as the following:

- surplus business equipment
- surplus furniture
- paper of all sorts
- equipment that creates a learning environment that simulates a workplace

A Systemwide Approach to Rigor, Relevance, and Relationships

Why Business–Community Involvement?

To continue to run a business successfully, employers will need employees who are team-oriented problem-solvers, are articulate, possess functional writing skills, understand human nature, and are fully versed in applied technology. With this range of skills, employees will perform at the level necessary to keep a business competitive. In educational terms, this means that adults must be lifelong learners. It is our responsibility to show students that education only begins in school. The presence of business emphasizes how real that aspect of lifelong learning is.

Business leaders know that if they are not learning something new all the time and applying that knowledge to their business daily, someone else will. The enormous technological expansion that the world is experiencing means that innovation is necessary to give the United States the ability to compete.

The outcome of high-quality education is a work force that can provide better services and products for the consumer, both in the community and beyond. Today, the academic skills and knowledge required of entry-level employees are often at a higher level than those that are required for college entrance.

Business leaders have a unique position in the community: They are admired because of their financial success, and this status gives them an opportunity to influence people. Their influence can help young people become better prepared for their first steps into a career.

Businesses often relocate to find a more suitable work force. A world-class work force in any community strengthens the economy of that community by providing more employment. Business is supported by the community. It is the responsibility of business, therefore, to support the endeavors of the community, among which the education of its children is a primary concern.

Service Learning/Community Service

Many schools provide students with opportunities to engage in community service programs. Community service programs consist of volunteer efforts to make a positive impact on the school or community at large. In some schools, a number of hours in community service are required for graduation. In other schools, this may be a voluntary requirement that gives students who complete a specified number of hours a special honor at graduation. Engaging in these programs gives students an opportunity to gain life skills as they experience the real world through hands-on work. Some schools tie community service requirements to students' areas of career interest, so that the community service lends additional opportunity for students to explore a possible career choice.

Another benefit of a community service program is the opportunity to meet a variety of people in the workplace. These community members can be a source of insight to students about the field or profession associated with the community service. Participating in these programs indicates to future employers and college admissions personnel that a student has made a meaningful contribution and is willing to "give back" talent, time, and expertise. Volunteering has many other intangible benefits; for example, it allows students not only to explore personal areas of interest but also to learn much about others while gaining personal satisfaction from giving.

Community service programs may also create effective school partnerships with city and town governmental agencies; churches and synagogues; and many volunteer, service, and civic organizations. Examples of community service projects include developing local tourism brochures, rehabbing and refurbishing housing; processing recyclables; collecting items for food banks; producing and reporting a television news program; creating business displays; painting murals on community property; planting trees; developing reading/literacy programs; and teaching computer courses to senior citizens.

The significant difference between a community service program and a service learning program is that the latter combines active learning from real-world service work in the community with academic content and competencies. Meaningful service to the community is directly linked to student learning. The community service becomes the means for students to reach academic goals. Academic credit is offered for the service learning because the curriculum is integrated into the volunteer work. The following areas receive attention in an effective curricular model for service learning:

- **Preparation:** This involves determining the need, matching students' skills and knowledge, collaborating with community partners, and integrating curriculum into the service.
- **Action:** This involves determining what the student will be doing; combining meaningful service with relevant learning experiences; building upon the student's skills and knowledge; and ensuring that the work is significant, that it is performed in a safe environment, and that it allows the student to experience success and learn from failures.

- **Reflections:** This involves having students review and evaluate their experiences. Using seminars, journal writing, and role-playing, students note what occurred, what impact their actions had, what their reactions and feelings were, and what they learned or rediscovered.
- **Demonstration and Celebration:** This involves having students show what they have learned through the service learning experience by presenting reports, writing articles about their experiences, and developing ongoing projects to benefit others.

School-Based Enterprises

School-based enterprises are a model of work-based learning. This type of career and technical education consists of a high school course or program that functions as an actual business that serves the school and/or larger community. Academic and technical instruction gives students the background needed to understand and run the operations of the business, as well as to produce the product or service being sold. In most instances, students receive academic credit for their participation in the enterprise. Typical examples of school-based enterprises are bookstores, restaurants, print shops, and auto repair services.

The school-based enterprise functions as a real business. The profit earned is reinvested in the business; in some cases, students may earn income. The school-based enterprise gives the students a new context to relate to their teacher. This shared business venture creates many opportunities for teachers to model acceptable business standards and behavior, to get to know students in a different role, to observe students' abilities to perform in real-world applications of learning, and to build a collaborative spirit of learning and working in a joint venture. Research has shown that work-based learning reinforces academic and technical skills, improves students' self-esteem, exposes students to career options, develops an understanding of workplace culture and expectations, and engages and motivates students through real-world applications of skills and knowledge.

School-based enterprises are a mirror of work-based learning. In the school-based enterprise, students assume a greater responsibility for the success of the business enterprise than they would assume in a work-based learning program. Through the school-based enterprise, students experience a greater sense of accomplishment, satisfaction, and pride as the business prospers.

At Excelsior Education Center in Victorville, California, students in career academies may participate in school-based enterprises. Academic requirements are incorporated into the specialty of the business organization. The business enterprises are student-run businesses on the school campus. Excelsior brings the business application model to the student and provides internships in the field as an adjunct to the enterprise. Specialty students spend a minimum of 50% of their time on campus taking courses and working in the enterprise. The business enterprises are directly partnered with and supported by local businesses involved in the same type of production or service. Across the career academies, student-run businesses exist in insurance and investment, banking, travel and tourism, construction, and computer repair. These internal businesses provide goods and services to Excelsior and the community while providing students with valuable field experiences.

In order for school-improvement efforts to be successful and sustained over time, it is critical to engage the community, families, and all stakeholders actively in the initiative. The following methods can help ensure that the school-improvement plan directly addresses the needs of the school and its district. They also ensure that the energy of community members and stakeholders is aligned in the same direction, and toward the same goal. Successful school-improvement initiatives may be enhanced by:

1. Assessing the current status of community engagement
2. Creating a collaboration plan to bridge the school and community
3. Developing support from community, family, and business members to promote student achievement
4. Involving parents and families in academic goals
5. Supporting the collaboration plan between the school and community

WE™ SUPPORT Parent/Community Surveys

As part of a comprehensive communication system, the WE SUPPORT *Parent/Community* survey was developed by means of a partnership between the International Center and the Successful Practices Network to help schools gauge the level of support and engagement among external stakeholders. Specifically, these surveys measure perceptions of the school experience as well as the community's expectations of the school system in terms of rigor, relevance, and relationships. Results from this survey can, for example, help answer the following kinds of questions:

- How well does the community think students are prepared for the future?
- Do they think students have the skills and knowledge to be leaders in the community?
- Do they think students of all abilities are encouraged to learn?

Creating a Community, Family, and Stakeholder Collaboration Plan

After collecting data from parents and community members, schools must collaborate with key stakeholders to develop and implement a comprehensive plan to maximize engagement. The plan can be based on the results from the WE SUPPORT survey, but these results, however they are acquired, should define clear expectations, establish specific policies, identify resources, and make recommendations for maximizing community engagement. The central component of this plan will be to develop a focused communication initiative that will ensure a common focus, and buy-in from, all external and internal stakeholders. To achieve these goals, the effective use of technology to drive interactive communication is a key component.

Community Engagement Presentations and Forums

Another effective method for collaborating with key stakeholders involves delivering a series of presentations to a wide range of community members and groups, including: business groups, Chambers of Commerce, parent and family groups, religious leaders, not-for-profit organizations, political organizations, Parent-Teacher associations, and more. These presentations provide a two-way communication forum for establishing an ongoing dialogue between the school and important stakeholders. The presentations should focus on the goals of school improvement, and be designed with the objective of ensuring buy-in and active participation from all stakeholders.

Supporting the Collaboration Plan

The data collected from the surveys and from conversations with leadership teams and community members will guide how the relationship between the school and community takes shape. These data will also inform the partnership's vision for future collaborations. With an adequate survey of needs in hand and a healthy working relationship with key stakeholders established, schools should leverage their resources and support structures to sustain a strong and meaningful relationship between a school and its community, being sure to develop those relationships in ways that are specific to the needs of the school and district.

Three Examples of Successful Partnerships in Model Schools

Douglas Taylor Elementary School, Chicago, IL

Relationships and Parent/Community Involvement

Chicago Public Schools, the largest school district in Illinois, with 589 elementary schools, and is the third largest school district in the United States. Within this massive district, you can find Taylor Elementary — an urban, high-poverty school — in the southeast side of Chicago, in the 10th Ward.

In spite of its challenges, Taylor has established strong ties to various stakeholders in the community. For instance, Taylor staff members reach out to the community through such events as Family Math Night, Family Literacy Night, and the Taylor Family Fun Fair. Each event brings out over five hundred students, parents, staff, community members, and the 10th Ward Alderman, John Pope. In addition, members of the East Side Chamber of Commerce support the school by advertising their businesses in the Taylor Assignment Notebook. These ads reduce the cost of the assignment notebook for families. The Chamber also offers mentoring and internship programs at Taylor.

Parents are also highly involved at Taylor. The Taylor Parent Patrol, for example, is a unique group of 35 parents who help ensure the safety and well-being of the students as they arrive and depart from school. During the day, the Taylor Parent Patrol serve as greeters in the main entrance of the school. In May 2008, at his safety luncheon, Mayor Richard M. Daley recognized the Taylor Parent Patrol as one of the best parent patrols in Chicago Public Schools. In addition, the Taylor Parent Patrol was asked to be part of a parent focus group sponsored by the United States Department of Education.

Taylor has also involved parents through its No Child Left Behind Parent Committee and its Bilingual Advisory Committee, both of which advise the principal by sharing community concerns. All communication from the school is distributed in both English and Spanish, to reach as many parents as possible. In addition, Taylor offers computer classes on site for parents. Parents commend Taylor for its structure and clear rules, and they appreciate the school for its discipline and its emphasis on safety. The parents also commend the teachers for their willingness to work with students and listen to parents' concerns. A supportive, caring environment at the school, coupled with a cooperative home-school-community link, is Taylor's formula for student success and lifelong learning.

Harris Hill Elementary School, Penfield Central Schools, NY

Leadership

Our District Curriculum Council

Through our general strategic planning process, we identified a need to focus on having our students achieve NYS standards at high levels (rigor). We also idenitified a need to ensure both that our educational program was preparing them for the future (relevance) and that we were addressing the whole child, with an emphasis on character education (relationships). As part of our planning, we included the following goals: to educate ourselves about education needs of the future, to look at research on rigorous educational programs and implementation, and to identify high-priority educational areas for rigor. Since we wanted to engage all stakeholder groups in the process, our council members included teachers, administrators, Board of Education members, parents, community business representatives, and students.

As we learned about future education needs and rigorous educational programs, our Council identified the behavioral indices for use in our learning criteria as indicators of student progress district-wide. Additionally, we mandated our building-level improvement planning processes to require building goals that would foster rigor, relevance, and relationships, and we charged the Curriculum Council with the task of reviewing each building's school improvement plan on an annual basis. The goals we established for our council were as follows.

Objective 1: Defining Rigor, Relevance, and Relationships Through the Learning Criteria. Achieving this objective would comprise several of the following tasks:

- To define rigor and implement rigorous programs in the district
- To identify and implement educational programs with increased rigor and relevance, including but not limited to K–12 gifted education, accelerated core courses, HS electives, AP, SUPA (Syracuse University Project Advance), and other college courses

- To identify behavioral indices for each of the learning criteria
- To identify and implement student-support programs and services that promote student-school-community relationships, including expanded extracurricular and community-involvement opportunities.

Objective 2: Community and Constituency Curriculum Input. To seek community and constituency input that will advise the district's education program goals and outcomes regarding needs and perspectives of the community, staff, and students (local and world).

Objective 3: District Shared-Decision Plan Review. To collect, and review progress toward achieving each school's School Improvement Plan as developed by their building's Shared Decision-making Teams, and to do this every year.

A. J. Moore Academy, Waco, Texas

With its career focus, A. J. Moore Academy strives to provide a rigorous curriculum that meets state standards and helps students apply skills and knowledge to the real world. It operates six career academies: Information Technology, Finance, Engineering, Hospitality & Tourism, Environmental Technology, and Health Sciences. The variety of offerings at these academies is a strength of the A. J. Moore curriculum and students at their academies take pride in their achievements. Partnerships are strong and include business partnerships, agreements with area colleges, along with active parent involvement. Moreover, the school has done an excellent job of integrating technology. By means of several initiatives, it has achieved a very low student-to-computer ratio. As a result, technology can be integrated effectively by teachers in the classroom and by administrators of the school. One of the school's most recent technology initiatives involves providing all students in math classes with a graphing calculator for homework assignments. This program allows each student to receive a calculator for use at home. Consequently, this "Graphing Calculator Initiative" promotes increases in student proficiency by giving them a tool that is invaluable for solving complex math problems. Waco is not a wealthy district and A. J. Moore is not a wealthy school, but it has, nonetheless, achieved a truly remarkable school culture and level of achievement.

A. J. Moore Academy is a small magnet school, one of three high schools in the district, and is a school of choice, meaning that any student from the district can attend. In grades nine through twelve, it serves 700 students. At A. J. Moore, students closely reflect the diversity of the larger community, with 34% of its students being African-American, 50% Hispanic, and 16% white. Approximately 22% are students with disabilities and 84% of students come from families designated as economically disadvantaged. The school day is divided into eight periods of 45 minutes each, and staff are organized into departments. The building is about 37 years old and was built according to an "open classroom" floor plan, so many classrooms adjoin one another and lack doors or walls.

One aspect of excellence at A. J. Moore is the high degree of community involvement. The school's shared decision-making team forms a key part of school leadership and decision-making. The school also maintains three active postsecondary partnerships with a local university, community college, and technical college. A. J. Moore's Business Advisory Board is active and has not only influenced curricula but has also, by means of several partnerships, improved the quality of teaching and learning. The work of the group's 60 active members is substantial and involves several subcommittees. To assist with newer academies, new members are recruited throughout the year.

Students and staff mention frequent school-to-parent and school-to-student communication as an important element of the school's initiatives. This year, a new technological messaging system, School Messenger, has been added to help provide instantaneous communication with parents and students. Students also indicate that attendance and counseling staff develop close relationships with their parents. Counselors send daily e-mail updates on scholarships and grants as well as congratulatory messages when students receive word that they have been accepted to colleges. Students report, in fact, that because they received up-to-the-minute information via e-mail, the were able to apply to many scholarships about which they would have otherwise been unaware. Counselors at A. J. Moore are always available to give that "personal touch" in assisting students as they navigate the numerous college and financial aid applications. A "Go Center" has also been developed to give students access to technological resources that will help them explore their post-secondary options. To address different aspects of high school and college readiness, A.J. Moore is also designated as a "Gear-Up" campus, which entails maintaining a liaison from Baylor University on campus. Parents, too, are assisted in every way to eliminate any barriers that may stand in the way of their children's post-secondary education. FAFSA (Free Application for Federal Student Aid) nights, along with additional college readiness programs, are implemented to help make the process as easy as possible for parents.

Chapter 7: Community Partnerships

Review Questions

1. Do you partner with any local businesses? If so, which ones? If not, why not?
2. How might you go about developing a community or business partnership?
3. Compare partnering activities with students with those of teachers.
4. How might you use partnerships to address the need for community service in your district?
5. What are some ways in which you might use school-based enterprises to create rigor and relevance?

Chapter 8

Creating a Culture of Rigor, Relevance, and Relationships

Among the attributes of human dynamics and organization development, leadership is one of the most studied. Ancient Chinese philosopher Lao Tzu reminded us, "A leader is best when people barely know he exists, when his work is done, his aim fulfilled, they will say: we did it ourselves." Noted leadership author and speaker, John Maxwell, adds this thought, "A great leader's courage to fulfill his vision comes from passion, not position."

As we have examined in previous chapters, the DSEI frames instructional leadership as the shared responsibility of educators in many different roles. The DSEI emphasizes, in fact, that the laser-like focus of leaders on effective instruction is the life-blood that fuels organizational coherence and empowers both teachers and students.

The DSEI envisions successful instructional leadership as having a systemwide focus on: using research to establish urgency for higher expectations; aligning the curriculum to standards; integrating literacy and math across all content areas; facilitating data-driven decision-making to inform instruction; and, providing opportunities for focused professional collaboration and growth. These are the things — when done collaboratively and relentlessly — that move school systems toward success in student learning.

School administrators are under a spotlight that is brighter than at any previous time in education. The research is consistent: School leadership is key to school and student success. Every move by administrators is highly visible; more than ever, administrators are being held accountable for school performance. The intense pressure to have students achieve may influence some school leaders to become conservative and avoid taking risks. However, merely maintaining the status quo in procedures and policies will not raise student achievement. While most schools are not under a state or federal mandate to improve school performance, any school that is not moving forward will find itself in a formal "needs improvement" status.

The work of the International Center for Leadership in Education has shown that exemplary schools are out ahead of the curve, anticipating challenges and innovating. Becoming an exemplary school requires dynamic leadership. The Rigor/Relevance Framework can be an excellent tool for administrators to focus their staff on improvement and to engage teachers in reflective practice. The following pages provide suggestions about how administrators for instructional leadership can "take action" on improving student achievement.

Instructional Leadership

Educators often talk about the important role in their schools of principals as instructional leaders. But as we have shown in previous chapters, successful schools have realized that instructional leadership is never solely vested in an instructionally savvy principal, but requires everyone in the school and system to play a unique and specific role in creating powerful learning opportunities for all learners.

Rigorous and relevant instruction is achieved by teachers who make changes in the way that they plan and conduct instruction and assessment. They cannot, however, accomplish these tasks alone. All school staff, but particularly administrators, must play an important role as well. The philosophy, culture, policies, and procedures of the school can provide an incentive to change, or they can be significant barriers.

The research consistently shows that the principal is key to any instructional change in schools. In fact, the principal should be the instructional leader of a school, helping to guide, encourage, and support teachers in making a change.

Wilma Smith and Richard Andrews define nine characteristics of an instructional leader. Such a leader:

1. places priority on curriculum issues.
2. is dedicated to the goals of the school and the school district.
3. is able to rally and mobilize resources to accomplish the goals of the district and the school.
4. creates a climate of high expectations in the school, characterized by a tone of respect for teachers, students, parents, and community.
5. functions as a leader with direct involvement in instructional policy.
6. continually monitors student progress toward school achievement and teacher effectiveness in meeting those goals.
7. is able to develop and articulate a clear vision of long-term goals for the school.
8. consults effectively with others in school decisions.
9. recognizes time as a scarce resource and creates order and discipline by minimizing factors that may disrupt the learning process.

The Council of Chief School Officers has developed "Standards for School Leaders," which articulates the knowledge, dispositions, and performances that school leaders must have in order to be effective in their role in school. The standards defined for a school administrator call for an education leader who promotes the success of all students by doing the following:

- facilitating the development, articulation, implementation, and stewardship of a vision of learning that is shared and supported by the school community
- advocating, nurturing, and sustaining a school culture and instructional program conducive to student learning and staff professional growth
- ensuring management of the organization, operations, and resources for a safe, efficient, and effective learning environment
- collaborating with families and community members, responding to diverse community interests and needs, and mobilizing community resources
- acting with integrity and fairness, and in an ethical manner
- understanding, responding to, and influencing the larger political, social, economic, legal, and cultural context

It is the responsibility of the principal to show leadership by focusing educational planning, reinforcing changes, working for outside support, and modeling the characteristics of learner-centered instruction. Key responsibilities of principals include following through consistently in classroom observations, creating public awareness and support, changing the paradigm of instruction, and facilitating effective professional development.

Classroom Observation

Classroom observation is a vital link among the student, teacher, and principal. It brings the principal closer to the real action: instruction and learning. It places the principal in a resource role, in which his or her ideas can really affect teachers, students, and learning. The International Center's Collaborative Instructional Review includes a set of rubrics focused on the work of the students. There are four rubrics focused on rigor, relevance, learner engagement, and literacy. Each rubric is based on a continuum, from "Beginning" to "Exceeding." Instructional leaders and coaches can use the rubrics as part of a needs assessment or as part of instructional coaching to support teachers in raising the levels of rigor, relevance, engagement. and literacy in daily practice.

The following rubric is focused on rigor. Thoughtful work, high-level thinking, and oral extended student responses are the three areas of rigor as defined by the International Center.

Chapter 8: Creating a Culture of Rigor, Relevance, and Relationships

Collaborative Instructional Review—Classroom Visitation Rubric for Rigor

Evidence of Rigor	Beginning	Developing	Meeting	Exceeding
Thoughtful Work	Student work is easy, usually only requiring a single correct answer.	Student work occasionally requires extended time to complete, stretches student learning, and requires use of prior knowledge.	Student work requires extensive use of prior knowledge, is frequently creative and original, and requires students to reflect and revise for improved quality.	Student work requires extensive creativity, originality, design, or adaptation.
High-Level Thinking	Student work requires simple recall of knowledge.	Student work requires explanation and understanding of knowledge and/or limited application. Students occasionally use higher-order thinking skills.	Students demonstrate higher-order thinking skills, such as evaluation, synthesis, creativity, and analysis. Students evaluate their own work and identify steps to improve it.	Students routinely use higher-order thinking skills, such as evaluation, synthesis, creativity, and analysis. Students skillfully evaluate their own work and the work of others.
Oral Extended Student Responses	Students' oral responses demonstrate simple recall and basic understanding of knowledge, as evidenced by single-word responses or recital of facts.	Students' oral responses demonstrate comprehension by explaining information in their own words and occasionally by expressing original ideas and opinions. Students participate in discussions with peer groups.	Students' oral responses demonstrate an ability to extend and refine knowledge automatically, to solve problems routinely, and to create unique solutions. Students are able to facilitate class discussions.	Students' oral responses demonstrate logical thinking about complex problems and the ability to apply prior knowledge and skills when confronted with perplexing unknowns. Students are skillful in discussions with peers and adults.

© International Center for Leadership in Education

A Systemwide Approach to Rigor, Relevance, and Relationships

The next rubric is focused on relevance. Relevance, as defined by the Application Model of the Rigor/Relevance Framework, is about making interdisciplinary connections and/or real-world predictable or unpredictable situations. Three criteria have been established: meaningful work, authentic resources, and learning connections.

Collaborative Instructional Review—Classroom Visitation Rubric for Relevance

Evidence of Relevance	Beginning	Developing	Meeting	Exceeding
Meaningful Work	Student work is routine and highly structured, reflects knowledge in one discipline, and usually requires the memorization of facts and formulas or an assessment of content knowledge.	Student work is structured and reflects a basic application of knowledge (and, occasionally, interdisciplinary applications). Students practice using the steps in a procedure and drawing from previous knowledge to solve problems and create solutions.	Students have choices for work that is challenging and often original, that reflects application of knowledge, and that requires performance that is consistent with real-world applications.	Student work reflects real-world, unpredictable applications of knowledge that have unknown factors, as well as individual and unique solutions to problems.
Authentic Resources	Students rely on the teacher as their primary resource to complete work.	Students use and rely on the teacher as their primary resource but also use textbooks, references, and secondary reading material to complete work.	Students use real-world resources such as manuals, tools, technology, primary source documents, and/or interviews to complete work.	Students select and use multiple real-world resources, as well as new or unique resources, perhaps unknown to the teacher.
Learning Connections	Students see learning only as a school requirement, unrelated to their future or their outside lives.	Students begin to see connections between their learning and their lives as it relates to personal examples and applications to solve problems.	Students see connections between what they are learning and their lives, and they can make links to real-world applications.	Students are committed to the learning experience as something that is an essential part of meeting their future goals and life aspirations.

The learner engagement rubric is focused on verbal participation, body language, focus, and breadth. The engagement level of students is not necessarily indicative of how deeply students are thinking. A highly engaged student in a low-rigor task does not make for effective instruction. Instructional leaders may be able to see correlations between high engagement and high relevance.

Collaborative Instructional Review — Classroom Visitation Rubric for Learner Engagement

Evidence of Learner Engagement	Beginning	Developing	Meeting	Exceeding
Verbal Participation	Students rarely share ideas, ask questions, or answer questions.	Students follow classroom procedures but may be reluctant to share ideas or to ask or answer questions.	Students are eager to share ideas and to ask and answer questions.	Students confidently share ideas and ask and answer questions related to the learning experience.
Body Language	Students exhibit negative body language.	Students exhibit some negative and some positive body language.	Students exhibit positive body language and make eye contact with others.	Students' body language shows their commitment to learn.
Focus	Students lack focus on the learning experience.	Students are focused on the learning experience, with limited distractions.	Students are focused on the learning experience.	Students are committed to high-quality work in the learning experience and persevere to completion.
Breadth	Few students are fully engaged in classroom instruction and activity.	Some students are fully engaged in classroom instruction and activity.	Nearly all students are fully engaged in classroom instruction and activity.	All students are fully engaged in classroom instruction and activity.

A Systemwide Approach to Rigor, Relevance, and Relationships

The final rubric is focused on literacy. As an important aspect of the Common Core State Standards, the following rubric addresses the expectations set with regards to literacy. Five criteria are included in the rubric below:

- Text Complexity
- Digital Use
- Speaking, Listening, and Collaborating
- Document and Quantitative Literacy
- Written Communication

Collaborative Instructional Review—Classroom Visitation Rubric for Literacy

Evidence of Literacy	Beginning	Developing	Meeting	Exceeding
Text Complexity	Students comprehend simple text at an information retrieval level, using texts or teacher read-aloud materials.	Students comprehend simple text for main idea, summary, and initial analysis of information. Students understand familiar vocabulary, clear cause-effect relationships, and simple sequences of events. Students can respond to basic questions for which answers are implicit or directly implied.	Students comprehend complex texts, determine meaning of virtually any word; understand subtle cause-effect relationships; understand simple sequences of events; and summarize, evaluate, or analyze the text.	Students comprehend complex texts, understand implied and complex cause-effect relationships, understand the meaning of context-dependent words, analyze a complex set of ideas or sequence of events, and explain multiple interpretations of the story or event. Students can explain how specific ideas develop over the course of the text. Students are able to integrate information from primary and secondary sources.

Collaborative Instructional Review—Classroom Visitation Rubric for Literacy (Continued)

Evidence of Literacy	Beginning	Developing	Meeting	Exceeding
Digital Use	Students' work often consists of copying directly from other sources. Use of digital tools is rare and most often involves lower levels of rigor and relevance.	Students' use of digital sources is limited to demonstrating awareness, comprehension, or basic application of knowledge.	Students demonstrate effective integration of single and multiple digital sources to understand, infer, and act upon knowledge; to facilitate communication; and/or to create solutions. Students demonstrate the ability to apply information to relevant, real-life scenarios. Students demonstrate an ability to use basic citation.	Students integrate multiple digital sources, independently evaluating the credibility and accuracy of sources. Students skillfully use this information to create solutions; to offer justifiable points of view; to apply to relevant, real-life, and complex scenarios; and/or to create a new project. Students correctly cite information and demonstrate the ability to teach digital strategies to others.

Collaborative Instructional Review—Classroom Visitation Rubric for Literacy (Continued)

Evidence of Literacy	Beginning	Developing	Meeting	Exceeding
Speaking, Listening, and Collaborating	Students work in isolation. They demonstrate limited ability to apply their language skills to communicate effectively, frequently, and persuasively in academic and/or social communication.	Students collaborate and communicate integrated information to demonstrate awareness, comprehension, or basic application of knowledge.	Students collaborate and communicate integrated information to adapt, create, solve, justify, and apply knowledge. Students are given an opportunity to evaluate other points of view and present their own information.	Students collaborate in person and virtually to contribute fully to point-of-view conversations, debates, problem solving, and integration of the ideas of others to achieve a common goal. Students are able to present information, reasoning, and supporting evidence. Students understand and use language, culture, and verbal and nonverbal communication methods.

Collaborative Instructional Review—Classroom Visitation Rubric for Literacy (Continued)

Evidence of Literacy	Beginning	Developing	Meeting	Exceeding
Document and Quantitative Literacy	Students have few or no opportunities to utilize strategies for comprehending information in tables, charts, graphs, and other visual modes of presenting information.	Students can comprehend simple information contained in tables, charts, graphs, and other visual modes of presenting information.	Students compare or combine information contained in tables, charts, graphs, and other visual modes of presenting information, using inference, analysis, synthesis, and evaluation skills. Students use new information to make predictions based on the data.	Students use complex visually based sources of information, as well as numeracy-based sources to develop solutions, to analyze the correctness and usefulness of data, to determine how to use the information to complete complex tasks, and to evaluate the results of actions or predict outcomes.

Collaborative Instructional Review—Classroom Visitation Rubric for Literacy (Continued)

Evidence of Literacy	Beginning	Developing	Meeting	Exceeding
Written Communication	Students' writing skills are underdeveloped and/or interfere with the ability to communicate in writing for a purpose and audience.	Students use basic writing skills to communicate. Writing demonstrates limited development of ideas, some evidence of organization, minor errors in sentence structure, and acknowledgement and basic justification of point of view.	Students use the skills and characteristics of good writing to communicate simple ideas for a purpose and audience. Writing demonstrates clear ideas, effective organization, complete sentences, and acknowledgement and basic justification of point of view. Students demonstrate a limited ability to edit their work.	Students use the skills and characteristics of good writing to communicate complex ideas and concepts in multiple formats for a variety of purposes and audiences. Writing demonstrates clarity of analysis, use of complex sentence structure, effective organization, acknowledgement and justification of point of view, and creative solutions or insights. Students demonstrate an ability to edit their work and/or the work of others.

Using the rubrics to help describe the learning environment is not an easy endeavor. Having a deep understanding of rigor and relevance as well as literacy is critical to establishing this process and keeping it reliable and valid. Observing students' work in a 30-minute period of time can also be challenging. The rubrics are effective tools for having quality discussions with teachers and instructional leaders about how students should be thinking and working.

Strategies for Moving to the Next Level of the Rubric

Interdisciplinary Curriculum Work

Creating interdisciplinary teaching teams or designing interdisciplinary projects for students has a significant impact on instruction. The dynamic of teachers working together creates new ideas and new perspectives on teaching. Interdisciplinary work also fosters a climate in which teachers can support and encourage one another as they attempt to make changes in teaching and learning.

Lengthen Time

A recent trend in secondary schools is to change the master schedule in order to lengthen class periods. Schools are rapidly moving away from 45-minute periods to time blocks of 60, 90, or even 120 minutes. These longer blocks provide opportunity for more in-depth instruction and group projects. Although it may be possible to get by with a weak lesson plan and to keep students entertained for 45 minutes, longer classes require much better planning to include a variety of instructional activities. Student work is definitely a focus when more time is available in class.

Multilevel

On the elementary level, interdisciplinary instruction is often not a problem because teachers typically teach more than one subject. However, the barriers at the elementary level can be the connections between grades. Creating multigrade teams in elementary school has changed instruction. It also creates the dynamic of two or more teachers collaborating and then supporting one another. Multilevel teams improve the ability of teachers to reinforce and continue skill development over time.

Technology Applications

Schools that rely heavily on instructional technology for student work and problem solving have had remarkable success in engaging students in challenging instruction. Accomplishments are even greater in schools that have all students using laptop computers. These students do not use educational software but rather business, design, and communication software to solve real problems.

Embedded Assessment

Another way to make significant changes in instruction is to change the timing of assessment. Traditionally, testing comes after instruction, often in the form of a chapter test on a Friday or an end-of-year test on a hot day in June. As teachers seek to design more performance-based assessment, they make the assessment part of the instruction. As students do the work, they receive direct feedback in the form of self-evaluation and peer, teacher, or external evaluation. Seeking ways to embed assessment within the instructional time results in a significant change in the way that instruction and assessment are provided.

Small Learning Communities

Many large high schools and middle schools are using innovative redesign to create smaller schools. The intent is to make learning more personalized by having teachers work with fewer students, whom they get to know better. Moving to a small learning community organization can create positive changes. It is easier for staff to collaborate and teachers to develop strong relationships with students in a small school. It is essential to focus on changing the curriculum and increasing professional collaboration, or the small school will result in no higher student achievement than the large school.

The following questions are also helpful in classroom observation. Principals may also want to conduct brief interviews with the teachers in order to answer each question fully.

- Does the teacher support high student achievement by high expectations, challenging work, respect for students, and assistance for students?
- Does the teacher use open-ended questions during presentations or on tests/quizzes?
- Are questions directed at individual students during presentations? Is the wait time provided by the teacher sufficient for students to respond to questions? Are students asked to justify/explain their responses?
- Is student discourse/discussion encouraged during class? Does the teacher invite extended student explanations and stimulate student discourse?
- Does the teacher have a "system" for making sure that each student is called on during the class and that there is full participation by all students?
- Are multiple instructional strategies included in every class?

- Does the vocabulary of the teacher and students align with high rigor/high relevance key verbs?
- Does the teacher make frequent connections and references between what is being learned in the classroom and the real world and/or student experiences?

The National Association of Secondary Principals (NASSP) recommends the following procedures for classroom observations by principals. The procedures were compiled by Dustin A. Peters, principal at Elizabethtown (PA) Area High School.

- Give every staff member the option of a pre-observation conference, although new staff members might be the only ones who show interest. The conference provides new staff with insight into the complex process and thus relieves tension. It also enables you to lay a groundwork of expectations for the teachers.
- Use the pre-observation conference to set the stage for the teacher and you to share ideas about teaching and learning. Make it a positive and supportive experience. From these planned and focused beginnings can spring a tremendous opportunity for teacher growth and improvement.
- Include the assistant principals in the process by assigning them to make observations and asking them to provide intensive assistance to teachers in need of extra help.
- Spend a day observing a particular department, rotating each period. In some cases, you might observe a teacher twice. By the end of the day, you will have completed several observations, improved your knowledge of that department, and formulated specific ideas for improvement in the department as a whole.
- Provide each teacher with your usual observation report and write a one- or two-page draft of your total day, describing what happened period by period and including general comments particular to the department staff members. Offer four or five suggestions, ideas, questions, or considerations for the department as a whole.
- You have now established a better link with this instructional area and can offer yourself as a well-informed resource. Keep in touch with the staff to get their reactions to your observations/comments. Schedule a day or half-day every week for this kind of observation.
- Make your post-observation report count. Take some time to prepare your suggestions for improvement. It is better not to write down any suggestions than to come up with ones that are not meaningful and helpful.

- In your post-observation conference with teachers, keep the atmosphere positive. Avoid distractions during the meeting; keep the lines of communication open. Remind teachers to invite you into the classroom when they think you would find a particular lesson interesting. When you do receive an invitation, be there.
- Observation need not be limited to the classroom. Effective observation involves everyone in every school setting.
- Follow a student around the building for an entire day and interview him or her at the end of the day. In addition to observing the student, you will have the opportunity to observe six or seven teachers. Write teacher observation reports and one- or two-page reports about the student, the student interview, and the happenings in each class.
- Spend the first 30–40 minutes each morning wandering around the building. Meet the substitutes and visit teachers; check out the library, lobby, or other areas where students congregate. By being out and about, you can take care of problems that might have otherwise been brought to your attention later in the day when someone "just dropped in" to discuss a situation with you.
- This "walking around" concept is good at any time. Visit a few classrooms during the day and do not forget art, technology, physical education, library, and family and consumer science classes.
- Find other ways and times to make observation reports. Write one about the play rehearsal, concert, math convention, career day, or special effort made by a counselor on parent night. Use any meaningful situation to observe, record, reinforce, and give feedback. Use your time effectively, and generate a positive response and some new ideas.
- Observation can be one of the more pleasant aspects of the principal's role. It allows you to spend more time with students — which should be a priority — and to have positive, constructive contact with teachers. Observation also improves classroom activity and instruction. For those occasions when you need to be critical, your new observation approach will provide you with more background information, time-on-task, and, ultimately, better documentation.
- Instructional leadership is an important responsibility. Accept it. Enjoy it. Your time will be better spent, and you will soon be far more knowledgeable about what is going on in the building and in the classroom. As you spend more time with your teachers and students, you will gain a new perspective on your school — one beyond your office walls.

Student Work

Focusing on student work is a powerful way to change the paradigm of instruction. Too often in school the focus is on the quality of the teacher's performance in the classroom. The real test of the effectiveness of an education program, however, is what students are able to produce that demonstrates their fundamental skills in communication and problem solving, as well as the quality of their thinking.

Significant changes have occurred in classrooms that emphasize critically evaluating the quality of the work in which students are engaged. Is it challenging? Is it interesting and meaningful? Do students understand the measure of high quality?

Principles for Principals

The following principles are useful for reminding principals of their educational leadership role in implementing rigorous and relevant instruction.

- The primary purpose of school is to teach students to use their minds well.
- There is a strong sense of a common learning community among staff and students.
- The school atmosphere is safe, trusting, concerned, and caring.
- Students are the workers in school; teachers and administrators facilitate and support that work.
- There are clearly defined outcomes for students to achieve.
- Expectations are high, and there is a commitment to high-quality work.
- All staff model the self-discipline, self-motivation, and commitment that they hope to develop in students.
- Everyone is treated with dignity and respect.
- The focus is on the learner; decisions are based on sound knowledge of learning research and effective organizations.
- The school celebrates life and learning.
- The school is a happy place where humor is a positive force.

Supervising Learning

Good Reflective Questions

- What do you intend students to learn?
- What is the level(s) of rigor and relevance?
- How do you know that students understood the lesson?
- Are you meeting the needs of all students?
- What data are you using to determine that you are meeting the standards?
- What can I do, as instructional leader, to support your efforts?
- What was the most successful part of the learning experience, and why?
- If you teach this lesson again, how might you change it?
- What evidence can you share regarding achievement of standards?
- How do you know that learning has occurred?
- What strategies do you use to address individual learning styles?

Public Awareness Support

Success with these initiatives requires support outside the classroom. Creating awareness of the need to change is a critical first step that should not be ignored. The responsibility for initiating public awareness falls to the administration. Parents, students, educators, and the community must be made aware of the pressing need to restructure U.S. schools. It is no longer enough to prepare our young people for good citizenship and higher education; schools also must help all students develop the basic skills needed for an increasingly sophisticated workplace. Only when parents and community leaders are convinced that schools need to change can administrators generate the political and community pressure necessary to support moving the curriculum to a more relevant base.

Creating awareness is a long-term, ongoing process. School districts that have successfully created a culture and environment to support change have used a variety of awareness techniques. Here are some suggestions that can get parents, students, educators, and the community thinking about the need for change in school.

- Provide information on the changing nature of work and the new skills that all students need for the workplace as part of back-to-school nights and open houses conducted for parents in the fall.
- Use the school newsletter to provide parents and the community with ongoing information about the inability of U.S. children to compete against international standards, the changing nature of the U.S. workplace, and so on.
- Encourage students to challenge the relevancy of curriculum by writing the following question in the front of classrooms: "Where will I use what you are teaching me today?"
- Make awareness of the changing world of work part of the students' ongoing curriculum.
- Ask community employers to bring in lunch for their employees and to use the time to discuss the importance of restructuring schools and the need for higher-level skills.
- Request that community groups and community leaders expand their regular meeting structure to include information about the need to upgrade and expand the curriculum in American schools.
- Create partnerships with business leaders, other education leaders, and the local media to help coordinate an ongoing awareness program on the need for change in schools.

While awareness efforts must emphasize areas in which U.S. students are not competitive internationally, they should also note areas in which we are truly world-class. When it comes to developing creativity and self-esteem in students, U.S. schools do extremely well. In the area of equity — including gender equity, racial/ethnic equity, and equity for students with disabilities — the United States is a world leader.

International comparisons are useful for reflecting on current standards. The United States does not need to duplicate other countries' education systems, but this country must ensure that its students can compete internationally.

Focus on Adult Roles

Once an ongoing awareness program on the need for change in the schools is underway, it is time to engage the public actively in the process. The International Center has found that an excellent way to do that is to approach a broad cross-section of the community and seek advice on what high school graduates should know and be able to do when they leave school. The key to this process is shifting thinking away from what students do in school to what people expect them to be able to do after they graduate.

To break the traditional preoccupation with courses, grades, and test scores, it is important to refocus the attention of educators, parents, and the general public on the adult roles for which graduates must prepare. Adult roles identified independently by various school districts and states include citizen, worker, lifelong learner, consumer, family member, and good user of personal health care and leisure time. It is interesting to note that these six adult roles were first identified in 1917 as part of the Cardinal Principles of Education, which governed the first wave of school reform in the United States.

Many communities have succeeded in reaching agreement on adult roles. Districts could simply provide everyone with a list of adult roles, but that is not recommended. To restructure our schools so that they focus on what we should expect graduates to be able to do instead of on courses and tests, experience has shown that school staff, parents, and the community must discover for themselves what they want for the current generation of children. The process of coming to agreement through the power of discovery creates a sense of ownership that can help sustain the entire effort. Without it, the strong tendency is for everyone to drift back to the old paradigm of courses and tests.

Checklist for Rigorous and Relevant Teaching and Learning

The Teaching Design

- ☐ Is planned using data on students and curriculum.
- ☐ Is clearly linked to the Common Core State Standards.
- ☐ Has an expectation for levels of rigor and relevance.
- ☐ Uses appropriate assessments aligned with the rigor and relevance of expectations.
- ☐ Is clearly guided by big ideas and essential questions.
- ☐ Uses strategies that are aligned with the rigor and relevance of expectations.
- ☐ Includes the knowledge and skills necessary for expected student performance.
- ☐ Uses authentic performance tasks that call for students to demonstrate their understanding and apply knowledge and skills.
- ☐ Uses clear evaluation criteria and performance-standards evaluations of student products and performances.
- ☐ Uses a variety of resources. The textbook is only one resource among many.

Checklist for Rigorous and Relevant Teaching and Learning (Continued)

The Classroom

- ☐ Has student work as central to classroom activities.
- ☐ Has high expectations and incentives for all students to achieve the expected performance.
- ☐ Has a culture that treats students and their ideas with dignity and respect.
- ☐ Displays evaluation criteria or scoring guides.
- ☐ Has samples of high-quality student work on display.

The Teacher

- ☐ Informs students of the expected performance, essential questions, performance requirements, and assessment criteria at the beginning of the lesson or unit.
- ☐ Engages students' interest when introducing a lesson.
- ☐ Uses a variety of strategies that match the expected level of rigor and relevance and the learning styles of students.
- ☐ Facilitates students' active construction of meaning (rather than simply telling).
- ☐ Effectively uses questioning, coaching, and feedback to stimulate student reflection.
- ☐ Facilitates student acquisition of basic knowledge and skills necessary for student performance.
- ☐ Differentiates instruction to meet individual student needs.
- ☐ Adjusts instruction as necessary on reflection and feedback from students.
- ☐ Uses information from ongoing assessments to check for student learning and misconceptions along the way.
- ☐ Uses a variety of resources to promote understanding.

The Students

- ☐ Can describe the goals (student performance) of the lesson or unit.
- ☐ Can explain what they are doing and why (that is, how today's work relates to the larger unit or course goals).
- ☐ Are engaged throughout the lesson or unit.
- ☐ Can describe the criteria by which their work will be evaluated.
- ☐ Are engaged in activities that help them to apply what they have learned.
- ☐ Demonstrate that they are learning the background knowledge and skills that support the student performance and essential questions.
- ☐ Have opportunities to generate relevant questions.
- ☐ Are able to explain and justify their work and their answers.
- ☐ Use the criteria or scoring guides to revise their work.

Public forums are a good way to seek the public's advice both on the adult roles for which graduates should be prepared and on the skills they will need to fulfill those roles. These forums offer another excellent opportunity to get out the message about the need to restructure curriculum for the sake of the students and the country.

It is relatively easy to set new standards and institute different assessments, even to say that teaching will change. It is much more difficult for a teacher actually to break out of the "comfort zone" of current habits. Habits are strong forces to overcome. Initial attempts to change even the simplest of habits make us uncomfortable and cause us to doubt our own competence. By recognizing that change is difficult and may not "feel right" initially, principals can encourage teachers to keep focused on the goal and to support one another so that the change can be a lasting one.

Pitfalls When Making Change

In addition to considering recommendations for creating change, it is also helpful to pay attention to pitfalls to avoid. The following problem areas must be addressed in any schoolwide change.

Lack of Consensus

The area where school leaders are most likely to fall short in bringing about change is in building consensus on the beliefs and values that should guide teaching and learning. Educators need to communicate their goals clearly to others. From the start, any proposed educational change should include a broad-based group of individuals in order to attain a critical mass of people who are committed to reform. Once involved in the process, these individuals can become important advocates for the reform, especially when the going gets tough (and it will get tough).

Lack of Commitment

Another area of difficulty is in the implementation of the change. Most administrators have seen too many innovative education reform plans that end up going nowhere. This happens because everyone underestimates the complexity of changes required, the length of time it will take, the intensity and frequency of professional development required, and the necessity to significantly reform the school culture. If we accept this reality, we can better commit the patience, energy, and time that are required to bring about a genuine, lasting transformation of learning and teaching. One way to maintain the commitment is to create a detailed plan for implementation and to revisit, evaluate, and revise it periodically.

Lack of Trust

Change requires taking risks. Competent professionals do not want to fail, particularly with the education of someone else's children. There is a feeling of safety in staying with the status quo. In order to risk attempting something new, people need the support and encouragement of others. A key ingredient of a climate of risk-taking is trust. Any school attempting change needs to do a self-analysis of the level of trust in the school and in the community. If trust is low, then efforts must be made to open communications and build common expectations in order to establish a higher level of confidence in the school administration.

Testing Mismatch

Testing and assessment programs that are not aligned with the curricular goals can become significant barriers to change. For example, mathematics tests may focus more on computational skills than on the reasoning and problem-solving skills that might be part of the new curriculum. Still, teachers and administrators will feel significant pressure for their students to perform well on these tests. When a mismatch like this occurs, teachers are teaching to a test that differs from the stated goals of the curriculum. Changes in assessment practices must therefore be a key part of any curriculum reform effort.

Facilitating Effective Professional Development

Moving instruction to more rigor and relevance requires that staff members learn new skills and habits. This learning must be provided through professional development activities. The principal's leadership is critical in facilitating professional development.

Professional development is most effective when it is done on a school rather than district basis. Professional development activities should be planned in a way that strengthens the sense of a united community within a school.

Professional development should focus on areas that are likely to improve student achievement. Teachers and other staff may find a variety of topics of great personal interest, but professional development time provided by a school must focus on building skills directly related to increasing student achievement. These professional development requirements can be spelled out in a coherent plan that includes a needs analysis, skills to be developed, activities, follow-up, and timeline.

One area that is frequently overlooked is including all staff members. Teachers are key to developing rigor and relevance in instruction, but all adults in school play a supporting role. A professional development plan should incorporate, as appropriate, all staff and parents as well.

Professional development days are often seen as an opportunity to offer workshops or presentations conducted by outside experts. While there are times when this is a useful way to introduce new information or to motivate staff, the most powerful professional development occurs through a collaborative and coaching model. After establishing clear goals within a school, staff members can work together to develop the necessary skills. Through reflective observation and coaching in one-to-one situations, teachers can make significant and lasting changes in instruction. It is not easy to establish this type of collaborative culture. It also is more expensive in the use of time — but it works.

Professional development is typically looked upon as a frill. Schools do it if they have time and spend money on it if they have money. When time or money becomes tight, it is often the first item on the budget to go. Schools need to build professional development into their everyday operations as an ongoing, indispensable component. The level of rigor and relevance in the curriculum will not increase if teachers continue to teach and schools continue to operate in the same way.

Characteristics of Effective Professional Development

Professional development programs that are most successful in changing instruction and learning:

- focus on teachers as central to school reform yet include all members of the school community.
- respect and nurture the intellectual capacity of teachers and others in the school community.

- reflect the best available research and practice in teaching, learning, and leadership.
- are planned principally by those who will participate in them.
- enable teachers to develop expertise in content, teaching methods, and other strategies to reach high standards.
- enhance leadership capacity among teachers, principal, and others.
- have ample time and other resources to enable educators to develop their individual capacities in learning to work together.
- promote commitment to continuous inquiry and improvement of the culture and daily life of the school.
- are driven by a coherent long-term professional development plan that is built on needs assessment.
- are evaluated on the basis of student learning and guide subsequent professional development efforts.

Resources for Teachers

Effective leaders need to put support structures in place to provide professional development, but teachers need to develop high rigor/high relevance experiences. Teachers do not need to be in Quadrant D of the framework all the time; there should be a balance. The following resources are tools that instructional leaders can use with teachers to increase student achievement and meet the expectations set by the fewer, clearer, and higher expectations of CCSS.

What's a Gold Seal Lesson?

Gold Seal Lessons are tasks or activities that are strategically designed to teach to specific academic standards/performance indicators/objectives/benchmarks. It is these standards that are assessed by high-stakes state and national tests, which are then used to evaluate individual student, school, and district educational effectiveness.

Each Gold Seal Lesson centers on a highly motivating theme, activity, or project. The lessons are almost always multidisciplinary and deal with real-world situations or problems. Each lesson includes a scoring guide to assess learning progress.

A lesson may take as little time as a class period or as much as a year to complete. The task may run concurrently with other class activities, or it may be the exclusive activity for a period of time. Students sometimes work individually, but more frequently they accomplish the task in a small work group.

Gold Seal Lessons require students to learn and perform in a number of different ways. Students may research, write, compute, model, demonstrate, build, survey, or report in a variety of academic, technical, work, and community environments.

Gold Seal Lessons:

- ensure academic rigor and prepare students for success after schools.
- are easy to search and sort through the use of an online database.
- provide a vehicle for bringing teachers from different subject areas and grade levels together to talk about common ideas for improving instruction.
- are multidisciplinary and can point the way to effective collaboration among faculty members.

Description of a Gold Seal Lesson

The following information is included in a Gold Seal Lesson:

- The **title** is intended to pique the student's interest and to give some clue as to what the lesson is all about.
- A **Grade Level** span for which the lesson is most appropriate is indicated. This designation is not cast in concrete! Often, the lesson can be modified easily for other grades.
- The **Subject(s)** is designated for organizational purposes, but rarely does a Gold Seal Lesson include knowledge and skills from just one subject area. Most lessons, because they deal with real-world tasks, are interdisciplinary.
- **Common Core State Standards** (or state standards) are aligned to the lesson.
- The **Rigor/Relevance Framework** is a guide to the difficulty of the lesson, based on two variables: rigor and relevance. The vertical axis indicates the level of knowledge (rigor) required, with 6 being the highest. The horizontal axis indicates the level of application (relevance), with 5 being the highest.

- The **Instructional Focus** lists statements that indicate where the lesson fits within the curriculum. The statements should reflect the subject areas included in the lesson. These statements usually align with state standards.
- **Student Learning** is a list of what the students will be able to do as a result of completing the activities in the lesson. It also serves to provide a quick overview of the objectives prior to implementing the lesson.
- The **Performance Task** is a clear and concise description of what the student is asked to do, usually within the context of a real-world situation. These instructions may be written to the teacher, the student, or both. The Performance Task may also include lists of materials and equipment needed; reference sources such as books, articles, and Web sites; suggestions for grouping students to do the task; and prerequisite knowledge and skills needed to perform the work.
- The **Essential Skills** section contains the specific English, math, science, and/or social studies knowledge and skills that students should acquire and demonstrate as a result of the lesson. Those Essential Skills should be reflected in both the Performance Task and the Scoring Guide. One way to judge the quality of a lesson is by being able to identify this correspondence among the three sections.
- The **Scoring Guide** is the "measuring stick" used by both teachers and students. Students see the Scoring Guide ahead of time, so they know exactly what is expected of them. Teachers use it to determine how well the student has mastered the skills and knowledge required and how well the lesson has been taught. Scoring Guides come in several forms and can be used for both diagnostic and assessment purposes. The teacher decides which form is most appropriate.
- **Attachments/Resources** may be included at the end of the lesson or as separate attachments.

The following are examples of Gold Seal Lessons.

A Systemwide Approach to Rigor, Relevance, and Relationships

Gold Seal Lesson—Justify Your Purchase

Subjects: Math, ELA
Grade Level: 7–8

Common Core State Standards (or other state-specific references)
ELA
- Write arguments to support claims with clear reasons and relevant evidence.

Math
- Summarize numerical data sets in relation to their context, such as by reporting the number of observations.

Student Learning
- Students will work cooperatively.
- Students will share oral information and give feedback.
- Students will construct a Semantic Feature Analysis (SFA) grid to display product evaluations.
- Students will rate products and share justifications.
- Students will record and interpret data on SFA.
- Students will organize and summarize results.
- Students will draw conclusions based upon ratings.
- Students will justify purchasing one product over another.
- Students will write letters explaining justifications.

Performance Task
Overview
Students will compose a letter to a manufacturer recommending one product (cereal, chips, cookies, etc.) over another and include a rationale.

Description
This activity may be a good for students to demonstrate the significance and power of real-world argumentative writing and data collection.
Prior to the start of the activity, the teacher will need the following materials:
- Mints, candies, and gum for Entrance Ticket Activity
- LIKE/DISLIKE signs on table for hook
- SFA organizer (large for classroom use; small for individual student use)

Gold Seal Lesson—Justify Your Purchase (Continued)

- Labels to identify roles for each member
- Generic and brand-name products (no peanuts), pre-sorted into small sandwich bags, labeled *A, B, C*, to use in Taste Test
- Thesaurus or connection to www.dictionary.com
- Chart paper for draft of e-mail or letter

Upon entering the classroom on the day of the lesson, the teacher will present each student with the same treat (a mint, piece of gum, a mini candy bar, etc).

On the board, the teacher will have the following directions: *Examine, eat, and evaluate your treat. Decide if you like or dislike it and why. Decide if you like or dislike it and why. Place the wrapper in one of two groups: LIKE or DISLIKE.*

Upon completing this introductory activity, the teacher may stimulate a discussion by asking students to share their feedback. The teacher may also ask how their judgment might change if they received the snack at a different time of day.

The teacher will continue to guide the learners to brainstorm and prioritize "criteria" used to evaluate the snacks, and record possibilities on board as features in a pre-created SFA (Semantic Feature Analysis). The teacher will poll the class and record numbers for each feature of the focus treat.

Since semantics deal with different meanings of words or symbols, the teacher may pose this question: Why do you think researchers call this organizer a Semantic Feature Analysis grid?

The teacher will then assign students into cooperative groups. Within each group, each student will select a color to represent a role. (The teacher will have the list on the board and on sheets at each table.) Examples include:

1. Red—Discussion Director
2. Light blue—Timekeeper
3. Yellow—Materials Manager
4. Pink—Product A Distributor
5. Orange—Product B Distributor
6. Brown—Product C Distributor
7. Navy blue—Noise Monitor
8. Green—Recorder for SFA
9. Grey—Scribe for Letter or E-mail
10. Black—Peace Keeper

A Systemwide Approach to Rigor, Relevance, and Relationships

Gold Seal Lesson—Justify Your Purchase (Continued)

Next, before distributing snacks for the taste test, the teacher will direct each group to list two verbs that explain what a quality (*insert snack here*) does. The teacher may want to supply a thesaurus to assist students in selecting the best word choice. In an Idea Wave, record one response from each group to record on class SFA. To further stimulate conversation, the teacher may ask: If you were creating a graphic or cartoon about this snack, what actions would you use to "personify" the snack?

Now, groups will construct a list of two adjectives that describe what a quality (*insert snack here*) looks, smells, feels, sounds, or tastes like. Again, the teacher may want to recommend that students use a thesaurus to enhance their lists. And again, the teacher will use an Idea Wave to collect one response from each group to record on class SFA. The teacher may possibly pose this question: If you were describing this snack to a person wearing a blindfold or earplugs, what words would you use to explain how it looks or sounds? What if the person couldn't taste or feel or smell? (An optional extension at this time could include assigning each group one of the five senses to focus on for word search.)

The teacher will then instruct students to record class list of verbs and adjectives on the horizontal features row of their SFA. Each member then records SNACK A, B, and C vertically on SFA.

Objective #1: Design a Semantic Feature Analysis (SFA) grid to evaluate products.

The teacher will distribute snacks in marked A, B, C bags, and students will analyze the three products, completing the SFA as they examine each one. Recorder completes the SFA chart with (+) if the product has the characteristic and (–) if it does not have characteristic. All members are responsible for completing individual SFA grids. The recorder will acknowledge the consensus of the group, although individual members may mark differently on individual grids. A possible teacher question might be: How will your group compromise to settle disagreements and reach a consensus?

Objective #2: Rate products. Record data on SFA. Draw conclusions based on ratings.

Each group will interpret SFA to determine which product is the best representation of a quality (*insert snack here*). The Discussion Director will share the group's consensus with whole class and reveal the name of manufacturers for tested products.

Next, using the verbs and adjectives from the SFA, each group will compose an e-mail or letter to the manufacturer. The scribe will record a draft on chart paper, but each individual will be responsible for recording the e-mail or letter. The teacher can prompt students by asking: What tone will you use in your letters, and why does tone matter?

Gold Seal Lesson—Justify Your Purchase (Continued)

Objective #3: Justify purchasing one product over another via an e-mail or letter. For the closing (N.E.W.S. Brief), the teacher will direct each group to reflect on today's lesson and complete the following statements: • We noticed . . . (What did you discover?) • We enjoyed . . . (What parts of lesson were most engaging?) • We wonder . . . (What questions do you still have?) • We suggest . . . (How would you do this differently next time?)
Essential Skills M1   Perform operations fluently with positive and negative numbers, including decimals, ratios, percents, and fractions, and show reasoning to justify results. M10 Understand and apply a systematic methodology or procedure (e.g., direct or indirect measurement, direct or indirect proof, inductive or deductive reasoning) to model and solve problems. M14 Understand and apply measures of central tendency (mean, median, and mode, and representative sampling of a population). M16 Apply pattern recognition in data sets and series to reason or solve problems involving arithmetic, geometry, exponents, etc. M21 Evaluate and employ accurate and appropriate procedures for statistical data collection, organization, analysis, and display including making estimates and predictions, critiquing data, and drawing inferences (e.g., using the normal curve and z-scores, line of best fit). M31 Understand and apply measures of dispersion (range, mean deviation, variance, and standard deviation). E16 Locate and gather information such as data, facts, ideas, concepts, and generalizations from oral sources. E10 Participate in (sometimes leading) one-on-one or group discussions by asking questions, asking for clarification, taking turns speaking, agreeing and/or disagreeing courteously, making informed judgments, and working toward a common goal.
Assessments Checklist, Written questions
Attachments/Resources (list here) Checklist

Student Checklist—Justify Your Purchase

Name			
Criteria	Yes, Without a Doubt	Almost	Not Yet
Construct Semantic Feature Analysis grid to evaluate products for taste test.	Features and products organized in an easy-to-read format and ready for data analysis	Parts of grid require clarification to use for data analysis	Grid construction difficult to use for data analysis
Rate products and record data on SFA.	All products rated and data recorded correctly on SFA	Most products rated and/or most data recorded correctly on SFA	Few or no products rated and/or data is incorrectly recorded on SFA
Draw conclusions based on ratings (assessed as group).	Group consensus correlates to data recorded on SFA	Group consensus has limited correlation to data recorded on SFA	Group consensus does not correlate to data recorded on SFA
Justify purchasing one product over another via an e-mail or letter.	E-mail or letter demonstrates strong connection to taste test results	E-mail or letter demonstrates limited connection to taste test results	E-mail or letter demonstrates no connection to taste test results

Chapter 8: Creating a Culture of Rigor, Relevance, and Relationships

Gold Seal Lesson—
Chemistrymatch.com

Subjects: Chemistry, English
Grade Level: 10–12

Common Core State Standards (or other state-specific references)
ELA
- Integrate and evaluate multiple sources of information presented in different media or formats (e.g., visually, quantitatively) as well as in words in order to address a question or solve a problem.
- Write informative/explanatory texts to examine and convey complex ideas, concepts, and information clearly and accurately through the effective selection, organization, and analysis of content.
- Use technology, including the Internet, to produce, publish, and update individual or shared writing products in response to ongoing feedback, including new arguments or information.

Math
- Interpret expressions that represent a quantity in terms of its context.

Student Learning
- Students will conduct Internet research.
- Students will demonstrate the ability to use Windows Live Movie Maker to create an advertisement.
- Students will edit a piece of music using Audacity.
- Students will create a PowerPoint presentation.
- Students will demonstrate knowledge of the periodic table.
- Students will describe real-world uses for the element.
- Students will relate the bonding of an element to the relationships of people.

Performance Task

Overview

Students will work individually to create a dating advertisement for an element. The dating advertisement will be in multimedia format and will include pictures, text, and audio. Students will use the information they have learned about families, valence electrons, oxidation numbers, and bonding to create this advertisement. Students will also conduct Internet research for any assistance they may need.

A Systemwide Approach to Rigor, Relevance, and Relationships

Gold Seal Lesson—Chemistrymatch.com (Continued)

Description

Pretend you are an element and you are looking for a date for the big dance. You must create a multimedia dating advertisement in order to find this date. Your advertisement must include the following:

1. the name of the element and its symbol
2. the family the element belongs to
3. four characteristics of the element
4. the number of valence electrons the element has
5. the oxidation number of the element
6. the type of ions the element is looking for to make a bond
7. the type of bond the element will make to become stable
8. several examples of things the element can be used for in elemental or compound form in our everyday life
9. works cited for any information derived from the Internet
10. sources documented below any pictures used from the Internet
11. smooth flow between slides into the closing
12. credits

The final project must include 13 or more slides covering each of the above topics as well as audio in a Windows Movie Maker format.

Essential Skills

E9   Organize supporting details in logical and convincing patterns that focus on audience and purpose.
E15 Demonstrate ability to select and use appropriate technology or media for presenting information to the target audience for the specific purpose.
E31 Apply an understanding of graphics, layout, white space, italics, graphs, charts, and other visual aids to enhance informational reading, writing, or presenting.
S57 Know the symbols that represent one atom or one mole of atoms of an element. Name and write molecular and empirical formulas of chemical compounds.
S73 Explain chemical bonding in terms of the transfer or sharing of valence electrons.

Attachments/Resources

Dating Advertisement

Submitted by Alison W. McCauley, Central High School

Scoring Guide—Chemistrymatch.com
The following rubric will be used to score your final project.

Elements Looking For	Possible Points	Points Earned
Title for movie	3	
Includes name and symbol of element.	3	
Includes family name of element.	3	
Characteristic 1	3	
Characteristic 2	3	
Characteristic 3	3	
Characteristic 4	3	
Includes the correct number of valence electrons.	3	
Includes the charge of the element.	3	
Includes the type of ion the element is looking for to make a bond.	3	
Includes the type of bond the element will make to become stable.	3	
Includes what the element can be used for in elemental or compound form in everyday life.	3	
Sources are properly cited on pictures.	5	
Sources for information are properly cited at the end.	5	
Includes credits.	3	

Scoring Guide—Chemistrymatch.com (Continued)

Technical Design Components		
Final movie provides evidence of research and understanding of concepts related to the objective of the assignment.	10	
Vocabulary is appropriate to the content and the audience.	3	
Movie is complete (includes visuals, audio, and sources).	7	
Music has been edited to fit the movie from beginning to end.	10	
Each picture enhances the text used.	10	
The sequence of slides has a clear theme/focus.	10	
The sequence of slides is well organized throughout the movie.	5	
Enough time is allowed to read the text on the slide before moving to the next, creating a smooth a flow between slides.	10	
Titles and other statements throughout the movie contribute to the objective of the movie.	7	
All components of the movie fit together and achieve the stated objective.	10	
Final Score	120	

Portions of the rubric were adapted from the following Web sites:
http://www.bcps.org/offices/lis/models/tips/video.html;
http://www.bcps.org/offices/lis/models/tips/rubrics_sec/slide_photo.html

Chapter 8: Creating a Culture of Rigor, Relevance, and Relationships

Gold Seal Lesson — To: Cinderella

Subjects: English Language Arts, Social Studies
Grade Level: 3–4

Common Core State Standards (or other state-specific references)
ELA

- Recount stories, including fables, folktales, and myths from diverse cultures; determine the central message, lesson, or moral and explain how it is conveyed through key details in the text.
- Refer to parts of stories, dramas, and poems when writing or speaking about a text, using terms such as chapter, scene, and stanza; describe how each successive part builds on earlier sections.
- Distinguish their own point of view from that of the narrator or those of the characters.
- Write opinion pieces on topics or texts, supporting a point of view with reasons.
- Write narratives to develop real or imagined experiences or events using effective technique, descriptive details, and clear event sequences.

Student Learning

- Students will be able to compare and contrast Cinderella stories from several different cultures.
- Students will be able to identify problems and solutions in fairy tales.
- Students will be able to write their own version of a fairy tale.
- Students will be able to use inferencing skills.
- Students will write with correct grammar, spelling, and punctuation.

Performance Task

Overview

Students will compare and contrast Cinderella stories from different cultures. Students will then decide what gift could be given to Cinderella that would help her. Students will then write their own version of Cinderella using this gift.

A Systemwide Approach to Rigor, Relevance, and Relationships

Gold Seal Lesson—To: Cinderella (Continued)

Description

1. Students will read several different versions of Cinderella from different cultures.
2. As a class, students will complete a chart with story information from each book. They will identify the problem, solution, magic, and what happened to the stepmother and stepsisters. Using this, students will compare and contrast different versions of the story.
3. On a map, students will locate the country of origin for each story and mark it with a pin or sticky note. Students will discuss these points and their geographic relation to each other. Students will reflect on the similarities and differences between the stories and how these may be driven by geographical location.
4. Students will reflect on Cinderella as a character and decide on a gift that would have helped her. Students will then reflect on how this would have changed the story.
5. Students will then write their own version of the Cinderella story, including the gift they chose to give her. The story should be altered to show how this gift would have helped her in some way.
6. Students will then prepare a tag for Cinderella's gift. They will include a poem of at least two lines, hinting at what the gift is.

Essential Skills

E1 Apply writing rules and conventions (grammar, usage, punctuation, sentence structure, and spelling).

E2 Read for main ideas and supporting details and discriminate important ideas from unimportant ideas to aid comprehension.

E6 Collect and focus thoughts about the writing activity (brainstorming, listing, drafting, etc.).

E9 Organize supporting details in logical and convincing patterns that focus on audience and purpose.

E10 Participate in (sometimes leading) one-on-one or group discussions by asking questions, asking for clarification, taking turns speaking, agreeing and/or disagreeing courteously, making informed judgments, and working toward a common goal.

E16 Locate and gather information such as data, facts, ideas, concepts, and generalizations from oral sources.

E18 Apply rules of appropriate diction and grammar in formal and informal speaking situations.

Gold Seal Lesson—To: Cinderella (Continued)

E23	Create a connection to a text by understanding the personal, social, cultural, and historical significance of it.
SS1	Employ geographic tools (maps, globes, photographs, models, satellite images, charts, databases, GPS, etc.) and other visual images (physical, mental, and electronic representations) to acquire, process, and report information about people, places, and environments from a spatial perspective.
SS19	Compare and contrast the physical, human, and cultural characteristics of places and regions on Earth.

Attachments/Resources
Scoring Guide
To Cinderella Story Comparison Chart

Submitted by: Lisa Pyck, James R Watson Elementary

Rubric for To: Cinderella

Category	4	3	2	1
Story Understanding	The student is able to identify main story events and details. The student can provide accurate comparisons of different versions of Cinderella stories.	The student is able to identify most main story events and details. The student can provide some comparisons of different versions of Cinderella stories.	The student is able to identify some main story events and details. The student can provide vague comparisons of different versions of Cinderella stories.	The student is not able to identify main story events and details and/or the student cannot provide accurate comparisons of different versions of Cinderella stories.
Creativity	The story contains many creative details and/or descriptions that contribute to the reader's enjoyment. The author has really used his or her imagination.	The story contains a few creative details and/or descriptions that contribute to the reader's enjoyment. The author has used his or her imagination.	The story contains a few creative details and/or descriptions, but they distract from the story. The author has tried to use his or her imagination.	There is little evidence of creativity in the story. The author does not seem to have used much imagination.
Spelling and Punctuation	There are no spelling or punctuation errors in the final draft.	There is one spelling or punctuation error in the final draft.	There are 2–3 spelling and punctuation errors in the final draft.	The final draft has more than 3 spelling and punctuation errors.
Inference	Student showed inference skills. The ending makes sense with the gift given.	The ending mostly makes sense. Evidence of inference is clear.	Student used some inferences to write the ending. The ending makes some sense with rest of story.	Inference is not evident. The ending does not make sense.

Rubric made using RubiStar (http://rubistar.4teachers.org)

To: Cinderella Comparison Chart

Book	Country of Origin	Problem	Solution	Magic Used	Stepmother	Stepsisters

A Systemwide Approach to Rigor, Relevance, and Relationships

Gold Seal Lesson—We Can Change Our World

Subjects: English Language Arts, Social Studies
Grade Level: 7–12

Common Core State Standards (or other state-specific references)
ELA
- Cite strong and thorough textual evidence to support analysis of what the text says explicitly as well as inferences drawn from the text.
- Delineate and evaluate the argument and specific claims in a text, assessing whether the reasoning is valid and the evidence is relevant and sufficient; identify false statements and fallacious reasoning.
- Analyze seminal U.S. documents of historical and literary significance (e.g., Washington's Farewell Address, the Gettysburg Address, Roosevelt's Four Freedoms speech, King's "Letter from Birmingham Jail"), including how they address related themes and concepts.

Student Learning
- Students will analyze some of the problems they think the U.S. is facing.
- Students will work cooperatively and collaboratively to develop a bill with group consensus.
- Students will justify their choice through careful research and statistics.
- Students will research how lawmakers write laws.
- Students will revise and analyze different forms of the bills and then vote on the version of the bill that they feel is the best policy to address their concerns.

Performance Task
Overview
In groups of three to four, which will represent one of the current congressional committees, students will brainstorm about problems they feel the United States is facing. They will work to develop a bill that they believe will effectively solve the proposed problem. Once the research is completed, students will work cooperatively to develop a bill that will either eliminate the problem or decrease the impact the problem is having on the United States. Once the bill is written, the group will create an effective presentation to help ensure the bill will pass a full 'House' vote. Each group will present its bill and there will be a full House (class) vote.

Description
1. Prior to this assignment, students will have learned how a bill becomes a law. Students will also be familiar with the importance and functions of congressional committees.
2. Students will be broken up into groups. The group will choose a problem and then determine which congressional committee would be used to address their problem.

Chapter 8: Creating a Culture of Rigor, Relevance, and Relationships

Gold Seal Lesson—We Can Change Our World (Continued)

3. As a group they will decide which member will chair the committee. The committee chair will assign research tasks to each member.
4. After each member completes the research task, he or she will present the findings to the group.
5. Based on the research, the group will compose a bill to address the problem.
6. Once the bill is written, the group will work collaboratively to develop a dynamic persuasive presentation, using a variety of visual aids.
7. Each student in the class will vote on the bill. Each student will be responsible for providing the teacher with a written explanation of why he or she either supported or rejected the bill.
8. Students will then write a reflective essay about the project. They will grade each group member as well as themselves. They will also write about the high and low points of the project and what they would do differently for the next project.

Essential Skills

SS3 Examine the purpose of rules and laws, explain how governments enact and enforce them, and assess ways to evaluate rules and laws.
SS4 Examine the purpose of rules and laws, explain why government is necessary.
SS35 Understand and evaluate the role of political parties and interest groups in the United States and other nations.
SS40 Make and communicate decisions by identifying alternatives and consequences and satisfying constraints.
SS44 Distinguish valid arguments from fallacious arguments in historical interpretation.
E7   Research information from a variety of sources and draft a well-organized, accurate, and informative report or essay that engages an audience and addresses its needs.
E10 Participate in (sometimes leading) one-on-one or group discussions by asking questions, asking for clarification, taking turns speaking, agreeing and/or disagreeing courteously, making informed judgments, and working toward a common goal.
E16 Locate and gather information such as data, facts, ideas, concepts, and generalizations from oral resources.
E19 Analyze and evaluate a speaker's opinions, personal values, and persuasive techniques.
E36 Define a position on a controversial topic and make an oral presentation likely to persuade a specific audience to change an opinion or take a particular action.

Assessment

Rubric for evaluating group work
Rubric for evaluating group presentation

Submitted by: Joyce Gilly, Mooresville High School

Rubric for Group Presentation: "We Can Change Our World"

Criteria	Distinguished 4	Proficient 3	Basic 2	Unacceptable 1
Organization	Extremely well organized.	Generally well organized.	Somewhat organized.	Poor or nonexistent organization.
	Introduces the purpose of the presentation clearly and creatively.	Introduces the purpose of the presentation clearly.	Introduces the purpose of the presentation.	Does not clearly introduce the purpose of the presentation.
	Effectively includes smooth, clever transitions that are succinct but not choppy in order to connect key points.	Includes transitions to connect key points, but better transitions from idea to idea are noted.	Includes some transitions to connect key points, but there is difficulty in following the presentation.	Uses ineffective transitions that rarely connect points; cannot understand presentation because there is no sequence for information.
	Student presents information in a logical, interesting sequence that audience can follow.	Most information is presented in logical sequence; a few minor points may be confusing.	Student jumps around topics. Several points are confusing.	Presentation is choppy and disjointed; no apparent logical order of presentation.
	Ends with an accurate conclusion that shows thoughtful, strong evaluation of the evidence presented.	Ends with a summary of main points, showing some evaluation of the evidence presented.	Ends with a summary or conclusion; little evidence of evaluating content based on evidence.	Ends without a summary or conclusion.

Teacher Comments:

Total Points _____

Chapter 8: Creating a Culture of Rigor, Relevance, and Relationships

We Can Change Our World

Name: Teacher:

Date: Title of Work:

Skills	Criteria				Points
	1	**2**	**3**	**4**	
Helping: The teacher observed students offering assistance to each other.	*None* of the Time	*Some* of the Time	*Most* of the Time	*All* of the Time	_____
Listening: The teacher observed students working from each other's ideas.	*None* of the Time	*Some* of the Time	*Most* of the Time	*All* of the Time	_____
Participating: The teacher observed each student contributing to the project.	*None* of the Time	*Some* of the Time	*Most* of the Time	*All* of the Time	_____
Persuading: The teacher observed students exchanging, defending, and rethinking ideas.	*None* of the Time	*Some* of the Time	*Most* of the Time	*All* of the Time	_____
Questioning: The teacher observed students interacting, discussing, and posing questions to all members of the team.	*None* of the Time	*Some* of the Time	*Most* of the Time	*All* of the Time	_____
Respecting: The teacher observed students encouraging and supporting the ideas and efforts of others.	*None* of the Time	*Some* of the Time	*Most* of the Time	*All* of the Time	_____
Sharing: The teacher observed the students offering ideas and reporting their findings to each other.	*None* of the Time	*Some* of the Time	*Most* of the Time	*All* of the Time	_____
Total Points:					_____
Teacher Comments:					

© International Center for Leadership in Education

Personal Portfolio

The Personal Portfolio is designed to be a working document that you can use to plan and reflect on the progress that your school is making to achieve rigor, relevance, and relationships. This is your document; you may modify it to meet your needs. Print out the portfolio and create your own notebook of progress on rigor, relevance, and relationships. Keep in mind the continuous efforts necessary to envision, discover, build, create, develop, and support.

The Personal Portfolio has four parts: Benchmark Tasks, Implementation Actions, Evidence, and Reflection.

- **Benchmark Tasks** is a checklist of the major tasks related to each phase of the change model. Use this checklist to identify what to do and what steps to take. Rate the current progress of school staff periodically to reflect on where progress is being made and what remains to be done.
- Use **Implementation Actions** to record your personal goals and your actions to further implementation.
- In the **Evidence** section, place examples of school success. Consider this your rigor, relevance, and relationships scrapbook. Insert copies of good examples of high rigor, high relevance lessons or practices. Any specific examples of relationship development should be kept here as well. As a result, when you want to show progress to new staff, district leaders, or visiting educators, you will have convenient examples of rigor, relevance, and relationships in your school.
- **Reflection** is a place to periodically make notes of your progress and needs. The reflection questions will guide you to the important aspects of change. In the space provided you can make notes, organize thoughts, and leave reminders of future work.

Benchmark Tasks

Use the following checklist of benchmark tasks to reflect on the various aspects of progress in implementing rigor, relevance, and relationships in your school.

Exceeding	Meeting	Developing	Beginning	Absent	Envision *"Vision without action is a dream. Action without vision is simply passing the time. Action with vision is making a positive difference."* —Joel Barker
					Share information on WHY rigor, relevance, and relationships are important.
					Collect ongoing evidence of the need for rigor, relevance, and relationships.
					Engage staff in discussions to understand, embrace, and reflect on the need for rigor, relevance, and relationships.
					Establish common definitions of rigor and relevance.
					Establish common definitions of relationships to support student learning.
					Establish common definitions of relationships to support staff collaboration.
					Share examples of rigor and relevance in the school.
					Connect rigor and relevance with instruction and assessment practices.

A Systemwide Approach to Rigor, Relevance, and Relationships

Exceeding	Meeting	Developing	Beginning	Absent	Discover *"The real act of discovery consists not in finding new lands but in seeing with new eyes."* —Marcel Proust
					Analyze local assessments for levels of rigor and relevance.
					Identify examples of Quadrant D lessons in the school.
					Share examples of high rigor and high relevance learning.
					Analyze state assessments for levels of rigor and relevance.
					Conduct student focus groups on rigor and relevance.
					Conduct student focus groups on relationships.
					Survey students as to the current levels of learning support and relationships.
					Share examples of good learning support and relationships with staff.

Exceeding	Meeting	Developing	Beginning	Absent	Create *"The goal isn't to live forever; the goal is to create something that will."* —Chuck Palahniuk
					Design interdisciplinary lessons.
					Design new activities to strengthen learning relationships among students.
					Design activities to strengthen support and relationships for students in the transition year into the school.
					Create new instructional activities that increase rigor and/or relevance.
					Create new assessments that increase rigor and/or relevance.

Chapter 8: Creating a Culture of Rigor, Relevance, and Relationships

Exceeding	Meeting	Developing	Beginning	Absent	**Build** *"You lead today by building teams and placing others first."* —Jeff Immelt
					Share the Rigor/Relevance Framework with students.
					Explain the Rigor/Relevance Framework to parents.
					Engage staff members in applying the Rigor/Relevance Framework to their instruction.
					Explain the Relationship Framework to staff and reflect on current levels of relationships.
					Create consensus on priority standards for learning.
					Map instruction at each grade and in each course to state standards.
					Agree on a common lesson format for high rigor/high relevance instruction.
					Reflect on positive and negative staff behaviors that influence learning relationships.
					Analyze strengths of extracurricular activities that contribute to positive learning relationships.
					Establish student learning criteria and data measures for school that relate to foundation and stretch learning.
					Establish learning criteria and data measures for school that relate to learner engagement and personal skill development.
					Improve staff collaboration through team-building activities.

A Systemwide Approach to Rigor, Relevance, and Relationships

Exceeding	Meeting	Developing	Beginning	Absent	**Develop** *"When you shift people's perceptions, their actions follow."* —Rayona Sharpnack
					Develop staff skills to create, adapt, and use performance assessments.
					Develop staff skills to identify and write good test questions.
					Develop common performance tasks for typical student performance (for example, writing and presentations).
					Develop staff skills to write high rigor/high relevance performance tasks.
					Develop staff ability to select and use instructional strategies appropriate for high rigor/high relevance.
					Develop staff skills in building positive learning relationships.
					Develop staff ability to create classroom procedures that build learning relationships.
					Create structures and support for daily professional learning.
					Create a model of peer teaching and coaching.

Chapter 8: Creating a Culture of Rigor, Relevance, and Relationships

Exceeding	Meeting	Developing	Beginning	Absent	Support *"Some people change when they see the light, others when they feel the heat."* —Caroline Schoeder
					Conduct frequent walk-throughs to observe instruction.
					Include rigor and relevance as a part of the observation protocols for classroom walk-throughs.
					Provide opportunities for peer review of instruction.
					Conduct peer review of learning experiences for rigor and relevance.
					Conduct celebrations of achievement of rigor and relevance.
					Conduct celebrations of developing learning relationships.
					Analyze data of student learning criteria on foundation and stretch learning related to rigor and relevance.
					Analyze data of student learning criteria on learner engagement and personal skills development related to relationships.
					Encourage staff members to give each other feedback on positive relationship behaviors.

A Systemwide Approach to Rigor, Relevance, and Relationships

Implementation Actions

In this section of the portfolio, plan your specific actions. What will you do?

Action Planning Form

Identify the objective of what you intend to do as a follow-up action. Then, brainstorm to identify actions to be taken, the person or people who will take responsibility, and date to be accomplished. Finally, identify the data or measure that will be used to evaluate the effectiveness of actions taken.

Action Planning Form

Identified Objective: What do you plan to accomplish?		
Actions to Be Taken: What do you plan to do?	Who will do this?	By when?
Data to Measure Effectiveness: What will be different, and how will you know?		

Evidence

This is your section to keep a scrapbook or journal of your progress toward rigor, relevance, and relationships. Place copies of written materials, model lesson plans, memos, photographs of student work, descriptions of students, and other items that have been created in your school and that are great evidence of the progress you are making toward the goal.

Reflection

In this section of the portfolio, you can reflect on progress. Use the reflection questions to guide you in considering various aspects of making the change to rigor, relevance, and relationships.

The New 3 Rs Powered by Aligned School Systems

The chapters of this handbook have made numerous references to the "3 Rs." The original use of that phrase is attributed to an Englishman, Sir William Curtis, who gave a toast in Parliament in 1825 referring to the 3 Rs: reading, writing, and reckoning (a Victorian term for being able to do mental arithmetic). Since that time, in this country, we have translated that third R to 'rithmetic."

The expression focuses on the three elements that, for a century, have defined a basic education. During the last century, as teachers and administrators have tried to bring those subjects to life in the classroom, they have often gotten stuck on the content of the curriculum — in other words, 'what' should be taught, or 'how' to teach those subjects.

Now, however, we have a coordinated vision for education. As you have read in the previous chapters, 21st-century learning will be fueled by a new vision for empowered student learning and powerful instruction, a vision that can be completely refocused and sharpened by the new 3 Rs — *rigor, relevance,* and *relationships.* As schools and educators step into 21st-century learning, they will work together to implement the fewer, higher, clearer Common Core State Standards, as well as the related Next Generation Assessments. In the new century, these are the standards and benchmarks that will define the 'what' and the 'how high' dimensions of rigorous and relevant learning and teaching. But, even beyond that, the new 3 Rs will also provide a way to shift the learning process — from teachers to students, and from the four walls of the classroom to the broader world in which those students live and work.

The vision of a world in which the perceived boundaries between school and life disappear was articulated powerfully by Willard Wirtz, the Secretary of Labor in President John Kennedy's cabinet. He said, "There aren't two worlds — education and work. There is one world — life." As we move into the new century of American education, Wirtz's statement challenges us to consider how we might refashion the artificial learning environment called school that we have developed and refined for 100 years.

This handbook has provided insights, examples, and the tools of the new 3 Rs, as well as the systemic context in which they can be effectively nurtured and efficiently implemented. DSEI provides a valuable framework for envisioning and implementing the systemic elements that support powerful learning — effective instruction (teaching), strong instructional leadership, and supportive organizational leadership.

As with any framework, or mental model, DSEI helps us understand those components and how they work together. The critical factor that will determine our success in leading and moving our school systems toward outstanding results, however, is alignment. For all human systems or organizations — such as schools or school districts, for example — alignment is almost always the factor that determines how effectively the system operates.

So as we think about the new 3 Rs, we should think about another expression we often use — "get your ducks in a row." Although a few competing explanations for the origin of the expression do exist, most agree that it refers to young ducklings swimming in a row behind their mother, who cuts a path through the water and makes their swimming easier if they stay in her wake. We can glean a similar lesson from the ducks' flying cousins, the migrating geese that fly in their signature V-formation. Just as the baby ducks' efforts are aided by swimming behind their mother, geese, according to animal scientists, fly 71 percent farther by aligning their flight in that formation.

In order to achieve the new 3 Rs and create systems that strongly support student-centered, rigorous, and relevant learning that is built around meaningful relationships, we absolutely must align the efforts of the adults in the system. If we are to fly farther than we have in education before, we must first coordinate those adults, making sure that they empower students through their teaching, are guided by collaborative instructional leadership, and are inspired by supportive organizational leadership.

Chapter 8: Creating a Culture of Rigor, Relevance, and Relationships

Review Questions

1. What conditions might prevent teachers from changing the ways in which they plan and conduct instruction?
2. How often have you experienced effective classroom visitation? How might it be improved?
3. Are you involved in an interdisciplinary teaching team? If so, how useful has it been? If not, what advantages do you see to such a team?
4. Do you utilize assessment as part of the instruction? If so, how? If not, how might you go about making this change?
5. Do you see a public awareness of the need to restructure schools? If not, what suggestions might you offer about how your school might go about increasing awareness?
6. How might you benefit from the use of Gold Seal Lessons?
7. What steps can you take to take advantage of the Personal Portfolio?

Appendix

For Further Reading

Barth, R. *Lessons Learned: Shaping Relationships and the Culture of the Workplace*. Thousand Oaks, CA: Corwin Press, 2003.

Bereiter, C., and Scardamalia, M. "Intentional Learning as a Goal of Instruction," 1989. Online: http://ikit.org/fulltext/1989intentional.pdf.

Blanchard, K. *Whale Done!* New York, NY: Simon & Shuster, 2002.

Blankstein, A. M. *Failure Is Not an Option: Six Principles That Guide Student Achievement in High-Performing Schools*. Thousand Oaks, CA: Corwin Press, 2004.

Bransford, Brown, and Cocking (Eds.). *How People Learn: Brain, Mind, Experience, and School, Expanded Edition*. Washington, DC: The National Academies Press, 2002.

Caine, G. and Caine, R. *Making Connections: Teaching and the Human Brain*. Upper Saddle River, NJ: Dale Seymour Publications, 1994.

Calvin, W. *How Brains Think: Evolving Intelligence, Then and Now*. New York, NY: Basic Books, 1997.

Cambron-McCabe, N., Cunningham, L., Harvey, J., and Koff, R. *The Superintendent's Fieldbook: A Guide for Leaders of Learning*. Thousand Oaks, CA: Corwin Press, 2004.

Collins, J. *Good to Great: Why Some Companies Make the Leap . . . and Others Don't*. New York, NY: HarperCollins, 2001.

Conrath, J. *Our Other Youth*. Gig Harbor, WA, 1988.

Cotton, K. "School Size, School Climate, and Student Performance," 1996. Online: http://upstate.colgate.edu/pdf/Abt_merger/Cotton_1996_Size_Climate_Performance.pdf.

Crowther, F., Kaagan, S., Ferguson, M., and Hann, L. *Developing Teacher Leaders*. Thousand Oaks, CA: Corwin Press, 2002.

Cushman, K. *Fires in the Bathroom: Advice to Teachers from High Schools Students*. Providence, RI: Next Generation Press, 2003.

Daggett, W. "The Education Challenge: Preparing Students for a Changing World." Paper presented at the Model Schools Conference, 2006.

Davenport, P., and Anderson, G. *Closing the Achievement Gap: No Excuses*. Houston, TX: American Productivity and Quality Center, 2002.

Deal, L.B. and Deal, T. *Leading with Soul: An Uncommon Journey of Spirit*. San Francisco, CA: Jossey-Bass, 1995.

Deiro, J. A. "Do Your Students Know You Care?" *Educational Leadership*, 60 (March 2003), 6. Online: http://www.ascd.org/publications/educational-leadership/mar03/vol60/num06/Do-Your-Students-Know-You-Care¢.aspx.

DuFour, R. *Creating the New American School: A Principal's Guide to School Improvement*. Indianapolis, IN: National Education Service, 1996.

DuFour, R., and Eaker, R. *Creating Professional Learning Communities*. Indianapolis, IN: Solution Tree, 1998.

Eaker, R., DuFour, R., and DuFour, R. *Getting Started: Reculturing Schools to Become Professional Learning Communities*. Bloomington, IN: Solution Tree, 2002.

Evans, R. *The Human Side of School Change: Reform, Resistance, and the Real-Life Problems of Innovation*. San Francisco, CA: Jossey-Bass, 2001.

Friedman, Thomas L. *The World Is Flat: A Brief History of the Twenty-first Century*. New York, NY: Farrar, Straus and Giroux, 2005.

Frome, P. "High Schools That Work: Findings from the 1996 and 1998 Assessments." Online: http://info.sreb.org/programs/hstw/ResearchReports/RTI_study.pdf.

Fullan, Michael. *Leading in a Culture of Change*. San Francisco, CA: Jossey-Bass, 2001.

Gambone, M., Klem, A., and Connell, J. *Finding Out What Matters for Youth: Testing Key Links in a Community Action Framework for Youth Development*. Philadelphia, PA: Youth Development Strategies, Inc. and Institute for Research and Reform in Education, 2002.

Gardner, H. *Changing Minds: The Art and Science of Changing Our Own and Other People's Minds*. Cambridge, MA: Harvard Business School Press, 2004.

Gardner, H. *Extraordinary Minds: Portraits of 4 Exceptional Individuals and an Examination of Our Extraordinariness*. New York, NY: Basic Books, 1998.

Glasser, W. *The Quality School: Managing Students Without Coercion*. New York, NY: HarperCollins, 1998.

Goleman, D. *Emotional Intelligence: Why It Can Matter More Than IQ* (10th Anniversary Ed.). New York, NY: Bantam Dell, 2006.

Hargreaves, A., and Fullan, M. *What's Worth Fighting for Out There?* New York, NY: Teachers College Press, 1998.

Harris, S. *Bravo, Principal! Building Relationships with Actions That Value Others*. Larchmont, NY: Eye On Education, 2004.

Harris, S. *Bravo, Teacher! Building Relationships with Actions That Value Others*. Larchmont, NY: Eye On Education, 2005.

High School Survey of Student Engagement. Bloomington, IN: Indiana University. Retrieved January 2006. Online: http://www.indiana.edu/%7Eceep/hssse.

Hodges, D. *Looking Forward to Monday Morning*. Thousand Oaks, CA: Corwin Press, 2005.

Hord, S.M. *Learning Together, Leading Together: Changing Schools Through Professional Learning Communities*. New York, NY: Teachers College Press, 2004.

Horsch, P., Chen, J., and Nelson, D. "Rules and Rituals: Tools for Creating a Respectful, Caring Learning Community," 1999. Online: http://old.originsonline.org/includes/files/Rules%20and%20Rituals.pdf.

Littky, D, and Grabelle, S.. *The Big Picture: Education Is Everyone's Business*. Alexandria, VA: Association for Supervision and Curriculum Development, 2004.

Marzano, R., Pickering, D., and Pollock, J. *Classroom Instruction That Works: Research-Based Strategies for Increasing Student Achievement.* Upper Saddle River, NJ: Prentice Hall, 2004.

Pink, D. H. *A Whole New Mind: Why Right-Brainers Will Rule the Future.* New York, NY: Riverhead Books, 2005.

Project Tripod, 2002. Retrieved January 2006 from www.ksg.harvard.edu/tripodproject/index.html

Schmidt, W., McKnight, C., and Raizen, S. *Characterizing Pedagogical Flow: An Investigation of Mathematics and Science Teaching in Six Countries.* New York, NY: Springer, 1996.

Schmidt, W. McKnight, C., and Raizen, S. *A Splintered Vision: An Investigation of U.S. Science and Mathematics Education.* New York, NY: Springer, 1997.

Sizer, T. R. *Breaking Ranks II: Strategies for Leading School Reform.* Reston, VA: National Association of Secondary School Principals, 2006.

Stevenson, H. and Stigler, J. *The Learning Gap: Why Our Schools Are Failing and What We Can Learn From Japanese and Chinese Education.* New York, NY: Simon & Schuster, 1992.

TIMSS. "Pursuing Excellence: A Study of U.S. Eighth-Grade Mathematics Teaching, Learning, Curriculum, and Achievement in International Context," 1996. Online: http://nces.ed.gov/pubs97/97198.pdf.

Wagner, T. "Rigor on Trial," 1996. Online: http://www.tonywagner.com/resources/rigor-on-trial.